P9-BJM-675

Date Due

PROVINCIAL SOCIETY
1690–1763

A HISTORY OF AMERICAN LIFE

Arthur Meier Schlesinger and Dixon Ryan Fox, editors

All 13 volumes are available as Quadrangle Paperbacks.

James Truslow Adams was born in Brooklyn, New York, and studied at Brooklyn Polytechnic Institute and Yale University. After an early career in business and finance, he became involved in the preparation for the Paris Peace Conference of 1919, and turned to writing. His books include *The Epic of America*, a three-volume history of New England to 1850, *Henry Adams*, and *Our Business Civilization*. He died in 1949.

PROVINCIAL SOCIETY
1690-1763

BY

JAMES TRUSLOW ADAMS

Q

Quadrangle Paperbacks
Quadrangle Books / Chicago

First QUADRANGLE PAPERBACK edition published 1971 by Quadrangle Books, Inc., 12 East Delaware Place, Chicago 60611. Manufactured in the United States of America.

CONTENTS

The first drudgery of settling new colonies, which confines the attention of people to mere necessaries, is now pretty well over; and there are many in every province in circumstances, that set them at ease, and afford leisure to cultivate the finer arts, and improve the common stock of knowledge. . . .

BENJAMIN FRANKLIN, *A Proposal for Promoting Useful Knowledge among the British Plantations in America* (Philadelphia, 1743).

. . . Whence came all these people? They are a mixture of English, Scotch, Irish, French, Dutch, Germans, and Swedes. From this promiscuous breed, that race now called Americans have arisen.

J. HECTOR ST. JOHN CRÈVECŒUR, *Letters from an American Farmer* (London, 1782), 32.

EDITORS' FOREWORD

SINCE the publication a few years ago of Professor Osgood's four volumes on *The American Colonies in the Eighteenth Century*, to say nothing of other works, it is no longer appropriate to speak of the years between 1690 and 1763 as the "neglected period" of American political history. The past generation had already become familiar with the striking features of the military conflicts of the times through the colorful pages of Francis Parkman. As yet no great historian like Parkman has written an epic narrative of the rise of American culture through these decades, nor has any scholar like Osgood made it the theme of an extensive systematic treatise. As in most periods, the materials of the social history lie obscure and scattered, and have been scarcely recognized when they came to light. In the present volume Mr. Adams has brought many of them together for rapid and summary review in a way attempted by few if any predecessors. There have been many single volumes on the social history of the colonists, but these for the most part have not only failed to trace the changes within the lifetime here to be considered, but most of them have grouped together practices of 1750 and those of a hundred years before as if, except for growth in numbers, time had not touched the daily round of American life.

It will be noticed that Mr. Adams not only presents a society in many ways sharply distinguished from that portrayed by Professor Wertenbaker in *The First Americans*,[1] but that he sees within these seventy-three years

---

[1] *A History of American Life*, II.

a steady evolution, an evolution marked more or less distinctly by three periods. Such factors as the sudden expansion both of the frontier and of sea-borne trade—made possible by the Peace of Utrecht—and the recognition about the same time that slavery and not indented service was to be the labor basis of society in the South, make it proper to close the first section about the middle of the second decade of the eighteenth century. Some thirty years later, in the author's analysis, the enrichment of the English stock with blood from other racial groups, the development of towns and especially the multiplication of contacts between American communities, hastened somewhat by the "Great Awakening," produce a third stage in the growth of American culture.

Critics of social history complain that too often it presents vast collections of facts, picturesque and entertaining in themselves, but discrete, unrelated and ungeneralized into any service to the great biography of man, or, at the other extreme, a speculative, theorized "interpretation," so thinly stocked with evidence as to make doubtful its claim to the name of history at all. Mr. Adams's richly furnished narrative will certainly exempt him from the latter charge, while his study of abundant data in the light of general human experience has warranted generalizations which will be valuable not only to students of American history but to those concerned with the history of society as a whole. His observations, for example, on the degradation of folk art in the face of the task of creating a condition of physical comfort, and the consequent development of "American materialism," will be profoundly interesting to the sociologist, as well as his analysis of the economic bases of growing class consciousness and sectional animosity. It may stimulate some philosophical reflection to find that improvements in the modes of life during this period were altogether in the homes of the rich and that the poor man of 1763 was in no better situation than his pioneer grandfather had been. Likewise one notes here how cultural accumulations such as libraries and colleges came into being and how they influenced American youth. New England culture has been the theme of many pens; perhaps no feature of Mr. Adams's book is more interesting than the attention which he calls to parallel achievements•in the colonies to the south.

He has made extensive use of materials not much exploited by general historians of the period, especially the early newspapers, and there most strikingly in the advertising columns and the shipping news. He has brought into synthesis the work of many monographs unfamiliar to the general reader. But this short book, like other volumes of *A History of American Life*, makes no claim to "covering" its subject—perhaps that is impossible; it will serve its purpose if it reveals the richness of the field.

A. M. S.
D. R. F.

PROVINCIAL SOCIETY
1690–1763

PROVINCIAL SOCIETY
1690-1763

CHAPTER I

THE STRUCTURE OF SOCIETY
1690-1700

IN 1690 along the entire length of the colonial shore, everywhere sweeping backward from the sea, creeping up the slopes of the mountain barriers and over their untrodden crests, lay the shadow of the virgin forest, illimitable, silent, starless. So thick was this covering in parts that an Indian trader two generations later reported that at times for miles he could find no place the size of his hand where the sunshine penetrated on the clearest day. The innumerable tree trunks, dusky beneath the green covering of summer or bare and gaunt above the winter's snow, formed a trackless maze save for the labyrinth of Indian trails. These were widened and trampled between certain of the more important English settlements into ways fit for the saddle horse or packtrain. For the infrequent wayfarer or trafficking merchant there were no highways of communication other than the sea and its arms, or the rivers which gave access to the interior up to the fall line where rock and cataract blocked further passage. It had been from over the sea that every new settler had come, tossing and plunging amid the waves in the track of the westward

1

faring sun.   It was across the same sea, to the islands of
the New World or the lands of the Old, that he now sent
the surplus products of his labor and from which he
received many of the necessities and luxuries of his
existence.

Two quests, indeed, had for some years been luring
him toward the interior.   These were the retreating fur
trade and the search for new lands where an untilled soil
would reward the wasteful farmer or where meadows
lying open to the sun, like green islands in the darker
green of the forest, would save the labor of clearing.
But whereas the picturesque and dissolute trader penetrated hundreds of miles, the settler went but tens.   Although in eastern Massachusetts, and to a slighter extent
in the other colonies, single plantations or small villages
were being planted in sections not served directly by a
waterway, the great bulk of the colonists as yet lived
within a few miles of ocean or tidewater stream.

It was a population sparsely scattered over great
stretches.   South of the Delaware River the unit of settlement was the solitary farm or large plantation, and that
section contained not a single town, with the exception
of the large village of Charleston which may have numbered two hundred and fifty families by 1700.   Philadelphia, laid out only in 1683, had but a few hundred
houses some years later and is said to have had not over
seven hundred at the close of the century.   New York
was slightly larger, its population being given as forty-
nine hundred persons in 1698, but it was the only community in that colony larger than a hamlet, for Albany
as yet was scarcely more than a trading post.   Newport
could count less than two thousand, and Boston, the
largest center of population on the continent, not over
seven thousand individuals, free and slave.   If we accept
the figure of two hundred and six thousand as the possible population of the twelve colonies in 1689, it is

evident that nearly two hundred thousand persons must have been living either on isolated farms or in little communities of a few score souls, at most a few score families.

The townsman or village dweller of today has difficulty in realizing the extreme narrowness and provinciality of outlook which resulted from such conditions. There was probably more communication between the colonists, and between them and the West Indies and Europe, even at this period than has generally been thought, but that is speaking comparatively. Actually, beyond limited economic contacts, there was little to enlarge the minds of the vast majority of the settlers. There was, indeed, more or less traveling by horseback between villages, and more rarely between the larger centers of different colonies. Moreover, owing to the small tonnage of the vessels of the day and the tidewater location of most of the settlements, almost every village was a seaport, even when far up the rivers. Vessels went from such interior villages as Hartford or Norwich in Connecticut, or the docks of plantations on the James River in Virginia, directly to the West Indies and England. Icebound streams or ocean storms suspended much of this traffic in the winter, however, and at best it was slow and subject to many vicissitudes. The voyage from the Northern colonies to Barbados or the other islands took, as a rule, about four weeks, that to England double that time and in extreme cases even longer. There were no newspapers and news traveled solely by word of mouth or by correspondence. Letters were dilatory and uncertain in delivery and expensive to transmit; although often sent in duplicate and triplicate form, it not infrequently happened that all the copies were lost on the way.

Under such conditions it is evident that the local interest would be the supreme interest and that the average small community would be a fertile field for the development of indifference, jealousy, prejudice or antipathy regarding the inhabitants of other colonies. Differences in history and in religious, economic and social conditions also contributed to emphasize and to perpetuate the separatist tendencies in spite of fundamental similarities. The differences were most marked between the several tidewater sections of the older settlements. The frontier, upland and mountain regions, to be settled later in the eighteenth century, offered much more uniform conditions and consequently a greater uniformity in feeling and social structure. But such frontier as existed between 1690 and 1700 was, for the most part, merely at the backdoor, so to say, of the tidewater settlements, and partook of their respective characters and prejudices. In spite, however, of excessive self-consciousness and inter-colonial jealousies, which are characteristic of all young commonwealths at a certain stage of their existence, there was a greater uniformity in the warp and woof of the social fabric in 1690 along the entire seaboard than at any subsequent time until perhaps our own. We shall have occasion to touch upon this uniformity later in some of its aspects—schools, culture, landholding, labor, morals—and here will merely note its racial one. Heterogeneous as the population of the colonies always was even from the beginning, it was to become far more so in the course of the eighteenth century, and it was less so, perhaps, in 1690 than at any other time before or after.

Of the numerous non-English stocks, many of which have made invaluable contributions to the economic and cultural life of the American people, only two founded colonies within the limits of the original English thirteen. The independence of one of these, the Swedes on the Delaware, was short-lived. Although in 1693 they were said to number nearly a thousand persons, they gradually abandoned both their language and national customs, and by another half century they had become almost completely absorbed by their English neighbors. Traces of this early Swedish influence, however, linger even to the present day in such matters as the type of local building and the red cattle of eastern Pennsylvania, the latter said to be the descendants of those brought over by the farmers who formed the bulk of the Swedish colonists.[1]

The influence of the other independent colony, that of the Dutch, was to be far more lasting. The colony had become English by conquest in 1664, but the Dutch language, architecture, culture and customs were still largely dominant in the cosmopolitan little town of New York, as they were almost wholly so in Albany and the villages along the Hudson. Nevertheless, in spite of efforts to trace Dutch formative influences in American political institutions, it would seem reasonably certain that those are derived directly from England and Calvinism rather than from Holland or the Dutch settlers in America. It is rather in social aspects and such arts as architecture that Dutch influence is to be found, and in these it was out of all proportion to the actual number of Dutch settlers. With regard to the framework of colonial society it must be remembered that, with the exception of a few hundred in Delaware, the Dutch were localized mainly in the Hudson Valley and the adjacent regions of western Long Island and northern New Jersey. The Hollanders had never been numerous as compared with the English, for the small population of their homeland neither required nor permitted emigration on a large scale, and New Netherland had always been regarded rather as a trading station than as a colonizing effort.

Mingled with the stream of emigration from England

[1] J. T. Scharf, *History of Delaware* (Phil., 1888), I, 57.

there had undoubtedly been many individual Irish and Scotch as well as what are known as the Scotch-Irish, but they nowhere formed a distinct element in the population of any colony. The important immigration of all three yet lay in the future, at the close of the seventeenth century. The dozen Presbyterian churches, however, scattered from New Jersey to South Carolina by 1700 were probably largely Scotch in membership. There were a few Jews, mostly in New York, where a congregation certainly established by 1706 may have been gathered some years earlier, but the Hebrews were as yet not important either socially or economically although they were to become so two generations later.

Another racial strain was that of the Welsh Quakers. These emigrated to Pennsylvania in several bodies from 1683 to 1699 and settled the towns of Merion, Haverford and Radnor, among others, in what was known as the "Welsh Barony" and the several "Welsh Tracts." Mostly skillful farmers, with a few doctors, they maintained for the first generation their own language and peculiar institutions but, although like the Swedes they have left their mark on local architecture and nomenclature, like them, also, they became absorbed in time by their neighbors, English and German. Their type was that of the small farmer, owning on an average not over two hundred acres each, but in a few instances, such as John Humphrey, even in the immigrant generation, they became rich as money lenders and business men.

Of far more importance in Pennsylvania, owing to the steady enlargement of their numbers from immigration in the following century, were the Germans. A second visit which William Penn had made to Germany in 1677 had coincided with an important phase of the Pietistic movement in that country and when, a few years later, he planned his settlement of a colony in America, some of the leaders of the movement with whom he had established personal relations on his visit, organized plans similar to his own for settlement on his lands. In 1683 Francis Daniel Pastorius arrived at the new hamlet of Philadelphia. He was followed some weeks later by the first band of German colonists, consisting of thirteen families, and with them established the neighboring settlement of Germantown. Each year brought additional immigrants until by 1700 a flourishing German population had been established, although in numbers it was but a trickling stream to the flood of the following century. Pastorius himself was, perhaps, the most learned man of his day in America—not forgetting Cotton Mather—and he was far in advance of the New England divine in the breadth of his education. Acquainted by travel with five of the most cultured countries of the time, he had been a student at a like number of universities in Germany. Although in his commonplace book he jotted down his thoughts in eight different languages he was no mere pedant, and both he and the colony of which he was leader at once began to make those contributions to our common life for which we have been so deeply indebted to Germany up to the twentieth century.

Most of the immigrants who have voluntarily come to America as permanent settlers have come as refugees from either economic, political or religious conditions in Europe. It was the last of these which caused the introduction of yet another important racial and cultural strain in the last fifteen years before 1700. The revocation of the Edict of Nantes in France in 1685 at once caused a vast exodus from that country of the Huguenots, many hundreds of whom found their way to the American colonies through England or the West Indies, following in the wake of a few who had come earlier. Settlements of groups, some successful and some not, were made in Massachusetts, Rhode Island, New York,

Virginia and South Carolina, and there were scattered individuals in other colonies. In proportion to their numbers, these French immigrants possessed a larger degree of culture and ability than, perhaps, any other racial addition to the mixed population then gathered here. Although, as was natural, the position attained by individuals in the second generation excelled that of most of the first, yet even among the first comers there were some in almost every colony who at once reached the highest point in the social and economic scale. Considering the comparatively small numbers of the total immigration in a dozen years as compared with the numbers of colonists already well established in the centers of colonial population, it is only necessary to note, before 1700, the presence of such names, already important in their respective communities, as Gabriel Bernon in Newport, the Faneuils and Bowdoins in Boston, the Boudinots, De Lanceys and Bayards in New York, and the Laurenses, Manigaults, Hugers and St. Juliens in Charleston to indicate the unusual character of the French contribution to our common life at that period. Most of them were not rich on their arrival but an unusual proportion showed an aptitude for becoming so, more particularly as merchants. Among the poorer elements a smaller number than among the other races became agriculturists, and there was a considerable proportion among them of handicraftsmen and workers in the minor arts who made a much needed contribution to colonial culture. Throughout the whole colonial period, moreover, the number of French physicians is notable.

In addition to these non-English stocks there were two which were non-European, the Indian and the Negro. We need only call attention to the fact that even in 1700 the whole back country extending along the entire seaboard behind the narrow fringe of white settlements was still the red man's, and there was not a town, with the possible exception of Boston, in which the savage was not even yet a familiar sight. Practically everywhere the frontier was but a few hours or a day's journey from coast or stream, and everywhere on the frontier the settler still lived under the menacing shadow of the toma-hawk. As a trader in furs, as a potential and frequently active enemy, and as the always uncertain ally against the French of Canada and the Mississippi Valley, the Indian was one of the fundamental facts to be reckoned with in colonial life.

The decade we are considering in this chapter marked the turning point in the history of the American Negro, and the greatly increased influx of slaves, now about to begin, was to have marked social and economic effects in the next few decades, but in 1690 they were not numer-ous enough to constitute a problem or to warp society in any colony. The fact that the Negro slave was not economically profitable, except as a house servant, in the North, whereas he was to become so in the staple colonies of the South, was pregnant with the most important consequences soon to become evident. These had not yet been markedly developed and in 1689 Negroes formed about twelve per cent of the population of the colony of New York as compared with only about eight per cent in Virginia. If, however, we estimate very roughly the total Negro population as about eighteen thousand in 1700 probably nearer two thirds than one half were in the colonies south of Pennsylvania.

Although one of the most important elements in the history of the succeeding half century was to be the enormous inflow of non-English stocks, it is evident that even at the close of the seventeenth century colonial life in all its aspects was already subject to important influ-ences from other than English sources. The little metropolis of New York probably contained a greater mixture of racial constituents in its permanent population than any European center of the day, and even the small village of Philadelphia, in only the second year of its brief existence, contained Dutch, French, Germans, Swedes, Danes, Scotch, Irish and Finns as well as the more numerous English.

If the human elements forming colonial society were thus complex, nevertheless the structure itself was simple. There was no hereditary aristocracy, and the only insurmountable barrier between classes was that between the slave for life and the freeman. There was, indeed, a certain hierarchy of wealth and occupation and discrimination in the voting franchise but the large amount of free or almost free land, the resources of a virgin continent, the insatiable demand for and limited supply of labor, and the absence of any permanent legal disabilities applying to any class above the slave, made for extraordinary opportunity and consequently a very mobile society.

The dominant note in this social life was that of domesticity. In the somewhat romantic atmosphere with which Americans clothe this early period, it is perhaps the peace, simplicity and unity of family life which contribute the elements of greatest charm. This domesticity afforded the most characteristic and appealing quality in colonial architecture even after passing into the more formal Georgian phase of the eighteenth century, and the most significant arts and crafts were those devoted to fashioning the furniture and utensils of the household. It is noteworthy that although American cultural life was woven of many ethnic strands, all of those which at the end of the seventeenth century were most effective —English, Dutch, French and German—were of races in which the solidarity of the family was strongly ingrained. To this home-making instinct, rooted in the inheritance of the settlers, was added the influence of environment. Under the conditions of a frontier existence the family tended to become greatly strengthened as a social, economic and even military unit.

The lack of accumulated resources, the scarcity of labor, and other factors in the life of a new country emphasized in a high degree the economic interdependence of all its members, and the family group in some of the colonies, at least, tended to include legally the wards, apprentices and servants as well as the children. The work of subduing the wilderness and establishing the economic position of the family was of necessity shared by the women and children to an extent that has not been adequately recognized. Indeed, the large number of offspring in the majority of households had a very close connection with the exploitation of child labor. This, of course, was not true of such families as had established themselves near the top of the economic scale, but the rich formed only a small part of the total population. Probably about ninety per cent of the colonists were engaged in agriculture. Of these in 1700 the vast majority, south as well as north, tilled small farms largely by their own labor and that of the members of their households. There were, everywhere, larger units of agricultural production, and some very large ones, but this does not alter the fact that numerically the great bulk of the people were living near the lower end of the social scale. At that end the necessity of utilizing the physical labor of women and children added its heavy weight to inherited instinct so as greatly to strengthen the position and organization of the family as a social unit.

The family was thus closely connected with another fundamentally important institution, land, which provided its economic base and to a large extent molded its social and legal aspects. The two most essential factors with regard to land were the tenure on which it was held and the ease with which it might be acquired, both of

which varied in the different colonies. Throughout all
of them the prevailing types of ownership were freehold
and leasehold, but with the exceptions of Massachusetts,
Connecticut and Rhode Island, no land anywhere was
held under any form of tenure save that from an overlord, either the king or proprietors to whom the crown
had granted the lands which they in turn either sold or
leased to the settlers.

The colonial land system was thus mainly feudal in
character but by the end of the seventeenth century the
strictly feudal tenures with the personal service exacted
from tenant to lord had largely disappeared and the quitrent had come to be the measure and fulfilment of most
of the tenant's obligations. Although its payment was
acknowledgment that the actual title to the property lay
in the overlord and not in the tenant, nevertheless, this
did not in the least limit the latter's entire freedom to sell
or bequeath his acres provided he had fulfilled his obligations to the overlord. Nor was this obligation, which
lasted until the Revolution, a heavy one, for not only
was it in many cases merely nominal, as in the example
of a red rose sent annually as the quitrent for a "manor"
in Pennsylvania, but even when the money payment was
exacted the amount did not bear, like ordinary rent, any
relation to the value of the land, and was frequently only
a fraction of a penny per acre. Moreover, the obligation
was not seldom left unenforced, although in some cases,
as the lands of the Penns, Baltimores, Fairfax and Granville, the sums annually raised were considerable.

In addition to this quitrent the overlord was also entitled to escheats and alienation fines. Under the former
in case of failure of heirs or of treason, the lands reverted
to the crown or proprietor, and under the latter as high
as one year's rent was sometimes required on every trans-
fer of the property. All of these incidents of feudal
tenure occasionally aroused opposition from the colo-

nists. This was not directed so much against the theory of the overlordship, which was almost of the order of nature to Englishmen on both sides of the water, as against occasional methods or abuses in connection with the collection of the several dues. Even in the New England colonies mentioned, Massachusetts herself imposed quitrents in Maine, and the theory was acknowledged in all three of them. In rarer cases even more interesting remnants of feudalism are found, as in the courts baron and courts leet of some of the Maryland manors, those of New York, and the attempted fantastic constitution for South Carolina.

Land, however, when once acquired by the settler was not heavily burdened, and more important as a factor in his content or discontent was the ease with which it might be obtained. In proportion to the population the supply of land may appear to have been practically unlimited but if we take certain factors into consideration we find that it was not so even physically. That lying remote from coast or river was as difficult of utilization as that which today is remote from any means of transport. Moreover, the pioneer was deterred from making too far a removal by the danger of isolating himself within the range of the Indian. The unscientific agriculture of the day and the lack of fertilizers quickly wore out much of the acreage used and prevented the use of much more which otherwise might have been brought under profitable cultivation. Not only was much of the richest land of the present then lying under innumerable undrained swamps, but these interfered with transportation and rendered still other lands inaccessible. Owing to the almost continuous forest, open tracts of meadow which could be used without the costly and toilsome work of clearing were comparatively scarce. The available supply of land at the beginning of the new century was thus by no means as ample proportionately as it had been a generation earlier.   Another factor even more important and more resented was the increasing tendency to segregate large holdings in the hands of fortunate individuals, as will be noted in a later chapter.

At the close of the seventeenth century all of the institutions of the settlers were yet in the formative stage, each of them being molded by environment and new conditions of life, and in turn acting upon one another.   Of none was this truer than of the law.   The accepted legal theory that the first settlers brought the English common law with them, using such portions as were applicable to the new conditions, is a view of the case which needs much qualifying.   During the seventeenth century there had been scarcely an English-trained lawyer in America. The codes adopted by the several colonies were largely the work of laymen and wholly administered by them. In 1700 the English professional lawyer Atwood became attorney-general in New York, but for several decades later the highest legal officers in many of the colonies and almost the entire bench in all of them, as well as the members of the legislative assemblies which constituted courts of appeal, were laymen.   In some of the colonies, notably New England, the common law was distinctly repudiated as a subsidiary system and the "law of God," which as one offender truly said admitted of many interpretations, was substituted in its stead.

Although some of the colonies had fundamental codes, these had been drawn early in their history for the most part and were adequate only to the simpler conditions then existing.   There was a good deal of similarity between these, but as the need constantly arose for new laws and interpretation of the old, the laymen-made law came to vary considerably.   Even when the English common law was not distinctly repudiated, the knowledge of it was by no means accurate; and in many cases in which the colonists thought they were following it, in fact they were not.   It was not until near the end of the first quarter of the eighteenth century that the attorney-general in England ruled as to the applicability of the common and statute law of England to its colonies. Meanwhile colonial law had entered upon paths in many cases divergent from those followed at home.   The resultant confusion had brought forth many bitter complaints.   "No one can tell what is law and what is not in the plantations," wrote an American at the beginning of the century.   "Some hold that the law of England is chiefly to be respected, and, when that is deficient, the laws of the several colonies are to take its place.   Others are of the opinion that the laws of the Colonies are to take the first place and that the Laws of England are in force only where they are silent." [1] An unfriendly report made upon the situation in Massachusetts declared that "as to the laws of England" the colonists "abhor the very thought of them, and Acts of Parliament they look upon to be only obligatory wherein the Province is particularly named, though they will use either of them to serve a friend, so that none can tell what is law and what is not." [2]   English merchants complained that they found "more security and better and more speedy justice in the most distant provinces of the Ottoman Empire from their Bashaws" than in the American colonies.[3]

However, the fact that colonial law was to so great an extent made and interpreted by laymen contributed greatly to its flexibility at this stage of its growth.   The lay judge cared little for consistency or precedent.   Like the attorney-general of New Hampshire, he believed that "every tub should stand on its own bottom."   But in any case both the law and those institutions from

[1] Cited by St. G. L. Sioussat, *The English Statutes in Maryland* (Johns Hopkins Univ., *Studies*, XXI), 30.
[2] "Larkin's Report," *Cal. of State Papers, Colon., Am. and W. I., 1701*, 576.
[3] "Larkin's Report," *Cal. of State Papers, Colon., 1701*, 512.

which in part it sprang and which in turn it molded and conserved, were bound to be strongly influenced by the conditions of colonial life. An instructive case, arising from the land situation and affecting the family, was that concerning the laws of inheritance. As we have already noted, the great mass of the colonists were small farmers, and the presence of ample free land had prevented the growth of a distinct wage-earning class. This, to a very great extent, had limited the size of a farm which could be operated profitably to one small enough to be tilled by the members of a family. The great majority had no other property than land, but land, without a supply of labor, was economically useless unless worked by the owner himself. Hence, in certain sections, there early arose the habit of dividing the land of a decedent among the several survivors in the family instead of allowing it to pass only to the eldest son. This was not at first statute law in the colonies but was recognized in many of them as the custom, and property was so divided in cases of intestacy. It was not until the final years of the seventeenth century and the very earliest of the eighteenth, as a result of fears aroused by the new colonial policy of England, that New Hampshire, Massachusetts and Connecticut all passed statutes embodying this customary mode of inheritance.[1]

Due partly to the conditions of life and partly to the lack of lawyers, other markedly original elements, in one colony and another, had also begun to creep into colonial law, which foreshadowed later American reforms and served to distinguish it from that of the mother country. The English legal distinction between real and personal property tended to lose its fundamental importance, and executions were allowed on land. Pleading was very much simplified. Evidence in some colonies was given

[1] A. M. Schlesinger, "Colonial Appeals to the Privy Council," *Political Science Quarterly*, XXVIII, 440-445.

in writing and made a part of the record. Here and there, to a minor degree, the effect of the legal conceptions of the non-English peoples were also of influence, as in New York where the Roman-Dutch law affected testamentary disposition. Moreover, aside from specific alterations of this sort, the absence of any well understood and accepted subsidiary system, such as the common law, strengthened the prevailing belief that such a system was to be found in the law of God or nature, and that positive law must be an expression of natural or moral obligation. At the close of the seventeenth century colonial legal development was thus already becoming something different from a mere transplantation of English law, both in theory and practice. Differences were already developing that were to become set and permanent with the rise during the eighteenth century of a colonial legal class and a trained bench.

The flexibility of colonial institutions was greatly aided by the division of the colonies into a dozen separate governments, which permitted a far greater number of experiments to be made than would have been possible had there been a single administration from Maine to Carolina. Although this political subdividing of the settlers had its obvious disadvantages in fostering a spirit of separatism, and in reducing at times the combined military strength of the colonies almost to a nullity, it had the advantage of permitting experimentation and of assisting the clarification of certain ideas.

Perhaps the most obvious example of the latter is that of the relation of church to state. In New Hampshire, Massachusetts and Connecticut the Congregational, or town, church was the legal ecclesiastical establishment to which the taxpayers were obliged to contribute support whether members of the congregation or not. In Rhode Island there was no establishment of any sort, and in New York the situation was an anomalous one. The

Dutch Reformed Church, as a legal establishment, had fallen with the Dutch government at the time of the English conquest. In 1693 the colonial legislature had finally been induced by English solicitations to pass an act establishing a church, but the act was of intention so vaguely worded as to leave it uncertain what church was established. In spite of efforts, the Church of England was never able to make its claim good and there was much confusion between the conflicting claims of the various sects. A somewhat similar situation prevailed in New Jersey where the crown had undertaken to establish the Anglican church by means of a royal decree. There were, however, no Anglican congregations and the provincial legislature never passed an act establishing that or any other church. In Pennsylvania and Delaware, which were separated in 1702, there was no establishment. In Maryland from 1692, and in the Carolinas, the Church of England became the state church, as it had been in Virginia from the beginning.

The most notable feature of the ecclesiastical situation was thus its extreme diversity. In America in 1700 none of the establishments had behind them that long history of achievement or service, the sentimental recognition of which may sustain an institution long after other props have fallen. Nor could the belief in a divinely appointed order fail to be regarded with scepticism in the face of such a heterogeneous jumble achieved by methods with which the colonists were all too familiar. There was still to be a long struggle for complete religious liberty, but at least there were forces at work tending to disintegrate the belief in the necessity or desirability of a union between church and state.

Just as the institutions briefly outlined showed local variety and yet a broad underlying uniformity, so also did the political framework into which colonial society was built. The units of local government in all the colonies had naturally developed from those with which the colonists had been familiar in England at the time of the beginning of emigration, but for a variety of reasons they had developed differently in different sections. Thus whereas in New England the town had gathered to itself functions performed in England by several local organs, so in the South the parish had developed in a similar way, and the town was there a later and always a much less effective division, as was also the county. As a result of the revolution in England and a somewhat altered colonial policy on the part of the mother country, there had been a number of changes in the framework of the several provincial governments, and by 1691 after some years of uncertainty in all of the colonies, and political upheaval in several of them, a new alignment emerged. Rhode Island and Connecticut resumed their charters and became once more practically independent republics. Pennsylvania and the Carolinas also retained their character as proprietary provinces, but New Hampshire, Massachusetts, New York, Maryland and Virginia were now all included in the list of royal governments.

It would be impossible in brief compass to give in detail the political structure of each of the colonies. Fortunately this is not necessary for our purpose, for in regard to the more important point as to the position of the people with relation to the governing power, they showed a marked similarity. In the dozen years or so following the Revolution in England there were changes made in the suffrage laws of every one of the colonies except Rhode Island. In all of them, of course, voting was limited to the male sex. In Massachusetts, based upon the charter of 1691, and in New Hampshire, under the act of 1699, the qualifications for a voter were identical, being the possession of a freehold estate of the value of forty shillings per annum or of a personal estate worth £50 sterling. Connecticut, in 1689, required a freehold estate of the same value in "country pay" but accepted in 1702 an alternative of a personal estate of £40. Rhode Island still only vaguely demanded that the voter should have a "competent estate" and be of "civil conversation." New York's requirements were identical with Connecticut's, the forty shilling freehold, which was the only qualification in 1691, having been made an alternative to a personal estate of £40 eight years later. In New Jersey by act of 1702 a voter was qualified if he owned fifty acres of which twelve were under cultivation; three acres and a house in a borough; or even if he only hired land provided that he had stock of his own valued at £50. Pennsylvania under the new act of 1700 required the same fifty acres of land with twelve under cultivation, offering as an alternative £50 personal estate but requiring a belief in Christ as the Savior of the world. In Maryland, by act of 1693, the requirement was fifty acres freehold or personal property amounting to £40. Although Catholics were not excluded from voting, the necessity of taking oaths precluded them from holding office. The Virginia act of 1699 definitely excluded them from the franchise and otherwise insisted upon a freehold estate as the only qualification. In North Carolina the requirements were uncertain, but in South Carolina the very loosely worded law of 1692 was altered in 1704 so as to limit the franchise to communicants of the Church of England possessing fifty acres freehold or a personal estate of £10. As a rule the requirements were still higher for an officeholder than for the voter. By 1700 it was generally recognized in America that, unlike the practice in the mother country, a member sent by the voters to the legislature should live in the district he represented.[1]

It is thus evident at the beginning of the century that,

[1] Hubert Phillips, *The Development of a Residential Qualification for Representatives in Colonial Legislatures* (Cincinnati, 1921), 244.

although a property qualification was the fundamental one, there was a tendency everywhere to broaden the suffrage by admitting personal property on an equality with land. Even so widened, however, the suffrage was an exceedingly limited one. In 1703, for example, out of a population of about seven thousand in Boston only two hundred and six voted for representatives. Throughout all the colonies the qualified voters were but a fraction of the adult male population, whole classes such as laborers, artisans, servants, fishermen, the smaller shopkeepers and others being automatically excluded. Limited as the suffrage was, however, it was a distinct advance over conditions in Europe, and by the end of the seventeenth century England had recognized the right of popular representation in the legislative branch of the government in all the colonies.

In each of them there was a governor and a legislature consisting of an upper and lower house. The governor, elected by the people in the corporate colonies of Connecticut and Rhode Island, was in the other colonies appointed either by the proprietary or the crown. In the two colonies just mentioned the upper house of the legislature was elected by the people, in Massachusetts by the lower house with the governor's consent as to each name, and in all the others was appointed in the same manner as the governor. In all of the colonies, however, the lower house was elected by the voters whose qualifications we have just considered. In most of the provinces the executive and judiciary were as yet beyond popular control and represented the external power of the British government.

As it was thus through the legislatures alone that the people could make their wishes felt, the story of the prerevolutionary years was, politically, to be one of persistent encroachment of the legislative upon the other two branches, dramatically shown by the constant struggles between the assemblies and the governors. This drama, played out in every colony with a royal governor, is so obvious that the characteristic political struggle has constantly been considered as one solely against external control. A study of conditions in the two colonies which elected their own governors, as well as a closer examination of the many influences at work in the others, indicate, however, that the struggle was not solely for home rule, but was incidental to a far wider movement designed to bring all power into the hands of the "people," understood in a steadily broadening sense. Not only do we find certain incidents of the contest repeated in the two corporate colonies in which there was no question of external control, but we also find economic grievances at work among certain classes and sections slowly tending toward expression in the form of political demands.

Voluntary organizations have been an increasingly important factor in American society. Of these we find scarcely a trace in the seventeenth century. The old guilds and labor organizations of England had been abandoned and no newer form had developed in their stead. Charity and education were functions either of the local governments or of individuals. Social clubs and artistic or scientific associations begin in a later period. There were no organized, or indeed sharply defined and continuing, political parties. On the one hand, certain social duties or obligations, such as education, were being grafted on to the governmental machinery. On the other, much was left to the individual which in the England of the day or later in America was assigned to some private corporate body. The great foundations, educational and charitable, of the old country had been left behind. The lack of accumulated wealth at this time in the colonies did not permit of new colonial ones. With the exception of a certain amount of group emigration to New England, the immigrants had all come as individuals or families, and time was required for a new social integration.

At the opening of our period, we thus have to deal with a widely scattered and mainly agricultural population leading a hard-working, narrow, parochial and sometimes dangerous existence in solitary farms, tiny hamlets, or at most in what would now be considered small villages. Few of these last, except in eastern Massachusetts and around Williamsburg, Virginia, were connected by even the shortest roads fit for wheeled traffic. It was a society in which all the conditions tended greatly to emphasize the solidarity of family life and that of the smaller political units. The collection of provinces with varied governments and religious beliefs was peopled by groups of differing nationalities yet, speaking broadly, all alike subject to the similar influences exerted by life in a new country and by fundamental similarities in the relations of the individual to his government. The eighteenth century was to be marked by growing differentiation in social and economic conditions, yet by an increasing tendency toward intellectual and political unity.

The young American society, or rather the collection of societies, which we have sketched only in broadest outlines, was closely articulated with others overseas. Indeed, these connections with other communities across the water were in many cases closer than those which bound the several continental colonies to one another. Politically, of course, all the colonies, island and continental alike, centered in England, and as there were no intercolonial political bonds there were no reasons for the New Englander and the South Carolinian, for example, to consider themselves as bound to one another in any closer relationship than each was bound to the Jamaican or Barbadian. Each was but a resident in an English colony, and the closeness of the relationship between any two of them could be based only upon the closeness of their social or economic ties. In fact there was far more intercourse between Boston and the West Indies, and between the West Indies and Charleston, than there was between Charleston and Boston. The absence of political ties binding a group of any of the colonies served to bring out more clearly the relationship of each to the only political entity of which it formed a part, the British Empire. That term, indeed, as used to include the overseas possessions, makes its first appearance in the decade we are discussing.[1]

With England herself the relations of the colonists were of the closest sort and embraced every field of political, economic and social life, although the closeness of these relations varied to some extent in the different colonies. She was not merely the source of protection, the seat of power, the center of empire, but was still "home" in the speech of all Americans of English descent. At the opening of the eighteenth century there was no fully differentiated American life, no American people. There was merely a loose group of English colonies in the West Indies and on the American continent. The latter possessed, it is true, certain fundamental institutions in common and were subject to certain common influences, but as yet they were without any common consciousness, common culture or even a vague premonition of a common destiny.

[1] See J. T. Adams, "On the Term 'British Empire'," *Am. Hist. Rev.*, XXVII, 485.

CHAPTER II

THE ECONOMIC BASIS

1690-1713

As we have already noted, the fundamental basis of the economic life of the colonies was agricultural. In England in the seventeenth century there was little that was scientific about farming methods and it was only after the middle of that century that improvements introduced from Holland were used and then sparingly and in scattered districts. In the colonies the fertility of the new land led to even more wasteful treatment than at home, and both in the North and the South the farmer thought it more profitable to move on, when possible, to new acres than to fertilize the old, either by the judicious use of certain crops or by that of manures. Nor was this due wholly to ignorance, for in all the colonies there were among the more wealthy and intelligent cultivators men who were abreast of the latest developments in Europe. Many books on agriculture were imported, among them such works as John Worledge's *The Mistery of Husbandry Discovered* and *The Art of Gardening*, both of which were sold by Micah Perry in Boston.

Everywhere, however, we hear the same complaints of the rapid wearing out of the soil and the need for bringing new lands under cultivation. These complaints were even more emphatic in the South, where tobacco proved an exhausting crop, than in New England where the soil itself was much poorer.[1] The Southern system of operating the larger estates by the employment of an

[1] A. O. Craven, *Soil Exhaustion as a Factor in the Agricultural History of Virginia and Maryland, 1606-1860* (Univ. of Ill. *Studies*, XIII), chap. ii.

overseer, who was paid by receiving a considerable percentage of the crop, was coming more and more into vogue about 1700, and this used up the soil with amazing rapidity as the overseer's only interest was to get as much out of it annually as possible with no thought of the future. After three or four years or even less, fields were abandoned to a second growth of woods, and new lands cleared from the virgin forest. In the older part of the settled South it was this constant need of enlarging the extent of cultivated lands, quite as much as speculation, which in this period created the demand for enormous estates.

The implements employed were few in number and almost wholly of types which had not altered for centuries. Spades were used to some extent but the almost universal instrument was the hoe, of several sorts and occasionally colonial made. The plows were heavy, clumsy wooden affairs, frequently, by the end of the century, shod with iron, and almost always drawn by oxen. The harrow was also used. Wheat was cut both with sickle and scythe, and apparently about this time the flail began to replace the treading of the grain by the hoof of the ox. The sieve for separating the chaff was also being introduced here and there, New England exporting these implements to the South. Not only were the methods employed wasteful of the land but the tools used were almost equally so of man power, and the physical effort required to cultivate a few acres would appall the modern farmer.

By the end of the century most of the vegetables and some of the grains and grasses with which the settlers had been acquainted at home had been introduced into the several colonies. Only a few years after the settlement of Pennsylvania, a writer there found "Wheat, Barley, Oats, Rye, Pease, Beanes, Squashes, Pumkins, Water-Melons, Musk-Melons and all Herbs and Roots that our

Gardens in England usually bring forth," and this list could be far extended.[1] It has often been stated both that potatoes were brought to America by the Scotch-Irish who settled in New Hampshire in 1719 and that they were not much used until the Revolution. Several writers, however, on New Jersey, Pennsylvania and Carolina speak of them before 1700 and they are so frequently mentioned in many of the colonies during the period covered by this volume as to indicate their common use.[2] More important as a food crop, nevertheless, was still the Indian corn, or maize.

Most of the English fruits, such as apples, plums, pears, cherries, peaches, apricots and quinces, were found in many varieties throughout the colonies, and in Carolina, figs, oranges and pomegranates were added to the list. In the latter colony a traveler reported peaches as so numerous that the principal use made of them was to feed them to the hogs. There were, indeed, large orchards in all the colonies, although they were apt to be neglected and little effort was made to improve quality. This was not always so, however, and Colonel William Fitzhugh's twenty-five hundred apple trees in Virginia were carefully grafted and tended as early as 1686. Three years later Judge Growden had a famous orchard of a thousand trees in Pennsylvania. In Rhode Island two new varieties of apple, the Yellow Sweeting and the Newtown Pippin, had been produced in the seventeenth century, and there was not a little scientific interest in fruit culture in New England in the opening years of the eighteenth.

[1] Nathaniel Crouch (pseud. R. B.), The English Empire in America (London, 1685), 111. Really, pumpkins and squash were indigenous to America.

[2] Thomas Ash (?) (pseud. T. A. Gent.), Carolina or a Description of the Present State of that Country . . . (London, 1682); same author, A Further Account of the Province of Pennsylvania . . . (London, 1685); Gabriel Thomas, An Account of Pennsylvania and West New Jersey (London, 1698)

Although the fields and gardens and orchards of all the colonies thus contributed in a more or less similar way to the food supplies of the settlers, nevertheless, before 1713, the southern boundary of Pennsylvania divided the seacoast into two quite distinct agricultural sections. North of that line there was a diversity of crops with no single staple, whereas to the southward the raising of tobacco in Maryland and Virginia and rice in Carolina dwarfed all other agricultural activity. It is true that in the early eighteenth century the tobacco raised in Connecticut had so far outrun the domestic demand as to become an article of export, and that, on the other hand, wheat was becoming an important factor in the exports of Virginia; but the distinction was a fundamental one and led in time to a marked social cleavage.

In New England, although the richer men were trying to accumulate land for speculative purposes and a unique community of very large farms was developing in the Narragansett country, what may be called the standard farm was a small one, made up of a comparatively few acres each of plowland, meadow and pasture in no constant proportions. Two factors tended to hold the raising of crops down to a mere subsistence level. One was the difficulty of securing labor at moderate wages, and the other the lack of a market for the produce, and this was true to a considerable extent of all the "provision colonies." In rural communities where even the minister and the occasional doctor "farmed it," and where there was little division of labor, there was no local market for the farmer's surplus as the only landless men were the servants or poor free laborers whose purchasing power was negligible or slight. The farmers within transporting distance of the larger villages or few towns had, indeed, some outlet. By 1698 in Pennsylvania, for example, Philadelphia held two markets a week, and

Chester, Germantown, Newcastle and Lewistown were also market towns, consuming some of the surplus produce of the immediate rural neighborhood.[1] But if division of labor has not proceeded far enough in the structure of society to create classes which are completely divorced from the soil, the farmer will have no broad market, prices will remain low, and there will be little incentive either for large-scale production or for the introduction of scientific methods. It is true that an export trade may replace the domestic market but Europe demanded none of the produce of the farms of the Northern colonies, and it was only the comparatively small intercolonial exchange which gave the farmer any market at all, outside his immediate neighborhood, until the expansion of trade with the West Indies. A most interesting "Invoys" for the town of Newbury, Massachusetts, in 1688, showing the property of its two hundred and sixty-nine citizens, gives the largest farm as one hundred and fifty-five acres, and the majority only from ten to thirty. Silvanus Plumer, for example, had a house, seven acres of plowland, fifteen of meadow and six of pasture. This, of course, was in one of the older and long settled parts of the colony but in the Northern colonies, even when the farmers owned several hundred acres, it is probable that they actually planted but a small part and that the rest remained in woodland or pasture.

In the staple colonies of the South, both tobacco and rice found their markets in Europe and although prices were at times disastrously low the position of the planter in relation to a market was entirely different from that of the small farmer of the North. Nevertheless, there, also, the average amount tilled was small, and if we may judge from such parts of Virginia as we now have accurate

[1] J. T. Scharf and T. Westcott, *History of Philadelphia* (Phil., 1884) I, 148.

figures for, the great majority of plantations were in reality small farms, comparable to those of the North, in spite of the large landholdings of individuals.   One of these, William Fitzhugh, described his plantation, when he was thinking of selling it in 1686, as a thousand acres, three hundred of which were "plantable" and seven hundred "rich thicket."   In another section of the county he had parcels aggregating twenty-three thousand acres additional, but of the whole twenty-four thousand only the three hundred named seem then to have been under cultivation.   He owned besides the large orchard already noted a mill, operated two stores, and possessed large numbers of hogs and cattle.   He was one of the rich men of the colony, yet had only twenty-nine slaves and a few white servants to help about the house, the plantation and his various enterprises.   In the next twenty years the enormous influx of Negroes, which we will discuss later, entirely altered the social and economic structure of the South; but, until that occurred, conditions in the North and South approximated one another far more closely than they have since then until perhaps our own day.[1]

In this earlier period, the farmer and planter, to a far greater degree than later, were also stockbreeders.   An epidemic in the South in 1695 is said to have carried off over a hundred thousand head of cattle, yet only a few years later in South Carolina travelers were amazed at the vast numbers and rapid increase.   The richer planters were credited with a thousand head and it was reported common for a man to have at least two hundred.   So rapidly did the half-wild cattle propagate in the woods that the colonial government found it necessary in 1703 to order hunters out to kill those that were unmarked. In Virginia large herds of wild bulls and cows roamed the forests and were hunted like elk or deer.   The lack of grass south of Maryland kept the cattle lean, and little

[1] "Letters of William Fitzhugh," *Va. Mag. of Hist.*, I.

effort was made to improve the breed which, unlike the pure bloods owned by the Swedish farmers of the Delaware, soon became indistinguishably blended. As we have noted, oxen were preferred to horses for much of the farm work and were probably more numerous. In the little village of Newbury, already alluded to, the farmers owned twelve hundred cows and calves, three hundred and fifty oxen and but two hundred and eighty-eight horses and colts.

Nevertheless, horses were rapidly rising in favor and in economic importance. In 1692 it was reported that about a hundred and fifty mares and some horses had been imported into Carolina from New York and Rhode Island, and that there was expectation of an excellent breed developing. In Virginia the number of wild horses running at large was almost as great as that of the cattle, and like the latter they were frequently hunted on horseback by the young Virginians with the aid of dogs. New England, however, was the great horse-raising district of the colonies. There, as elsewhere, there was little demand for the horse as a draught animal on the farm, the slower, stronger and less nervous ox being much better adapted for work on the rough lands. As the Indian trails from place to place began to develop into ways fit for horseback travel and even, here and there, into roads possible for clumsy wheeled traffic, the demand for the services of horses increased. Above all else, however, it was the export trade to the West Indies which rapidly stimulated the business of raising them. By 1700 this was going on throughout the entire New England area, and the importance of this sphere of the Northern farmer's labors steadily increased with the increase in the West Indian trade, tending gradually to become localized in particularly favored regions, such as the Narragansett country, the shores of the Sound and the upper Connecticut Valley.

Of the smaller farm animals, sheep, which were raised for their wool rather than for food, were exceedingly numerous in the North, the village of Newbury having about twenty-three hundred of them. Before 1690 mutton had been esteemed a rarity in the South but after that date the presence of sheep in plantation inventories becomes more frequent. Both north and south, hogs formed an essential factor in the farmer's economy, bacon being a principal article of export as well as of home consumption. There were not a few books for the stockraiser as well as the agriculturist, and as the raising of horses and sheep became more important probably many a copy of the recently published and handy little pocket volume, *The Countryman's Companion, or a new Method of ordering Horses and Sheep so as to preserve them both from Diseases and Casualties,* found its way to colonial shelf or mantel-corner. Butchering was an enterprise of neighborly coöperation.

In a day when the open fire was the only method of heating, and when coal was not as yet used in America, the wood-lot or trees in the commons were notable parts of the farmer's wealth. More important, however, from the standpoint of trade and of friction with the English government were the logging operations carried on all along the New England coast but particularly from Massachusetts northward. For a century or more the devastation of the forests in England had been proceeding rapidly. The amount of wood required for the iron trade alone was almost incredible, and early in the seventeenth century an iron master near Durham was accused of having cut over thirty thousand oaks during his life for his furnaces, and it was said that if he lived much longer he would not leave enough timber in the whole county to repair a church.[1] England was becoming de-

---

[1] T. E. Thorpe, ed., *Coal, Its History and Uses* (London, 1878), 232.

pendent upon the Baltic countries for her masts and naval stores but the magnificent forests of northern New England seemed to promise an alternative supply within the empire, and the mast fleet set sail annually for the supply of masts for the royal navy. All trees of a certain size not growing on lands granted to individuals were reserved for the crown and might be marked with the "broad arrow" of the king by the surveyor general. Not only, however, was shipbuilding becoming an important industry in America but the increase in the West India trade greatly enlarged the export demand for timber in various forms, and the depredations upon the "king's woods" were frequent and lawless, affording constant occasions of clashing with the royal officers. Not only were the loggers themselves an unruly lot but the capitalists and even the Massachusetts government connived at the felling of the royal trees for private gain. During the administration of Governor Samuel Shute of Massachusetts, Elisha Cooke, the leader of the "popular party" in that colony, propounded the convenient theory that the crown had no claim to the woods in Maine because that province had been privately bought by Massachusetts from the heirs of Fernando Gorges in 1677. The Massachusetts legislature created new towns in the wilderness for the purpose of making large tracts of land "private property" and thus circumventing the royal regulations. Most of the lieutenant-governors of New Hampshire were constantly breaking the law for their own advantage, and in the courts both judge and jury took the sides of the provincials in any case of depredation. By 1728 it was stated that scarcely any trees were still standing within six miles of the shore between Boston and the Kennebec, and the surveyors for the crown found themselves powerless to oppose the loggers, operators, and colonial courts and officials all leagued against them for the exploitation of the wilderness.[1] Imperial policy stood almost helpless in the face of local self-interest.

In the shadows of the forest there still lurked vast numbers of wild animals, or "vermin" as our ancestors called them, and the fur trade at the beginning of the eighteenth century was an outstanding economic factor, although it varied much in the different colonies, and the almost complete lack of statistics regarding it makes the task of determining its relative importance unusually difficult. In New England it had undoubtedly decreased from the days of early settlement but was still a source of wealth to some. The trade was almost wholly carried on through the medium of the Indian hunters, and in Maine the "trucking houses," where the whites met the natives and exchanged their goods for the red man's furs, were maintained throughout the entire colonial period. There is frequent mention of these, giving the impression of a trade of considerable volume. Even in the more southerly and better settled portion of New England neither the Indians nor the animals had entirely disappeared and a contemporary versifier wrote in 1720 of the Pequot country in Connecticut that

> Instead of Foxes, Wolves, and Hungry Bear,
> That oft the Massachusetts Herd do tear,
> Pequott has Beavers, Otter, and the wary Hare.[2]

It is possible to trace even in that section, and just before the opening of our period, the development of the fur trader into the overseas merchant. In 1650 Thomas Stanton had been granted the exclusive trade of the Pawcatuck River for three years. Some New London men became interested with him in the firm of Thomas Stanton & Sons and carried on a fur trade with the

[1] R. G. Albion, *Forests and Sea Power* (*Harvard Economic Studies*, XXIX), 256-259.

[2] *Connecticut's Flood on Merrymack's Ebb* (broadside, Library of Congress).

Indians. This was profitable and they tried business with Barbados. This also proved profitable and the firm developed as a West India house, Daniel Stanton later going to live there to represent the firm when its operations became more important and extensive.

Of all the colonies, New York was the most advantageously situated for the trade. That province had extended only to a slight degree into the interior and the white farmer had not displaced the Indian hunter. Within its borders dwelt the tribes known as the Five Nations who were united in the most powerful native combination on the continent, and who held the balance of power between the English settlers and the French of Canada. The beaver had disappeared from their territory by the beginning of the eighteenth century, but these Iroquois occupied the strategic position of middlemen between the white traders at Albany and the tribes in the Far West who brought skins for sale either to the French or English. For these western Indians to trade with the latter it was necessary to use the Five Nations as intermediaries but they could traffic directly with the French by means of the waterway of the St. Lawrence. Furs were the only goods which the savage could offer the whites in exchange for rum, guns and ammunition, and as the fur supply was scanty within the territory of the Iroquois it was to their advantage to divert as much of the western trade to Albany as possible. In this they were greatly aided by the fact that the English were able to purchase trading goods much cheaper than the French and therefore could give the Indians higher prices for their furs. Indian trade and Indian peace went hand in hand, and it was a matter of the utmost importance for all the colonies, from the standpoint of Indian policy, that New York, occupying such a position with respect to the most influential tribes of the continent, should do everything possible to foster the trade. This had naturally decreased to a considerable extent during the years of war preceding the Treaty of Utrecht in 1713, but it had become demoralized to an even greater extent on account of the short-sighted policy of the Albany traders. The low prices of English goods rendered it exceedingly profitable for the French to come to Albany, buy the goods, take them to Canada and use them in their own trade. The Albanians found this easier than trading with the Iroquois and greatly preferred lining their own pockets with the utmost speed and least exertion to pursuing a far-sighted, indeed an absolutely essential, policy with the savages.[1] Even a few years after the treaty it was said that they thus shipped from £10,000 to £12,000 worth of goods annually to Montreal, to the strengthening of the French alliance with the Indians and the weakening of their own. At the same time they were shipping about £8,000 a year in skins to England.

South of New York the trade was rather in deerskins than in beaver, and was pursued actively down to the Carolinas. In Pennsylvania it became more important later in the century and of the two hundred and fifty-three traders whose activities have been traced in that colony only fourteen are known to have been operating before 1713. In Maryland the Indian seems to have played little part in the trade, which mainly employed white men trapping in a small way for themselves, and which seems not to have exceeded about £600 or £700 a year. The trade in Virginia and the Carolinas, however, was much larger and involved serious intercolonial friction and contact with the French. By the end of the seventeenth century the Virginia traders were sending their pack trains as far as the Catawbas by way of the so-called "Trading Path," which extended four hundred

---

[1] Peter Wraxall, *An Abridgment of the Indian Affairs* (C. H. McIlwain, ed., *Harvard Historical Studies*, XXI), xlvi-xlviii.

miles into the wilderness.   One of these was William
Byrd the first, who, largely as a country merchant and
Indian trader, was then laying the foundations for the
fortune of his son who was to be one of the most distinguished planters of the next generation.   In 1715
Governor Alexander Spotswood organized the Virginian
Indian Company with a capital of £10,000 and a complete monopoly of the trade, but complaints to England
on the part of other traders forced the dissolution of the
concern.   The Virginians had to pass through the western parts of the Carolinas in order to reach the Indians
with whom they traded, and after the settlement of those
two colonies there was constant trouble over what the
Carolinians considered intrusion and what the Virginians
termed obstruction.   In defending himself to the home
government, Spotswood gave as one of the chief reasons
for forming the company and giving it a monopoly, the
fact that South Carolina was so persistent in interrupting
the Virginia traders on their way to the west that only
an important company would have the resources and
power to fight back.[1]   In 1705, the North Carolinians,
who depended largely on the trade, had complained that
the governor of their colony had engrossed it entirely to
himself and turned it into a business of slave raiding on
the natives.[2]   At that same time the traders from Charleston in South Carolina were said to be trafficking as far as
a thousand miles inland, and the town shipped seventy
thousand skins a year.

There can be no doubt of the enormous importance of
the trade from the standpoint of Indian relations in all
the colonies, but it is more difficult to gauge its economic
influence.   In 1719 James Logan estimated its value in
all the colonies at £40,000, and two years later a report to the British board of trade placed the figure for

---

[1] Alexander Spotswood, *Official Letters* (Va. Hist. Soc., *Colls.*, new ser.).
[2] W. L. Saunders, ed., *N. C. Colon. Recs.*, II, 904.

all furs exported from America at about £17,000 out of a total export trade of over £300,000.[1] Although the figures become more impressive later in the century, it must be remembered that just as there had come about as yet little clearly marked division of labor, so also there were few clearly marked distinctions in business. It is probable that not only was the fur trade of great importance in providing the settlers with much of their heavy clothing—a portion of the trade, it may be noted, which would not swell the export figures—but it was also one of the many minor ways that the settlers had of eking out a living. In some cases, such as the Stantons and Byrds, it was distinctly one of the main factors in founding fortunes later utilized for trade in the North and planting in the South.

As yet, no colonial fortune had been built upon manufacturing. The transporting of heavy raw materials by land routes was impracticable, and consequently a mill, forge or other plant could be advantageously located only at such points as united water power and water carriage, the latter both for raw material and finished product. These conditions combined with the colonial scarcity of skilled workmen at a time when the workman was of far more importance than the machine, the lack of accumulated capital seeking employment, and the ample opportunities for speculative exploitation of the country's resources in other forms, all tended to delay the establishment of manufactures. Iron forges had been started in several colonies quite early and were in successful operation in New Jersey before 1700 and soon after in Connecticut, Rhode Island and elsewhere. Spotswood and others, including Augustine Washington, father of the president, started forges in Virginia soon after the peace in 1713, and these were on a larger scale

[1] Cited by C. A. Hanna, *The Wilderness Trail* (N. Y., 1911), II, 321.

than anything else yet attempted in the colonies.[1]   On account of the amount of wood consumed for fuel, of which we have spoken, it was estimated that four square miles of woodland were required for every moderate sized furnace.   The amount of capital called for is indicated by the fact that one of these Virginia plants cost £12,000, including the furnace, over a hundred slaves for labor, fifteen thousand acres of forest, buildings, cattle and other necessaries.

As a rule, however, all attempts at manufactures were on a small scale, and the paper mills—such as the one early founded at Germantown—the grist mills, glass works, brickkilns, nail making, shoe making, the production of woolen goods and coarse cloths, the tanning of leather, making of candles, brewing of beer and a long list of other manufactures, each represented the investment of only moderate sums, and were carried on either in small plants or merely in the household.   The woolen industry in particular had made such important strides as to call forth hostile legislation from England in 1699, but none of these had reached the stage of large-scale production.   The total output undoubtedly added immensely to the comfort and aggregate wealth of the colonists, but the conditions of production and distribution did not yet permit of manufacturing being a rapid road to wealth.

Nor did the modest and somewhat amusing mining ventures of the day promise much more.   From the earliest days, searches had been made for the precious metals and occasionally false alarms were raised of their discovery.   Most of the mining was confined to bog iron ore, but at the beginning of the new century copper began to stimulate speculative interest and in 1707 a company was organized to operate a mine of that metal

[1] J. M. Swank, *History of the Manufacture of Iron in All Ages* (Phil., 1892), chaps. ix-xi.

which had been discovered at Simsbury, Connecticut. In typical New England fashion the technical management was placed in the hands of three clergymen who seem to have known more about the fires of hell than of smelting furnaces, and the enterprise languished, to be revived a little later under the management of New York and Boston business men. The difficulties of mining and transportation are well shown by the operation of the iron mines at Suckasunny in New Jersey where the ore had to be carried to the works in leather bags on horseback, and the finished iron by the same method over the Orange Mountains to Newark. There seems, however, to have been enough speculative interest in mining ventures to bring into the field the fraudulent promoter, and a company was projected which, according to their suggestion made to Stephen Sewall, was to "pretend by virtue of their charter to claim everything of that nature in the Plantations." [1] They offered Sewall an unlimited participation if he would further the scheme, but he proved honest and "spoilt the project." In 1704 William Byrd acquired several hundred acres near Manakin Town in Virginia, the "temptation" being coal, but although that fuel was beginning to be used in the forges of the smiths, it was to be several generations before the buried wealth of America's resources was to prove of commercial utility. As John Lawson reported of the Carolinas, "the Plenty of Wood (which is much the better Fuel) makes us not inquisitive about Coal Mines." [2]

Here and there, valuable mineral deposits of one sort or another were found and quickly worked for local benefit. In 1697, for example, limestone was found at Newbury, Massachusetts, and immediately thirty teams

[1] W. B. Weeden, *Economic and Social History of New England* (Boston, 1890), I, 396.
[2] John Lawson, *History of North Carolina* (London, 1718), 83.

a day were employed to cart away the stone for the making of building lime which before had been made wholly of sea shells.[1] All such operations, however, were either town affairs in which the material was free to all or else served to add to the income on a modest scale of the fortunate possessors of the land, much as a gravel or sand pit does in rural neighborhoods today. In the next period we shall find, as in manufacturing, a tendency toward larger-scale production, increased capital, and changes in method. In that treated in this chapter, no colonists made a fortune in mining any more than in manufacturing, although both added somewhat to the income of individuals and so helped the much needed accumulation of colonial capital.

In one industry, shipbuilding, there was an unusually favorable combination of raw material well located for utilization and of a ready market for the sale of the product. Consequently that business developed rapidly. Since the forests everywhere came down to the coast at this time, the building of ships was limited to no particularly favored localities until later in the eighteenth century. The small size of vessels employed even in the overseas trade, many of them only ten or twenty tons, permitted them to be built even at villages far up navigable streams, and thus we find ships being built in the upper Connecticut Valley. Occasionally they were built even at some distance from the water, as was the case with a vessel of ninety tons which was constructed on the common of Rowley, Massachusetts, and then hauled a mile to the water's edge by over two hundred oxen. Occasionally they were of considerable size, one as large as four hundred tons having been built at Boston in 1693.

Although New England led in the industry, boats were also built in all the colonies to the south, Virginia

[1] J. J. Currier, *Ould Newbury* (Boston, 1896), 421-423.

and South Carolina, however, finding it necessary to offer bounties. Between 1698 and 1701, in Maryland, which is usually thought to have possessed few vessels of her own, at least eighty appear in the naval office lists as locally owned. These were mostly built on the eastern shore. Fishing and the growing commerce of the colonies afforded a ready market for the building yards but in addition there was a steady and large demand from England for colonial-built ships. The names of many shipbuilders of the period have come down to us and occasionally we can follow the successful career of some of those who found the trade profitable. William Partridge, for example, contracted for ships on a large scale at Portsmouth, New Hampshire, grew in wealth and became treasurer and afterward lieutenant-governor of the province. All types of vessels of the day seem to have been built, and the colonial fleets included shallops, pinnaces, sloops, pinks, ketches, bilanders, brigs, brigantines, snows, ships and barks. That extremely useful vessel, the schooner, was purely a Yankee contrivance, the first being built at Gloucester by Captain Andrew Robinson in 1713. Although this industry was thoroughly established and highly successful before the Peace of Utrecht, the great increase in commerce and fishing after that date both made for a rapid development in shipbuilding, and like all other colonial business it entered upon a new era under the new conditions.[1]

In no branch of colonial enterprise was the change from the period we are now considering to the next more abrupt and marked than in fishing. That industry was for the most part limited to New England and mainly to Massachusetts. It had always been important both as a source of food supply and of com-

[1] John Robinson and G. F. Dow, *The Sailing Ships of New England, 1607-1907* (Maine Research Soc., *Publs.*, no. 1).

modities for overseas exchange, but from the Peace of Ryswick in 1697 to that of Utrecht in 1713 it had been in a languishing condition. This had been due to the advantages given to the French in the first treaty. Even as late as 1711 the fishermen of Massachusetts sent an address to the queen, thanking her for having provided a convoy for the fishing fleet and representing the great discouragement of the industry by reason of "the Fatall Miscarriage of Your Matys Glorious" design of reducing Canada.[1] On the coasts of Maine and New Hampshire fishing was almost wholly suspended, and the town of Salem saw its fishing fleet decline from over sixty ketches to only half a dozen. About the beginning of the period, in 1700, Bellomont reported to the lords of trade that Boston exported fifty thousand quintals of dried fish a year, of which three fourths went to Bilboa. As he gives the price as twelve shillings in New England, which was low as compared with previous years, and states that the shippers made a profit of fifty per cent on the direct Bilboa trade and a hundred per cent if their vessels returned by way of England with English goods, the trade would appear to have brought into that port a gain of from £15,000 to £30,000 annually, though this may well have been exaggerated.[2]

In merchandising, the main three channels of distribution were the shops, the markets and fairs, and the itinerant peddler. The first of these, the shops, formed the chief reliance of purchasers in the towns, except for food supplies, and by the beginning of the eighteenth century they had become fairly well differentiated as to the goods they sold, and need no special comment. In the country districts, the innkeeper was frequently the local merchant and his room contained that hetero-

[1] "Address of Massachusetts Fishermen to Queen" (n.d., endorsed Jan. 17, 1711-12), Colon. Office, Papers, 5, no. 10.
[2] E. B. O'Callaghan and B. Fernow, eds., *N. Y. Colon. Docs.* (N. Y., 1856-1887), IV, 790.

geneous jumble with which we are yet familiar in the "country store." In the South, however, the storekeeper was more apt to be a planter who frequently combined tobacco planting, stock raising, merchandising and the Indian trade, and who in a separate building on his estate kept a supply of the innumerable articles called for by those in the neighborhood who had no direct relations with England.

Owing partly to the objections of these merchants and partly to the scattered way of living, the use of markets, held several times a week and at which provisions and other goods were offered for sale under special conditions, did not obtain in the colonies south of Pennsylvania as it did from there northward, to some extent. The rules governing the markets were more or less the same in all cases, providing for a particular place where produce should be sold on certain days between hours named, and forbidding under penalty any dealer from buying until after the individual householders had had opportunity to make their purchases. The act establishing that in Boston in 1696 frankly stated that it was "principally intended for the benefit of housekeepers" and such markets undoubtedly facilitated the sale of country produce at reasonable prices and profits, although there was some fear on the part of the farmers that their being forbidden to sell goods at any other time and place might put them at the mercy of the town dwellers.[1] The fairs, which in some places were held from one to four times a year, were much like those in contemporary Europe and served as places for the exchange of goods for wider areas.

In the North, in the country districts, the itinerant peddler assisted in the work of distribution, much to the annoyance of the merchandising innkeeper and to the perpetual trouble of the authorities. But that the traffic

[1] *Acts and Resolves of Prov. of Mass. Bay*, I, 237.

was firmly established and served a genuine need is evidenced by the fact that it continued even when its total prohibition was backed up by such a heavy fine as £20, one half of which was to go to the informer.

The colonists had brought with them from Europe the belief that trade should be regulated by the governing power, and the statute books of all the colonies were filled with acts endeavoring to control one or another phase of the economic situation. In general, this mass of legislation was passed with a view to the benefit of the consumer rather than of the producer, and was directed toward controlling prices and quality of goods or services and securing an adequate supply of both for the community. In the attempts to keep down prices the efforts were crude, usually consisting merely in passing laws prohibiting sellers from charging more than specified prices for their goods, or workmen for their labor. Included in this group we may place the frequent laws as to weights and measures, such as the size and prices for loaves of bread. The efforts to define and protect standards of quality are somewhat more interesting, and the legislatures did not hesitate to restrict the workman's liberty of action with this end in view. In the attempt to maintain the quality of tanned leather, for example, Massachusetts passed an act forbidding butchers, curriers or shoemakers from being tanners, and tanners from engaging in any of these other trades. In the small colonial communities of the seventeenth century skilled workmen had not found enough work in their specialty to keep them busy and had had to turn their hands to other trades. Although this made for ingenuity and versatility, the standard of workmanship had undoubtedly deteriorated and at the beginning of the eighteenth century we find efforts to raise this by legally enforcing a division of labor.

The efforts to secure an adequate supply of goods

were directed either against their exportation—as by frequent embargoes of food stuffs at times of scarcity—or by offering inducements in the form of bounties, monopolies or exemption from taxation to stimulate their production.   The method of granting a monopoly to an individual for the public good had been an accepted one in England but had tended to fall into disuse there after the Restoration, and although it lingered long in America it often came into conflict with the spirit of individualism fostered by conditions there. Occasionally such conflicts reached the courts, and one of these cases, which we may cite, affords an interesting example of the conflict of the ideals of community interest when opposed to individualism at the opening of our period.   In 1683 a certain Pennsylvanian, Philip England, had been granted a monopoly of the business of keeping a ferry and inn at Schuylkill, one of the commonest forms of monopoly then granted in an effort to improve the means of travel.   Ten years later he complained that although he had spent much money in making landing places and buying canoes, nevertheless a Nathaniel Mullinax was ferrying people over at reduced rates and interfering with his business.   England asked for an order restraining him.   When interrogated by the court Mullinax replied that "most of the people of Harford and Marion, and some of Darbie, imployed and hyred him to ferrie them over, and that they were to pay him his wages, and that he knew no reason why he might not work for his Living as well as others." The court at once ordered him to jail until he gave security that he would ferry no more persons over, and the boats were seized until their owners should give like security.[1]

Many of the laws directed toward stimulating colonial production, such as the measures passed from time to

[1] *Minutes of Prov. Council of Pa.*, I, 437.

time in all the colonies, south as well as north, to encourage the production of wool, the weaving of cloth,
the making of hats, and so forth, were due to the poverty of the colonists and their inability to purchase these
articles in England, though both custom and fashion
led them to prefer the imported article when they had
money to buy it.   In spite of their being agricultural
communities and the extent of their household industries, the colonies were far from being self-sustaining,
and the articles imported from overseas were as numerous as they were varied.   Throughout the seventeenth
century and until well into the eighteenth, it was a constant struggle to find goods suitable for export from
America to pay for these imports.

Under the navigation acts all manufactured articles
had to be imported from England only, and in addition
to these the colonists had to meet their bills for slaves
and indented servants, for wines, for ocean freights, insurance and other matters.   In the direct trade between
England and the Northern colonies the balance was always and very heavily against the colonies, and even
in the case of the Southerners it occasionally went
against them on this direct business, being adverse in five
years out of the seventeen from 1699 to 1715.   When
to their purchases from England we add their slaves
and other imports from other sources it is easy to see
why the staple colonies as well as the Northern ones
were always hard put to it to find means to pay the
English merchants.   Here and there rich men might
have comfortable balances but for the colonists as a
whole it was a hand-to-mouth existence, and the necessary imports could be paid for only by the hardest
work and the display of much ingenuity in securing
the means of payment.

Locally, the needs of the small farmer in the country
were mainly met by barter at the country store.   He

would give his labor or some item of home produce or manufacture for the sugar or cap or bit of cloth imported from overseas. When these were insufficient he might go a little farther afield and take his produce to a market elsewhere, particularly his stock which could walk and thus avoid for him the problem of transport. Thus in the diary of Manasseh Minor, of Stonington, Connecticut, we read "sent My cow to Boston." [1] There was also considerable trade between the several continental colonies. In a description of the commerce of South Carolina in 1710 we find that that colony imported wheat, flour, biscuit, strong beer, cider, salt fish, onions, apples and hops from New England, New York and Pennsylvania, and in return sent thither hides, small deer skins, gloves, rice, pitch, tar and "slaves taken by the Indians in War." [2] Of the two hundred and fifty-nine vessels which entered at the port of Boston between May, 1704, and May, 1705, one hundred and forty-seven were from coast ports, including twelve from the Carolinas, fourteen from Virginia, twenty-three from Pennsylvania and twenty-five from New York. [3] The goods were sold on credit and the balances settled by bills of exchange provided by the larger merchants, such as Benjamin Faneuil of New York who advertised in the *Boston News-Letter* in 1708 that if any "merchants or others" who had money in New York wanted bills of exchange to remit to Boston he could supply them. [4]

Although this intercolonial trade was a source of profit and one of the innumerable ways in which capital was being accumulated as well as livings being made, it did nothing to solve the problem of paying for overseas imports in so far as the continent as a whole was con-

[1] Manasseh Minor, *Diary, 1695-1720* (n. p., 1915), 50.
[2] *A Letter from South Carolina* (London, 1732 [1st edn., 1710]), 17.
[3] Customs entries in *Boston News-Letter, passim.*
[4] Issue of April 26-May 3, 1708.

cerned. For this it was necessary to sell goods or services to communities outside the continent, and to an extent that would make up the difference between the value of the goods exported to England or other countries and the amounts imported from them. Otherwise the situation would too disastrously resemble that of the village in which the people lived by taking in each others' washing.

In developing such a trade the colonists were obliged to work within the framework of the navigation acts. These, in brief, required that all tobacco and certain other enumerated commodities be shipped to England only; that no goods, except wines from Madeira and the Azores and a few other articles, such as salt for the fisheries, could be imported from any country other than England or her colonies, without being landed in England first; and that all shipping must be either English or colonial manned and owned.[1]

Europe at this period had not become industrialized and as yet raised a sufficient supply for herself of the same food crops in the main as were raised in America, so that the only important agricultural market afforded there was the English one for consuming and distributing rice and tobacco. The European Catholic countries, it is true, did supply a large market for fish. On the other hand, the English West Indies, with a population which we may estimate in 1713 at a hundred and fifty thousand, of whom about one hundred and twenty-two thousand were slaves, demanded large quantities of horses, provisions and timber, which could be most easily shipped to them from the continental colonies. To these islands and Bermuda small vessels sailed forth from every port in America, carrying the refuse fish

---

[1] This is merely a very broad statement of the situation. There were several hundred statutes passed during the colonial period covering in detail the regulation of imperial trade, and altering it from time to time.

from New England for the slaves, shingles, coopers' supplies, planks, house frames, wheat, bacon, vegetables, horses and almost every article produced. Although the fish and horses went almost wholly from New England, the Southern colonies sent food in large quantities and even some household manufactures. South Carolina as well as the Northern colonies shipped to Curaçao, Barbados and the Leeward Islands pork, butter, tallow and myrtle-berry candles, cedar and pine boards, hoops, staves, barrel heads, as well as rice, pitch and tar. From the private docks of the Southern plantations and from the larger ports of the North, indeed from almost every village on ocean or stream, little vessels by the hundred were continually sailing or arriving from the islands. One of the most striking features of the trade was its wide distribution—and in the aggregate it must have been very large, for although the vessels were small they went heavily laden. For example in 1707, a merchant in Surinam gave orders for the building of a sloop at Salem which was to be nine feet deep, eighteen and a half wide, with a forty-five foot keel. This was to be loaded with sixteen horses "with long Tailes," fifty thousand oak staves, three thousand feet of boards, twenty-five barrels of onions, five thousand pounds of tobacco, the entire frame of another boat twenty-five feet long, and other items.[1]

In return for the goods carried to the islands, the vessels brought back sugar, molasses and currency or bills of exchange and other less important commodities. In many cases, however, circular voyages were made and the vessel instead of returning direct would sell the cargo, proceed next to the wine islands or Europe, purchase goods there and bring them back to the American continent. Others went to England first, thence to Africa

[1] John Robinson and G. F. Dow, *The Sailing Ships of New England, 1607-1907*, 16.

for slaves or the wine islands for wine, and on to the West Indies, where these would be sold and cargoes of West Indian produce or money be brought to America.

Men in remote villages were thus trading to the far corners of the world and learning the ways of a distinctly intricate commerce. As early as 1680, for example, George and Christopher Saunders at Windsor in the extreme northern part of Connecticut were already established as merchants trading direct from their little wharf on the river with England and the Indies. So energetic were such colonial traders and so great was the need for exchange with England that the English islands, great as was the market afforded by them, did not offer a sufficiently large one to take off all the surplus products of the continent, and the Americans found it necessary to trade with the French islands as well. This aroused the ire of the English West Indians who feared that such trading with their foreign competitors would tend to raise the price of the goods which the English islanders had to buy and lower that of those they sold. Consequently they brought every possible pressure upon Parliament in their efforts to force the government to confine the tropical trade of the continental colonies to the English islands only. During the wars this foreign island trade, although by no means suspended, had been illegal and the continental merchants had suffered in consequence. In this regard, as in so many others, colonial commerce was to feel the impetus given by the Peace of Utrecht.

This West India trade, including that with the French islands and a certain amount of clandestine trade with the Dutch and Spaniards farther south, together with the fish trade to southern Europe, seems just about to have enabled the colonists to keep their heads above water in paying their English balances. Some years it did not do so, and then the only way open to

them was to retrench their purchases and to live as far
as possible on home products and manufactures. As to
the average percentage of profit returned by the Indies
trade, it is impossible to estimate it with any accuracy.
That on goods imported from England at this time was
variously placed by contemporaries at from seventy to
one hundred per cent, even several hundred per cent by
occasional writers, but it is probable that from a third
to a half of this went in charges to England, insurance
and ocean freight. Even so, the overseas trades seem
to have been extremely profitable and it was almost
wholly due to them that liquid capital accumulated in
sufficient quantity to form the basis for a more varied
economic and a richer social life in the next period.

In that which we are now discussing, two temptations always lay before the astute and enterprising
traders and sea captains who were roaming the ocean in
their tiny craft and driving bargains wherever bargains
could be driven. One, of course, was the trade with the
French, which was illegal during the war but in which
profits had risen correspondingly; and the other was to
break the navigation laws in one way or another. This
might be done by trading with Scotland, by carrying
tobacco direct to the European continental countries, by
bringing French brandies or Holland goods directly from
their primary ports without calling at England, and in
divers other ways. We are without any statistics indicating the extent of this illicit trade for this period. The
fact that no colonial jury would convict in a smuggling
case renders the court records of little avail, and the
constant complaints of the English customs officers at
the close of the seventeenth century, such as Randolph,
are unsatisfactory testimony, and when individual cases
complained of by them are sifted down, the evidence
is not always very compelling. If, on the other hand,
we consider the character of the goods which are said to

have been smuggled from the continent, it would not seem likely that that portion of the illicit business bore a very large proportion to the whole body of legitimate trade—though this cannot be said of a later period. That there was a good deal of illegitimate trading at the time is, nevertheless, undoubtedly true.[1]

More serious at the opening of the eighteenth century was the situation with regard to piracy, both from the standpoint of public morals and of the fair trader. The peace of 1697 left numbers of privateersmen out of employment, and a swarm of desperate characters took to piracy and added to the number of those gentry who, war or no war, had always infested the seas to some extent. Had the pirates been merely parasites on society, forming an outcast class, the problem would have been one of extermination and the hazard merely another to be added to those of storm, shipwreck and other dangers of the sea. In many of the colonies, however, and notoriously in Rhode Island, New York and South Carolina, the pirates were leagued with merchants and officials ashore who shared in the gains and afforded protection. The English government attempted in vain to secure the coöperation of the provincial governments and finally in 1699 passed an act for the suppression of piracy, applicable to the colonies. In the letter of transmission to the Earl of Bellomont, then governor of New York and Massachusetts, it was said that this would teach those in New England that "where the public good does suffer by their obstinacy, the proper remedies will be easily found here," a statement of parliamentary authority which has frequently been overlooked.[2]

Bellomont's immediate predecessor in office and many of the leading families of New York were in league with

[1] G. L. Beer, *The Commercial Policy of England toward the American Colonies* (Columbia Univ. *Studies,* III), 107-108.
[2] *Cal. of State Papers, Colon., 1700,* 132, 164.

the pirates, and shared in the still more profitable trade
of supplying them with drink, ammunition and other
articles at their rendezvous at Madagascar. "When
Frederick Phillipp's ship and the other two come from
Madagascar," wrote Bellomont, "New York will
abound with gold." He added that wine which cost
but two shillings at New York sold at Madagascar for
£3, and that a pipe of Madeira which cost only £19
in New York had sold there for £300.[1] When the
protected pirates landed in the colonies, they swaggered
the streets with impunity, and the spending of the
money they brought and the cheapness of the captured
goods which they sold, brought them a following among
rich and poor. Although this phase of the situation became most acute about 1699, the pirates themselves as a
menace to commerce were of even more ominous importance in the next period, twenty years later.

The whole period which we have been discussing was
one of severe business depression for the colonists. It
was one of almost constant border warfare with the
French and Indians, of heavy losses, and, in the New
England colonies, of great additions to the public debt
and increase in taxation. We have already spoken of
the decline in the fisheries of that section. The West
India trade had also been adversely affected in various
ways, one of which was the low price of wheat in
England which enabled her to undersell the colonists,
and in 1701 Philadelphia reported that this trade was
dead. Inability to market their crops at prices which
gave a fair return, was nearly bankrupting the tobacco
colonies of Maryland and Virginia, and the cattle epidemic had temporarily distressed great numbers of the
smaller farmers. Everywhere there was great econo-
mizing, with the consequent stimulation of household
industry and decreased profits for the merchants. With

[1] *N. Y. Col. Docs.*, IV, 532.

the return of peace in 1713 the outlook and conditions rapidly changed, and there followed twenty years of great expansion and overinflation in currency and speculation. Before continuing the story in that aspect it is first necessary to consider some of the other elements in the life of the colonists at the opening of the new century.

CHAPTER III

THE ARISTOCRATS
1690-1713

FROM the very beginning of settlement there had been marked social distinctions between the colonists. Those who came as immigrants in every decade differed among themselves in wealth, family position, education and the various means of acquiring and maintaining influence. Although the icing may be said to have been left off the American social cake owing to the fact that none of the titled members of the aristocracy came as permanent residents, that merely created a vacuum in the accustomed social structure which was immediately filled to their own satisfaction by those whose claims or aspirations, buttressed by native ability or acquired capital, enabled them to rise to the top.

Compared with a later age or even with the England of the later Stuarts, the differences in social classifications were, indeed, slight. Instead of ascending by a multitude of gradations from the plowman or artisan through the yeomanry, several grades of gentry, large county families and a half dozen ranks of nobility to a duke, one climbed from indented servant to the middle gentry, and there one abruptly stopped. There never was an aristocracy, speaking strictly, in the colonies and perhaps never more than a few score at most of genuine aristocrats permanently domiciled there. Nevertheless, the term in its denatured form is a convenient one to use for colonial social figures of a certain type, for what is frequently, and obviously incorrectly, referred to as the colonial aristocracy was something more than a plutocracy. Breeding, learning, length of residence, political control and other factors all combined to establish a social position based upon something more than mere wealth. The fact, however, that the entire population of the colonies, English or foreign and practically without a single exception, were from the middle or lower classes was a social fact of great importance.

This abbreviation of the social scale did not prevent such distinctions as there were being taken with extreme seriousness. "Mr." and "Gent." were insisted upon in life and carved upon the tombstone in death. Place at table, position in the college class room in New England, seating in church, and many other minor matters were regulated with a nicety of regard for social status that was equaled only by the minuteness of the differences upon which it was based. This was probably due to the extreme rarity of the social atmosphere. Frontier existence always tends to obliterate certain aspects of social cleavage. In its simplest form, that of a wilderness which must be subdued by the hand of man and from which a subsistence must somehow be wrung by physical toil, claims of social consideration grounded on conditions existing in the country left behind suffer short shrift. Even the power of money goes under a partial eclipse where money no longer can buy service and where everyone works for himself. The trappings of every sort which in the complex society of the older settlement covered one so comfortably, and perhaps disguised one so conveniently, tend to fall away or be pulled off, and leave one socially naked to the critical eyes of one's fellow pioneers; and one clings to such shreds as may remain.[1]

In the first two generations of settlement along the

---

[1] D. R. Fox, *Caleb Heathcote, Gentleman Colonist* (N. Y., 1926), chap. i.

coast, this frontier tendency toward social denudation had been operative to a considerable extent, but had also been offset to some degree by the strong inherited sense of social stratification which the settlers had brought with them from Europe. Moreover, many of the leaders of the first settlements had been worthy pioneers as well as socially superior to the bulk of the colonists in their respective settlements. In addition, during the earlier part of the seventeenth century the enforced simplicity of life in America prevented to a large extent that flaunting of the advantages of wealth and privilege which is more irritating to the common man than the mere knowledge of their existence.

In a new country the possibilities of making a fortune are by no means commensurate with those of making a living. It might in a sense be true, as Franklin said a half century later, that any man who could bait a hook or pull a trigger could get food in America, but this brought him no nearer to becoming a mercantile magnate or an opulent planter. For that he needed political influence with the authorities, the luck of inherited capital or the always rare ability to acquire it rapidly for himself. For the first, he had in some way to gain access to official circles, which was not easy without some money or social position to begin with. For the last, the way then as always was much easier for those who had some capital to start with than for those who had none. This was obviously true of the increasingly mercantile North, and in the change soon to come over the agricultural South the way to wealth lay through the control of slave labor, and slaves cost money. By the first decade of the eighteenth century, therefore, the possession of money in the older seaboard settlements was becoming more effective, and the differences between the man who started with advantages and the man who did not, more definite and more fixed. On the other hand, the democratic and leveling tendencies of the frontier were also becoming more effective than had been the case earlier because the new frontier was two steps removed from the life of old England instead of one, and because the leaders of colonial life no longer lived among the people there but remained behind in the more comfortable seaboard districts.

The most important social figure in most of the colonies was the royal governor. In closer touch with the home country than the colonists because of his being a mere sojourner, frequently a member of the nobility with the glamor of a title and familiarity with London society, always, owing to his position, the source of political, social and frequently economic advancement, the governor himself and the "governor's set" naturally occupied the leading place in the social life of the provinces. Occasionally, as in the case of such a bankrupt rake as Lord Cornbury, the influence exerted was unmitigatedly bad. On the other hand, with governors of the better type, such as Spotswood of Virginia or William Burnet of New York, their culture, their close connection with the social or intellectual life at home and their genuine interest in the colonies which they governed, enabled them to bring to a focus in their small circle those ideals of a polished society that are lacking in the life of any new community concerned of necessity mainly with rapid commercial exploitation.[1]

At the opening of the eighteenth century two of the professions were in an interesting transition stage with regard to differentiation and social status. Throughout all the colonies it was customary for litigants to be represented in court by attorneys in fact but there was a strong feeling against attorneys at law, not seldom

---

[1] E. B. Greene, *The Provincial Governor in the English Colonies of North America* (*Harvard Historical Studies*, VII), 49. Jefferson in his "Notes on Virginia" testifies to the cultural influence of Governor Fauquier.

leading to statutes inimical to their pursuing their calling. This was true even in Maryland where they rose to prominence earlier than in any other colony. In 1700, and perhaps down to the Revolution, there was scarcely a single well educated colonial lawyer in all New England or, with a few brilliant exceptions, in New York. In the period covered by this chapter, the Marylander, Andrew Hamilton, who became attorney-general in Pennsylvania and whose later reputation was to become not only intercolonial but international, was first rising into prominence. The Welshman, David Lloyd, was also doing much in the Quaker colony to develop its crude legislation into a system of jurisprudence. At the beginning of the century, however, there was neither large fortune nor high fame to be won at the bar. Consequently that absence of specialization which is characteristic of all colonial life at this period is noticeable here as alsewhere. In Connecticut, for example, attorneys at law seem to have been first authorized in 1708, and such men as Roger Wolcott, Thomas Welles and Edward Bulkeley were admitted to the bar, but Bulkeley's grist and fulling mills were his primary concern, and the law occupied but little of the time of the others. In Virginia, William Fitzhugh had received a professional training in England and practised actively after coming to America, but his wealth and social standing were derived rather from his occupations as merchant, shipper and planter than from his legal work.

The period we are considering was one of transition in the medical profession as in so many other phases of colonial life. In New England it had early been the custom of the clergy to minister to the bodily as well as the spiritual ills of the parish and to apply mustard or hell fire according to the need. To the southward, the owners of large plantations included the care of their slaves, servants and poorer neighbors in their multifarious duties, and everywhere the women of the households practised the simpler forms of physic. Nevertheless, physicians who occupied themselves either mainly or wholly with their profession were becoming numerous. It is notable, however, that most of the leading men were not American-born but newcomers from Europe. Thus one of the ablest men who were connected with the profession was Dr. John Mitchell, a member of the Royal Society, who came to Virginia in 1700.[1] Dr. William Douglass, educated at Leyden and Paris, arrived in Boston in 1718. Dr. Cadwallader Colden, educated at Edinburgh, emigrated to Philadelphia a few years earlier, later moving to New York where he had a distinguished career as one of the most intellectual men in the colonies. The French were found practising in many places, and Doctors Porchier of Charleston, South Carolina, Jerauld of Medfield, LeBaron of Plymouth, Massachusetts, Pigneron of Newport, Rhode Island, and Gaudonnet of Newark, New Jersey, were only a few of those practising and teaching their apprentices along the whole seaboard. There were some native-born, however, such as Jared Eliot of Connecticut and Zabdiel Boylston of Massachusetts, who rose to prominence. The fame of both of these lay still somewhat in the future in this period.

If we can judge from the bills of a certain Dr. John King down in the Albemarle the physicians in the Carolinas did not do badly, as he seems to have charged ten shillings a visit. In 1702 a resident of Germantown wrote to Germany that a "student of medicine that well understands surgery . . . should find rich rewards of his money as soon as he had mastered the English language," and in the same year a traveler in Virginia reported that "doctors and surgeons are well-to-do and have a large

---

[1] Lyman Carrier, "Dr. John Mitchell," Am. Hist. Assoc., *Rep. for 1918*, I, 201-219.

income." [1] A decade earlier a doctor had been referred to
in the latter colony as "a considerable dealer here and an
able Practitioner in Physick, both laudable and profitable employs." [2] The more eminent men, however,
seem to have been less well satisfied. Not long after
their respective arrivals in Boston and New York, Douglass wrote to Colden that "you complain of the practice
of Physick being undervalued in your parts and with
reason; we are not much better in that respect in this
place; we abound with Practitioners though no other
graduates than myself." [3] "I have here practice," he
wrote in another letter, "amongst four sorts of People;
some families pay me five pounds per annum each for
advice, sick or well, some few fee me as in Britain, but
for the Native New Englanders I am obliged to keep a
daybook of my consultations, advice and Visits, and
bring them in a bill; others the poorer sort I advise and
visit without expectation of any fees." [4] Although we
still find frequently the combination of the pursuits of
clergyman, planter, farmer, lawyer and various political
offices such as sheriff with medicine, nevertheless the
physician is clearly beginning to emerge as an independent entity and, at least in the case of men who were
particularly successful, to occupy a social position of some
eminence due solely to success in his profession.

The clergyman had always done so, though his established position varied much in the different colonies, and
had been highest in New England. There, indeed, Cotton Mather was beginning to note mournfully how times
had changed since the people used to regard their ministers as "Angels of God" and how reverently they had

---

[1] Pa. German Soc., *Proceeds.*, XVIII, 1; "Journey of F. L. Michel,"
Virginia Magazine of History and Biography (to be cited as *Va. Hist.
Mag.*), XXIV, 287.
[2] *Va. Hist. Mag.*, IV, 71.
[3] Mass. Hist. Soc., *Proceeds.*, ser. 2, I, 44.
[4] Topsfield Hist. Soc., *Colls.*, XVI, 7.

formerly wished to have them provided for.[1] At the end
of the century he was right in believing that conditions
were altering and that many things had combined to
lower the prestige enjoyed by the clergy. In the South,
although there were, of course, many earnest men in the
church, nevertheless, it was too often considered in England that an inferior type was good enough to send out
to the colonies, and in many a parish the cloth received
no more respect than it deserved. In the Puritan colonies
of the North, the first fervor of religious enthusiasm had
long since evaporated, and the growth of other interests
tended to dislodge the ministers from the remarkable
position of leadership which they had occupied. It must
be confessed, moreover, that in the latter portion of the
century they had lamentably failed in the trust accorded
them, and by their attitude at the time of the Baptist and
Quaker persecutions and the witchcraft delusion, they
had lost enormously in influence. In the earlier decades
of settlement, the earnest and more or less intellectually
inclined New Englander who aspired to be a leader in
the community naturally turned to the pulpit as the seat
of power. With the broadening and secularizing of the
public mind, however, and the alluring opportunities for
the acquisition of wealth, men of marked ability tended
more and more to remain in secular life and to devote
themselves to business pursuits or to the nascent professions. As yet politics, other than royal officeholding;
offered no separate career.

More illuminating than the never very dependable
laments of the clergy is an example of a natural leader
who thus turned aside. In 1680 William Reed, a large
Connecticut land owner, had a son born who at first
promised to carry out the New England tradition. The
lad went to Harvard, graduated in 1697 and began to fit
himself for the ministry. He preached at East Hartford

[1] *The Good Old Way* (Boston, 1706), 70.

and Stratford for ten years but became greatly interested
in the law, and when the act of 1708 was passed was
admitted to the bar, and not long after was appointed
queen's attorney for the colony. In 1721 he moved to
Boston and became in turn the most noted jurist in that
colony, and the oracle of the council. Meanwhile, in
settlement of the intercolonial boundary dispute, Massachusetts had ceded to Connecticut one hundred and six
thousand acres known as the "Equivalent Lands," which
were sold for the latter colony by William Pitkin, the
commissioner, to a company of whom young John Reed
was one. The sum realized for the colony was only
£683, which created a scandal. Reed's share of the
purchase was ten thousand acres, which he developed
as an English manor, leasing the lands only and refusing
to sell any. Through inheritance and purchase he came
to have immense holdings and when he died in 1749
left vast estates in Connecticut, Massachusetts and New
Hampshire. In the career thus briefly outlined of the
studious lad, the young clergyman, the lawyer, crown
official, speculator and finally man of large business affairs, we can sense the change that was coming over the
life even of New England, and the magnetic attraction
of the vast potential resources of the continent.[1]

In all the colonies, land and ever more land was the
goal of those who wished to advance in the most rapid
way possible both their financial and social position.
For this, influence in the right quarter was absolutely
essential. It is a mistake to think that large landholdings were common only in the colonies from New
York southward and that all the corruption was in
royal officials. In the deal of which we have just spoken
in connection with the Equivalent Lands, such men as
Gurdon Saltonstall, Paul Dudley, Thomas Fitch, An-

---

[1] W. A. Beers, "John Reed, the Colonial Lawyer," Fairfield County
(Conn.) Hist. Soc., *Fifth Anniversary Volume*.

thony Stoddard and Addington Davenport were joined
with Reed to secure from the colony of Connecticut the
enormous tract of over a hundred thousand acres at the
even then absurd figure of about one pence half penny
an acre. To mention another case in the Puritan colony
of Connecticut, we find Major James Fitch in possession of almost the whole of Windham County which
had been transferred to him as guardian for the Indian
Owaneco. The interest of the redskin, however, seems
to have been lost to sight in the dispute over the title
between Fitch and the Winthrops. In 1706, the general court began to make grants in the disputed area
and Fitch moved rapidly to realize on his holdings
before the court could act. In 1707 he sold one tract
of fifteen miles square to a group and a little later another tract of over twenty-one thousand acres to others.
The elected legislature of that semirepublic was almost
as complacent at times to its favorites as were royal governors, and in 1714 it gave a quitclaim deed for over
ten thousand acres to Simeon Stoddard.[1]

For the acquisition of a rapid fortune in land merely
by standing well with the powers that be, New York
offered a rich field. Among Governor Fletcher's grants,
for example, was one to his favorite and right-hand
man, Captain John Evans, of an area of indeterminate
extent of between three hundred and fifty and six hundred thousand acres, at a quitrent of only twenty shillings a year for the whole, for which Evans alleged he
was later offered £10,000 in England. Bellomont indeed asserted that nearly three quarters of the available
land in the province had been granted to about thirty
persons, many of poor character, before Fletcher finished. Lord Cornbury's grants while governor from
1702 to 1708 were equally extravagant but were made

[1] E. D. Larned, *History of Windham County, Conn.* (Worcester,
1874), chap. xxii ff.

to companies of speculators rather than to individuals. They included such grants as that of the "Little Nine Partners" of ninety thousand nine hundred acres, Wawayanda of three hundred and fifty-six thousand, and Great Hardenburgh of two million acres, and were so loosely worded that sometimes the original intention as it appeared was so stretched as to result in claims of a hundred times the original acreage. Colden cites one ostensibly for three hundred acres under which sixty thousand were claimed later.[1] In the Southern colonies, more particularly Maryland and Virginia, political influence resulted in enormous grants to favored individuals, such as sixty thousand acres to Charles Carroll, and there were large grants in Carolina, in addition to the "Baronies," of twelve thousand acres each. The same influence which secured the grants also resulted in many cases in evading completely the payment of quitrents.

As has already been said, access to official society was a prerequisite to the securing of this influence, and as that society was comparatively limited, intermarriage among its members became increasingly frequent and everywhere added its weight to the building up of local aristocracies of wealth. The financial standing of their members thus increasing also enabled them to strengthen their position as merchants. In all the colonies, the councils were almost wholly made up of the members of these small aristocracies, or plutocracies, and as the suffrage was very limited, their influence extended to the assemblies as well. By means of their large land holdings, their possession of a considerable portion of the cash capital of America, their position as merchant creditors of the smaller people, their control of the councils, and their privileged situation with regard to the dispensers of patronage and favors, as well as the more

[1] C. W. Spencer, "The Land System of Colonial New York," N. Y. State Historical Assoc., *Proceeds.*, XVI, 150-164.

intangible influences always appertaining to a distinguished social position, the aristocrats by 1700 were fastening a firm grip both upon the political management and commercial exploitation of the New World.

About this time, the standing which they had attained, as well as the gradual enrichment of colonial resources, enabled them to increase the amenities of their existence, and the life they lived was one of very considerable charm. In many of its outward and visible trappings, however, it was as yet set off from the life of the somewhat less fortunate members of the community to only a moderate degree, as compared with a generation later. The contrast in size and type of dwellings, for example, was modest as compared with the period after 1720 when the introduction of the Georgian style and the increase of wealth permitted the building of the "great houses" both north and south. The architecture of the well-to-do was still strictly "colonial." It was of the type which had been known to the settlers in their native lands, occupied there by people of similar standing, and modified by the new local conditions.

In New England about 1700 the old type of lean-to, with its long sloping rear roof, tended to give place to one of full two stories. Brick was used to some extent in such towns as Boston where an unsympathetic observer noted that "the Buildings like their Women" are "Neat and Handsome, and their Streets like the Hearts of their Male Inhabitants, are Paved with Pebble." [1] Brick was rarely used in the country, however, and stone practically never, the lack of good lime, as well as the belief that such houses were not suited to the climate, acting as deterrents. Medieval English features, such as the overhang, were still retained, and the style was often the picturesque and rambling one which is familiar to us

[1] Edward Ward, *A Trip to New England* (G. P. Winship, ed., Providence, 1905), 38.

in the House of the Seven Gables.[1]   The better class houses were clapboarded, with shingle roofs, unpainted and severely plain.   In those which did not wander off into little additions and afterthoughts, beauty was a matter of proportion only.   In the Dummer house erected in 1715 we get one of the earliest hints of the coming change to Georgian, just at the close of our period.   This house was built for a wealthy family and gives us an idea of what a "modern" mansion for a New Englander of position was at that date.   It is perfectly rectangular, two stories and an attic, with five windows in front, two in the gable ends, and three dormers in the attic.   There is no porch, a feature rarely met with in this period, but the new elaborateness of the ornamentation of the doorway must have given it distinction in its day.   In our own time, it might be the home of a small farmer in comfortable circumstances.

In the Middle colonies, the styles were markedly influenced by the nationalities of the builders, and Dutch, Welsh, Germans and Swedes have left fascinating traces of their work and national predilections.   Stone and colonial-made brick were both much used, and in the little town of New York many of the houses were placed gable end to the narrow streets, some "very stately and high" with bricks of divers colors laid in checkers.   In the country the use of varied materials and the low sweeping roofs lent a charm and struck a note of appealing domesticity.   The larger houses were merely larger, for the most part, and in no way aimed at grandeur or flaunted the superior wealth of their inmates. Such survivals as the Welsh "Wynnestay" in Philadelphia or the German "Wyck" at Germantown, both dating from about 1690, and precursors of what is known as the Pennsylvania colonial farmhouse type, bespeak

[1] *Cf.* T. J. Wertenbaker, *The First Americans* (*A History of American Life*, II), chap. xiv.

the excellent craftsmanship of their builders and the solid comfort of their indwellers. There is an utter absence of pretension or of aim at effect which is characteristic of all the architecture of the period. Throughout all the North even the largest houses would be considered of very moderate size today, and probably few could boast of more than eight rooms at most.

In the Southern colonies this would also seem to have been true of most of those owned even by the wealthiest planters, although none of the largest houses of authentic date in this period have been preserved. The difference in climate, however, largely influenced the architecture in many minor ways. The chimneys, which in New England were built wholly within the house to keep in as much heat as possible, were placed at the ends in the South, just as the entry hall which in the North was small with the stairway frequently enclosed to prevent drafts, was broad and open in the South, tending to become a feature in the building. If we accept the date of 1712 as a possible one for "Tuckahoe," the seat of the Randolphs on the James River, that house, one of the few large frame ones in the tidewater section, would fall within our period, and in that mansion, elaborate for the times, we find ten rooms in addition to the hallways. William Fitzhugh, speaking of his own house, which he described in 1686 as "furnished with all accommodations for a comfortable and gentile living," said of the rooms that "four of the best of them" were "hung and nine of them plentifully furnished with all things necessary and convenient." [1] The kitchen was in a separate building and there were numerous outhouses of various sorts.

The smaller houses were frequently, if not generally, of wood but the larger ones after 1700 were almost invariably of brick, usually colonial-made but occasion-

[1] "Letters of Wm. Fitzhugh," *Va. Hist. Mag.*, I, 395.

ally imported.   In one respect the houses of the aristocrats were no better than the log huts of the pioneers—
there was no plumbing.   Sanitary arrangements were of
the simplest, and baths must have been of the scantiest.
Tubs for that purpose were unknown in America for a
century and a half after our period, and even large vessels are disconcertingly absent.   In the summer the young
men and boys went swimming and the number reported
drowned while thus "washing," as it was often called,
was not inconsiderable.   There is no record of feminine
bathing.

Such mansions as those spoken of above marked the
very summit attained by wealth in the colonies at this
time and although the contrast was not as striking as
that to be noted later, they were beginning to afford one
to the houses of the poor and the pioneers which we
shall note in the next chapter.   This contrast extended
to the furnishing with the same qualification.   When the
first William Byrd was building "Westover" in 1690,—
not the beautiful "Westover" of thirty years later but
the first house which marked his advancing fortunes,—
he ordered his correspondent in Rotterdam to send him
bedsteads, curtains, looking-glasses, tables, some Rússian
leather chairs and other furnishings, which he noted
with quite a New England spirit of frugality were "to
be handsome and neat but cheap." [1]   This importing of
household gear was characteristic of all those, North and
South, who had the wealth to do so, though the furniture was of English rather than of Dutch origin.   From
the cabinet-makers of London went forth a steady stream
of beautiful pieces—desks, highboys, chests, chairs, bedsteads—in oak, walnut, olive wood, lacquer or mar-
quetry to the houses of the rich in all the colonies.   The
introduction of mahogany just at this time was to prove
of marked influence on the style of eighteenth-century

[1] Col. William Byrd, *Writings* (J. S. Bassett, ed., N. Y. 1901), xxxi.

furniture, its strength permitting more delicate, even lacelike, carving, and from 1708 onward we find these new pieces taking their places somewhat slowly in company with the older ones in luxurious homes. With the beginning of the century also, china began to replace pewter on the tables, and as another indication of the refining of manners, forks, which had been laughed at as little instruments "to make hay with our mouths," came at last into general use among the genteel. Self-indulgent comfort was also increasing, and from about 1700 we can date the substitution of the upholstered wing "easy" chair for the somewhat Spartan wood or hard leather seats.

The furnishing of the homes of the rich and even the merely well-to-do at this time was indeed not only comfortable and in excellent taste but even extravagant. On the Tooboodoe Plantation of Joseph Morton in South Carolina, the inventory at the time of his death in 1723 shows the furniture in the "best chamber" as worth £195, that in the dining room as £126, in the parlor as £135, and in the other rooms to correspond. His linen was worth £217 and his silver plate £600. The last, of course, was not merely for ostentation but was generally considered as an investment or, as William Fitzhugh wrote to his London correspondent, it "gives myself the present use and credit, is a sure friend at a dead lift without much loss or is a portion for a child after my decease." [1]

Except in the very greatest houses, the small number of rooms still precluded too rigid a differentiation as to use, and we not infrequently find beds inventoried in halls in the South and in parlors in the North. The bed, indeed, both as to its high massive carved frame and costly hangings, and the feather mattress and pillows, was one of the most valued possessions in the

[1] *Va. Hist. Mag.*, II, 271.

house.   Springs for the beds, it may be noted, were unknown until well into the nineteenth century.   Carpets
had not yet come into use for floor coverings and the
"Turkey carpets" so often inventoried were merely table
covers.   Nor was wall paper introduced until the next
period, but in the houses of the very rich the walls were
hung with tapestry, frequently of considerable value.

In the year 1718 we have the inventory of the effects
of the ex-pirate, Captain Giles Shelley, of whom Bellomont had written in 1699 that he had "come lately from
Madagascar with 50 or 60 Pirates" and had "so flushed
them at New York with Arabian Gold and East India
goods that they set the government at defiance." [1]   With
the riches acquired in that profession, less what the authorities had taken from him from time to time, Shelley
later settled down to live at ease in the tolerant "Sion" at
the mouth of the Hudson.   The present writer is con-
vinced that one hour spent in drinking drams with the
genial old buccaneer would have told him more of colonial commerce than all of the monographs yet published.   The captain, moreover, was expectant of guests
for among his household goods were forty-five beer
glasses and no less than seventy chairs, among the latter
one of the new easy chairs, then coming into vogue, and
a cane couch.   That he was fond of novelties is shown
by the presence of two sconces, still somewhat scarce in
the colonies, although the lighting, of course, was as yet
done by candles.   A few Dutch stoves were in use, but
the customary heating for the houses of rich and poor
alike was from the open fire, and in Shelley's a "brass
hearth with hooks for shovel and tongs" reflected the
light from the blazing logs.   Over the mantel was "one
landskip chimney piece," for the former buccaneer seems
to have had a pretty taste for art and had seventy-four
pictures in all, perhaps the distinguishing feature of his

[1] N. Y. Col. Docs., IV, 551.

house. Some of the furniture was painted and, with the gay colors of the many cushions used on the wooden chairs, the curtains at the windows, and paintings or prints on the walls, must have lent a certain cheerfulness if not gayety to the occasionally somber thoughts of the captain. His pipe of canary in the cellar, his punch bowl, silver chafing dish, and gaming table for dice, all may have helped also. In his dashing about in the near neighborhood of town, where an improvement in the roads was beginning to permit such excursions, he may have driven his two fine coach horses over to the home of Colonel William Smith at St. George's in Suffolk County, who was also one of the few as yet possessing a coach. It is possible that the colonel may not have socially recognized the captain, but Long Island as well as New York was lenient to piracy. Moreover, that the rich colonel was somewhat sportily inclined is suggested by the inventory of his £2600 estate in 1705 which included one hundred and four silver buttons, a silver watch and gold buttons, over £100 worth of clothes, eleven embroidered belts worth £110, numerous firearms and swords, bottles, glasses and a fishing rod. His other tastes were represented by pictures, a violin and £40 worth of books. There were other establishments even by this time which were considerably more luxurious than either Shelley's or Smith's but such as these, rather than the extreme cases, represent the homes of the wealthy.

Perhaps the most striking visible contrast between moneyed and poor was the richness of the costume of the former as hinted in the items above. As the opulent or well-to-do gentleman walked abroad his clothes proclaimed aloud his bulging money bags or broad lands. They were advertised equally by the golden-laced hats, the powdered wigs, the patches on the cheeks of the younger dandies, the brilliantly colored coats, the velvet or satin waistcoats, the silver buckles and buttons, the silken hose, and the silver or gold headed cane. The ladies followed close upon the latest London fashions, which, indeed, were said to reach the colonies sooner than the outlying counties at home, and the deep maroons, brilliant blues, flaming scarlets, silver and golden embroideries and cascades of creamy lace used by both sexes make our modern assemblies drab by comparison, and this was as true of Puritan New England and Quaker Pennsylvania as of the supposedly more worldly colonies.

Breakfast was usually a light meal, more so in the Southern than in the Northern colonies, and was frequently not taken until nine o'clock, but it was a period of heavy eating and yet more heavy drinking. There were no kitchen ranges, and all the innumerable dishes had to be prepared by the open fire on the enormous hearth. Kettles sometimes held a dozen or more gallons, and iron pots weighed forty pounds, yet the task of preparing a dinner in a large household was as complicated for the number of dishes on the menu as arduous for the mere quantity of food. Sometimes a half-dozen different kinds of meat alone would appear, as the tripe, pork, beef, turkey, mutton and chickens served to Lord Cornbury, and this seems to have been the rule, at least for a meal of any formality. As we have noted in speaking of agriculture, most of the vegetables and fruits of the old country were grown here and served on the tables of the rich. Almonds, cloves, cinnamon, currants, figs, ginger, nutmegs, pepper, raisins and salt were imported, and the herb garden yielded many of the ingredients called for by the recipes of the day. These appeared in printed form but even more frequently in the manuscript volumes kept by careful housewives, such as that of Mary Doggett in which are jumbled together methods of making "cowslip wine," "fine cakes of lemons," "drinks to cause sleep," "Lemon Creame," "orange Biskett," "cheese cakes of oranges," "to candy double marygold, roses, and other flowers," "to perfume gloves after the Spanish manner," and how "to souse a pigg." [1] Desserts and sweets of all sorts were without number in the richer households but that American favorite, ice cream, seems to have come only with the next generation, when a traveler reports it as being served with strawberries and milk as a novel rarity at the governor's house in Annapolis.[2]

The favorite nonalcoholic beverage was chocolate, though coffee was used, and the first notice of the newly-introduced tea appears just at the close of the period in 1714. With the eighteenth century, rum became an increasingly favorite drink in New England, as beer was in the Middle colonies, but wines of several sorts were always on the tables of the rich. Madeira, canary, claret, burgundy, port, brandy and champagne were all imported, and—more particularly in the Southern colonies—the cherries, peaches and other fruits were all made into "flings" or "bounces" or brandies. Madeira, however, was the most popular of all and the foundation of a considerable trade. In the matter of drunkenness there was no difference observable between the classes or colonies, and not seldom as much liquor was consumed in the ordination of a minister in New England as at a barbecue in the South, while the velvet-coated dandy slipped under the table no less readily than the leather-jerkined plowman.[3] In smoking there was probably more distinction, for although all men smoked, the use of tobacco by women seems to have been mainly confined to the less aristocratic. Ward said of those in New England that they "smoke in Bed, Smoke as they nead

[1] E. S. Rohde, *The Old English Herbals* (London, 1922), 179.
[2] "Journal of William Black, 1744," *Pa. Mag. of Hist. and Biog.*, I, 126.
[3] See J. A. Krout, *The Origins of Prohibition* (N. Y., 1925), 26-50.

their Bread, Smoke whilst they're Cooking," and although he is not always a trustworthy reporter there is other evidence for the frequent indulgence by women.[1]

Certain aspects of the intellectual and moral life of the aristocrats will be considered in later chapters but we may here note that the lack of organized recreation had a deleterious effect upon them, and the absence of the theater, concerts and many outdoor sports narrowed their life down to less beneficial amusements. Driving was only just becoming a possible pleasure in some of the larger centers toward the close of the seventeenth century. In the North, particularly in the Dutch colony of New York, skating was popular in the winter. Somewhat improved firearms and a fair supply of game made hunting one of the recreations for the sportsman, and we have already noted the hunting of wild horses and cattle in the South. In the North, fishing was an amusement although the first fishing club belongs to the next period. Indoors, billiards were remarkably popular through all the colonies and by 1722, if not before, there was a public billiard room even in Boston. Men's clubs for social or intellectual purposes which became such a feature of colonial life in the next generation were as yet practically nonexistent. In New York about 1700 the first coffeehouse, on the model so popular in London, was established and became one of the fashionable places of rendezvous. Dancing was a favorite form of social entertainment and was rapidly gaining a foothold, even in New England, in spite of its teaching having been prohibited in Boston in 1685. The dullness of life, however, especially for those who had leisure and no longer had to labor with their hands, called for excitement. It was a period in England of brutal amusements and much gambling, and colonial life reflected these tendencies although in milder form. Card playing, com-

---

[1] *Trip to New England*, 51.

mon in the South, had also invaded New England and as early as 1686 Cotton Mather was preaching against it in Boston. The feeling there against all such games was of course strong on the part of the clergy and common people, and a decade later in the bond given for keeping the tavern at Marlborough it was specified that there must be no dice, tally bowling, nine pins, billiards, cards or other unlawful games. Backgammon was much played and was a frequent form of tavern gambling, as was also dice throwing. Cockfighting was much indulged in in the South, and, under the name of "cock scaling," Mather inveighed against it in Boston in 1705. There were occasional horse races, North as well as South, in the latter part of the seventeenth century, even in New England, but the great gambling fever in racing, as well as the interest in fancy breeding, belongs to later decades.

Travel offered little inducement for the rich to leave their comfortable homes save to visit others in the near neighborhood, for conditions in traveling were very little, if at all, more luxurious for them than for the poor. At sea the price of passage from England to the colonies, £5, was the same for master and servant and there was apparently little difference in the accommodations. The ships were small, the voyages long, and throughout the whole colonial period the conditions of food, water and sanitation indescribably bad. On shore, traveling offered no allurements for undertaking it purely for pleasure. A few roads were just being begun in the neighborhood of the larger towns, and Virginia in this respect was making more rapid strides apparently than any other colony, but before the Peace of Utrecht few important centers were connected by ways fit for wheeled vehicles. One must not be misled by the use of the term "road" in colonial days into believing that anything like a modern highway was intended, for a

contemporary writer states that in all America if the
trees were blazed from one point to another the route
thus indicated was given the name.   Boston, New York,
Philadelphia and the Southern colonies were linked only
by the sea with all its dangers of coastwise sailing by im-
perfect charts and almost no lights.   The first lighthouse,
at Boston, was not built until 1716, and there were only
three others erected on the entire coast during the period
covered by this volume.

All land travel between distant points was by foot or
horseback only.   The ways were not always clearly
marked and many of the inns were atrociously bad.
Travelers often reported the food to be uneatable, the
beds and houses dirty, and the landlords insolent.   As a
rule all guests ate at the same table of the same food, and
often slept four in a room regardless of acquaintance,
social position or sex.   Thus Madam Knight noted
without comment that at one of the inns on her way
from Boston to New York two men slept in her room,
and this was the custom for long after.   Of course, there
were occasionally better houses, but on the road one had
no choice as a rule except in a few of the largest towns.
In the South there were scarcely any good taverns and
it was the custom to stay at private houses where hospitality was usually freely offered.   Nevertheless we have
journals of travelers there who lodged at an inn practically every night of their journey and who had but
few good words to say for their entertainment.

The trip of Madam Knight from Boston to New York
in 1704 may be taken as typical of travel for rich as
well as poor, between two of the largest centers at that
date, in the most thickly settled portion of the colonies.
She left Boston on horseback at three o'clock one after-
noon with a kinsman who was to see her as far as Dedham, where she was to meet the post carrier.   She waited
there until evening and, as no post came, procured a

guide and went on to Billings where she put up for the night long after dark. There she was miserably lodged. At eight next morning she started off with the post. At noon she reached an inn where the dinner was so poor that it was impossible to eat it. Starting off again at three o'clock with a fresh guide she reached Providence Ferry which they generally rode through, she said, but which she had not the courage to attempt and was carried over in a canoe so cranky that she dared not "so much as to lodge my tongue a hair's breadth more on one side of my mouth than t'other." Later in the evening, long after the moon was up, she had to ford a swift river where her guide abandoned her and rode on fast ahead. Beyond, the "road" was so narrow that the branches brushed her on both sides as the horse threaded his way along. That night she lodged at an inn where the woman who kept it was neat, but in which her room adjoined the kitchen where a discussion between some drunken men kept her awake all night until she started again at four in the morning. In the course of the day's journey she came to a stretch of water to be crossed which she could not swim her horse over and so had to wait some hours for the tide to fall enough to be ferried across. That night she found a good inn at Stonington and the next day stopped at a private house at New London. The following day, however, at the place where she halted for dinner, the food was so bad that no one could eat it after having paid for it. The day after that, after five days' steady traveling, she reached New Haven, and on the following two days continued her journey, with similar discomforts and misadventures, to New York.[1]

By 1697 there were thirty carts or other vehicles in Philadelphia, a few in Boston and New York, and a

[1] Sarah Kemble Knight, *Journal of Madam Knight* (G. P. Winship, ed., Boston, 1920), *passim*.

number in the Southern colonies. None of the
"chaises," "chairs" or carriages had springs but were
merely slung on braces of wood or leather and the jolt-
ing over rough roads must have been bone breaking.
When a stream was reached the vehicle was set on two
canoes and ferried over while the horses swam. Whatever advantages the aristocrat possessed over the common man, and they were many, they did not yet include
that of traveling for pleasure and instruction. The sur-
prising part is not that the aristocrat, like his poorer
neighbor, tended to become narrow and parochial but
that he was not more so than he was, and that there was,
after all, considerable travel between the colonies, and
between them and England.

In regard to the influence of New World life upon
women we may note that in the case of those of the first
generation of immigrants, the transplanting had the effect which change to a new environment with new problems always has in quickening the action of mind to
meet them. The conditions of life in a new country also
tend to raise woman's position owing to her greater economic service and to the simple arithmetical fact that
there are not enough to go round as wives. In a number
of ways she attained a somewhat more independent
status in America in the eighteenth century. Her property rights were greater in a number of the colonies than
in England, as were rights of inheritance in case of intestacy. She was freer to move about without male es-
cort or chaperon of her own sex. It is true that in 1710
when young Sarah Hall, who had come with her maid
from Barbados to stay at her grandmother's in Boston
for her education, abruptly left the house and took lodg-
ings elsewhere, the old lady was scandalized and got
Sally's brother to insist upon her return, though a little
later she had to write that the young lady "is well and
brisk, says her Brother has nothing to do with her so

long as her father is alive." We have already found the sprightly Madam Knight traveling alone on horseback from Boston to New York, and the next year find two young Quaker maidens from Philadelphia making the trip thence through Virginia with two young men friends as a matter of course.[1]

Not only, however, is woman from her innate conservatism less subject to change in character than man from a change in environment, but it must be remembered that for her the change was not so great. Her work on both sides of the Atlantic was the same—running the household. Of the special trials and work of the poorer and pioneer women we shall speak briefly in the next chapter, but for all of them, rich and poor, the sphere of duty remained the same, nor was the door of opportunity opened much wider. For the aristocratic woman, the only career was that of wife and mother, which fortunately she did not attempt to evade, but performed with consummate grace and skill. Though her servants were frequently numerous, her duties were multifarious, either as the wife of a prosperous business man of the North or planter in the South. There she often lived an isolated life on a plantation which, not seldom, she looked after herself during widowhood or the absence of her husband. Enough contemporary travelers, particularly in the South, comment upon the superior industry, ability, and attractiveness of the women especially of the lower classes to the men to cause us even thus early to analyze a phenomenon which many have considered not limited to the eighteenth century. Possibly this is to be connected with what we have said as to the effect of colonial life with reference to strengthening the solidarity of the home, and that in this respect life under colonial conditions tended to bring out

---

[1] "Journal of Esther Palmer and Mary Lawson." Friends Hist. Soc., *Journal*, VI, 64.

woman's finer characteristics, whereas in many cases the new conditions of men's lives tended to have a contrary effect upon them.

For them the uprooting of their lives in emigrating wrought a far more complete change, and, in the winter particularly, time must have hung rather heavily on the hands of those of the richer class. The small farmer and the pioneer had their innumerable daily chores and, in addition, winter was the time when much of the household manufacture was carried on of tools, furniture and apparel. But the wealthy town-dwelling merchant, the land speculator, the hanger-on of official circles in the North, or the planter in the South whose overseer looked after many of the details of management, must have suffered not a little boredom with its consequences. As we shall see later, there were not a few men in all sections who loved and possessed books—John Locke, for example, found his way to many library tables—but after all the number who care for the things of the mind are always in the minority in any age and place.

Again, although the ways of life in the old country had been reproduced in many points, there had been nevertheless a break with established custom and hereditary duties. By 1700 the country had been settled in part for three generations but society was still in an inchoate state. Many of the newly-rich men had come, as it were, but yesterday. Capital which they had brought with them, a few years of lucky trafficking, privateering or piracy, a grant of an estate due to influence with the governor or in England had founded their fortunes. The relations which the grantee of a tract of ten thousand acres bore to those whom he settled on his land, the relations of a planter to his slaves or of a farmer or a merchant to the servants whose time he bought, the relations of everyone, in fact, to one another had little of that traditional mutual obligation which was one of the morally valuable elements in feudalism and which still to a considerable degree survived in England.

The possibilities of the limitless resources of the new land offered rich prizes to audacity. In spite of the aristocratic tendencies of the older families, the man who suddenly acquired wealth and stood well with the governor could not long be resisted in communities so small that such a man became at once a leading figure. In England not only was wealth accumulated more slowly in most cases, but even its acquisition did not bring to its new possessor the sudden social transformation which it did in America. Thus, on the one hand, the absence of the traditional relationships binding together the various elements in society, and, on the other, the opportunities for exploitation, and the results of economic success, all combined to make of the successful American a business man rather than a genuine aristocrat and to give a marked individualism to his outlook.

At the time of the signing of the Treaty of Utrecht in 1713, his position was unusually alluring. The colonial population had grown sufficiently to give stability to the older settlements and was increasing so rapidly as to assure markets for goods and lands in the future. The political and social framework had become set enough in form to enable him to count with some certainty upon the lines within which he could work out his plans and career. The routes and methods of commerce were established and the resources of the country had become known. Colonial capital, also, had begun to accumulate. There were not many, perhaps, who had done so well as Robert Carter of Virginia who when he died in 1722 was said to have left three hundred thousand acres of land, a thousand slaves, and £10,000 in money, but fortunes of from £5,000 to £15,000 were not infrequent all along the seaboard. That colonial capital was seeking investment is sufficiently indi-

cated by the fact that by 1720, if not before, South Sea
stock, bank stocks, lotteries and annuities in London
were quoted regularly in New York.   With the end of
the war and the prospect of some years of peace, the
outlook offered glowing opportunities to the rich American.   His surroundings thus already tended to make
him a little more daring than his cousin at home, a little
more optimistic, a little more individualistic, a little more
preoccupied with the problem, not so much of getting
rich as of getting rich with the utmost possible speed.

CHAPTER IV

THE COMMON MAN

1690–1713

ALTHOUGH the group described in the preceding chapter exerted great influence, it was, numerically, a small one compared with the total population. Economically, societies are always like a pyramid, and the mass of men at the opening of the eighteenth century was composed of those who had made only a moderate success or none at all in the art and practice of living. Outside the select group of the mercantile and landed "aristocracy" were the smaller merchants, shopkeepers, farmers, planters, artisans, mechanics, pioneers, fishermen, free day laborers, indented servants and slaves.

Although the "gentlemen" drew sharp distinctions, not seldom legal, between these smaller fry and themselves they could hardly be accused of snobbishness by the farmers, tradesmen and others who in turn insisted just as rigidly upon distinctions among themselves. In fact, perhaps, snobbishness has never been more rampant anywhere in America than it was in the small Puritan villages of New England, where it received an added and ugly twist of Pharisaism. This came out most clearly in the meticulous measurement of the personal and social qualifications of every member of a congregation before he or she could be assigned a sitting in church. Age, estate, "place and qualification," were weighed with the utmost care to determine the conflicting claims to precedence of the various small farmers who made up the bulk of every rural village. Infinite

85

were the rulings giving each seat its specific social rank, such as that the "fore seat in the front gallery shall be equall in dignity with the second seat in the body," the front seats in the gallery with the fourth seats in the body, and so forth, as was painstakingly worked out in Deerfield even while facing annihilation by the Indians. Not infrequently the settlement of such vexed questions, when disputed, was referred to the town meeting for decision. On the other hand, within the households of the tradesmen or small farmers there was little of that distinction between master and man or mistress and maid which developed later. Indeed, when crossing Connecticut, Madam Knight was somewhat scandalized to find the farmers were equally indulgent to the negro slaves, "permitting them to sit at table and eat with them, (as they say to save time), and into the dish goes the black hoof as freely as the white hand." [1]

Immediately below the "aristocrats" described in the last chapter were the richer town merchants or planters who had not yet fully arrived in a social sense but whose wealth and general position placed them between those above them and the smaller people of the descending economic scale. There was nothing essentially characteristic of them as a class, setting them off from others, and this chapter is concerned with those still lower for whom the New World offered special opportunities, and with those lower yet for whom it offered none.

Although luxury, of course, was limited to the wealthy, there was ample comfort for those who were able to do moderately well for themselves. The small shopkeeper or tradesman of the towns and the farmer or planter of the rural districts were well housed, clothed and fed. As was pointed out in the last chapter, their houses differed as yet in little but size from those of the ranks above them. The materials of which

[1] Madam Knight, *Journal*, 39.

they were built were, in most colonies, the same, although from 1700 there tended to be a distinction in the South, as we have noted. Within, of course, there was a noticeable difference. Pictures were naturally absent from the walls of the more modest homes. The several fireplaces of the rich were represented by the one great one in the poor man's kitchen. Although occasionally pieces of furniture might be found that had crossed the ocean, most, when not all, of the furnishing was colonial-made, if not, indeed, made by the owner himself and his family.

In fact such a household, particularly in the country, was self-sustaining to a remarkable degree. A few things, like the iron pots in the kitchen, the pieces of pewter—if the household boasted of them—the materials for the best clothes, a few of the necessities for the table, such as salt, came from outside but otherwise almost every article consumed or worn was the produce of the farm or the immediate neighborhood. The beef and bacon came from the owner's cows and hogs, slaughtered in the fall and salted down. The former also supplied his leather. The wool, which the women of the household carded and wove and spun, was from the sheep of his own fields. The cider was pressed from his own apples. The winter's fuel was from the woods of his own woodlots or the village commons. The candles were made from tallow, produce of the farm, or from bayberries gathered by the children. The clothes worn by the entire household were frequently made by the women and even sometimes by the men. During the long days of winter, the men and boys fashioned the wooden farm implements, made innumerable utensils for the kitchen or built and carved and painted the beds, chests and chairs which slowly filled the rooms and added to comfort.

In the diaries kept by such men at this period we get

a vivid impression, even from their extremely brief entries, of varied duties and manifold abilities. For example, in that of Manasseh Minor of Stonington, Connecticut, from 1696 to 1720, we find such entries as "I went a fishin to naraganset," "I mad Els coat," "Thomas begun to mak shoes," "I gelt lambs," "the whole town worked at the highways," "I help make Watson's coat," and others showing him as shearing sheep, hunting wolves, attending town meeting, making different pieces of furniture, training with the militia, carting hay, traveling on one errand and another to Rhode Island, Fisher's island, New London and Boston, and on one day, "I went to preson." [1] The diary of another Connecticut man, Joshua Hempstead, which begins in this same period, shows him leading an incredibly active life as farmer, sailor, trader, carpenter, shipbuilder, stonemason, surveyor and lawyer. Like Minor, he was continually moving about within a considerable field on his various activities. This multifold life was common to most of the small farmers throughout all the colonies. "Men are generally carpenters, joiners, wheelwrights, coopers, butchers, tanners, shoemakers, tallow-chandlers, watermen and what not," wrote a missionary of conditions in Carolina, and added a formidable list of the household occupations of the women.[2] Another observer, in the same colony, after noting that the women weave all the cloth and that some "are so ingenious that they make up all the wearing apparel both for Husband, Sons and Daughters," adds that "others are very ready to help and assist their Husbands in any Servile work, as Planting when the Season of the Year requires expedition: Pride seldom banishing house wifery." [3]

[1] Manasseh Minor, *Diary, passim.*
[2] Letter of Rev. Mr. Urmiston, quoted in *Doc. Hist. of Am. Industrial Soc.* (Cleveland, 1909-1911), I, 271.
[3] John Brickell, *The Natural History of North Carolina* (Dublin,

Urmiston's comment that house servants were not to be had at any price in Carolina is not quite accurate and certainly would not apply to the Northern colonies where even the modest households were better off in that respect than they are today. Almost all, except the very poor, in the older portions of the colonies, seem to have had at least one slave, indented servant or the "help" of the daughter of some neighbor. There was little if any stigma attaching to such a position as the last under the conditions of the time, and the unmarried girls of fairly good families frequently went out to service. In this grade of society, although woman's work in the house was heavier than for the wives of the aristocrats, she had rather more freedom of occupation, and there are not a few instances at the beginning of the century, rapidly increasing as it advanced, of women in various lines of small business, more particularly as shopkeepers, petty merchants and innkeepers.

The clothing of this class was in marked contrast to that of their wealthy neighbors. With the exception of a better suit for church or other high occasions, it was mostly made of coarse heavy cloths, such as "ozenbrig" which we find constantly in use throughout the whole eighteenth century. The skins of animals, particularly deer, were much used as furs and as tanned leather. Leather breeches, indeed, sometimes adorned even the legs of ministers in New England for their rougher work, and when the Rev. Mr. Buckingham went as chaplain with the expedition against Port Royal in 1710 he took such a pair with him. The stockings were heavy woolens and were worn to the knee as a rule, but in summer both these and shoes were discarded even by men and women throughout the rural sections. In Pennsylvania a writer noted that they could be worn only in the

1737), 32. Much of this is a mere compilation from Lawson's volume of 1710, cited earlier.

evening, and that by day the only costume of the men
was a shirt and "thin long pantaloons which reach down
to the feet." [1]   In the far South, the negro children went
naked and the men wore only a breechclout when working in the fields.   However, the passing of sumptuary
laws prescribing the economic or social position requisite
for the wearing of clothes of certain materials or cost
shows that there was a constant tendency on the part
of the poorer people, particularly in the towns, to adorn
themselves more elegantly, and to copy the fashions of
those who could better afford them.   The love of finery
is also indicated by the frequent offering of silk stockings
or other articles of dress as prizes at the country fairs.

Food was simple but abundant.   The West India
sugar of the rich was replaced in the poorer households
by that from the maple tree or by honey, and butter
seems to have been a luxury only for the wealthy.   In
New England for those of moderate means, including
the clergy, both breakfast and supper were often composed only of bread and milk.   The produce of their
own fields, the fish from nearby waters or game from
the forests insured a plentiful supply, though little variety.   There was no ice for preserving food in summer,
the spring house taking the place of the ice box, and in
winter salted meats or fish had to serve.   Cider and rum
in the North, beer in the Middle colonies, and homemade
drinks of one sort and another in the South replaced the
imported wines of the rich, though wine was drunk in
America by classes that could not have afforded it in
England.

Farther out on the frontier of all the colonies conditions of every sort were, of course, much more primitive, even the costume changed and the use of the Indian
hunting shirt was general.   Indeed, in the later years of

[1] Anon., "Diary of a Voyage from Rotterdam to Philadelphia, 1728,"
Pa. Germ. Soc., *Proceeds.*, XVIII, 23.

the Indian wars many of the younger pioneers adopted more of the native dress, making the leggings longer so as to reach over the thigh and replacing drawers with the Indian breechclout. On account of their costume the frontiersmen were called "buckskins" and it is a fact of no little significance regarding the relations between tidewater and frontier that the residents of the former used the term as one of obloquy.

The first shelters erected by the frontiersmen were merely temporary and need not be described, but the permanent homes were log cabins, usually about sixteen feet by twenty, and when done by community labor took only two or three days to build. The type scarcely varied either in different localities or decades, and Byrd has described it for us in southern Virginia at the time of surveying the boundary line between that colony and North Carolina in 1728. "Most of the Houses of this Part of the Country" he wrote, "are Log-Houses covered with Pine or Cypress Shingles, 3 feet long and one broad. They are hung upon Laths with Peggs, and their doors too turn upon wooden Hinges, and have wooden Locks to secure them, so that the building is finished without Nails or other Iron-Work." [1] In most places the shingles would have been considered luxurious, the chinks between the logs being filled only with mud and moss and plastered over with clay. The doors and windows were sawed out after the logs were laid, and there was no glass for the latter. When there was any covering at all for the windows, other than solid shutters, it was paper smeared with hog's lard or bear's grease. Light in the evenings came only from the blaze on the hearth or from pine knots which served as candles.

Sometimes there was a small room above the main one below, reached by a few slats fastened against the wall. When one passed from a mere dirt floor to the

[1] Byrd, *Writings*, 78.

next stage of luxury it was to broad slabs laid on the ground. The furniture was equally primitive, a section of tree trunk or a slab on three legs for chairs and a longer slab for the table. The bed, fastened against the wall, was a mere bunk or low shelf.

In one place where Byrd stopped, he says that "there was a dirty poor house, with hardly anything in it but children, that wallow'd about like so many pigs," and in another he had to sleep with ten or more people "forct to pig together in a Room . . . troubled with the Squalling of peevish, dirty children into the Bargain." [1] In fact, for a very considerable part of the population conditions must have closely approximated those obtaining today among the first generation of immigrants, such as the "Polacks" who take up abandoned farms in the East, or others whose standards of living we consider so totally "un-American." There was the same fierce and sordid struggle to obtain a foothold so as to secure the means of subsistence, the same squalor and dirt, the same annual addition to the number of children and the same working of women and children at field labor. Of the wife of one frontiersman we read in the contemporary account of a visitor that "she is a very civil woman and shows nothing of ruggedness or Immodesty in her carriage, yett she will carry a gunn in the woods and kill deer, turkeys, etc., shoot doun wild cattle, catch and tye hoggs, knock down beeves with an ax and perform the most manfull Exercises." [2]

How young the children were when set to hard physical toil we do not know, but when Deerfield was threatened by the Indians in 1703 the minister reported that they no longer dared to allow the youngsters under twelve to work in the fields for fear of the savages. Evidently, therefore, they were set to work earlier than that

[1] Byrd, *Writings*, 320, 323.
[2] "Boundary Line Proceedings, 1710," *Va. Hist. Mag.*, V, 10.

and a child of twelve was considered not only capable of heavy labor but of performing it in the face of possible savage attack. When the era of land speculation set in, it was the toils and dangers of such people as these that gave the speculators their profits, and these heroic, if often squalid and uncouth, figures should be traced on the reverse of that tapestry on the other and brilliant side of which are the gay and attractive figures of gentlemen and ladies in satin and brocade in houses where the light of abundant candles set in silver flickered across many a treasured portrait of today.

Still farther beyond this frontier region, which already lay behind the older settlements all the way from New England to the Carolinas, was the shadowy border land of the Indian trader. As we have said in an earlier chapter, the forest yet covered the entire land and if one could have looked down upon the Atlantic Coast from the air, he would have seen an almost unbroken sweep of tree tops from the sparkling waves of ocean westward, showing only here and there the glint of river and stream and the clearings of occasional solitary farms or, more seldom, the larger ones of village or town. But this forest, more and more being threaded with trails and narrow roads, was tenanted and known. Beyond the last fringe of settlement, however, the traders plunged into the depths of primeval woods where, except for themselves, there were no inhabitants but the savages and those wild animals whose skins were the object of their quest. There, far beyond the habitation of the hardiest pioneer, the traders built their "trucking house" or trading post where they stored their guns, ammunition, duffels, blankets, rum and other articles which they exchanged for beaver and other skins.

At the beginning of the century, both North and South, there seem to have been not a few substantial and honest men as traders, and the colonial governments all through the pre-Revolutionary period made spasmodic efforts to regulate a trade that was peculiarly difficult of adjustment to the satisfaction of white and Indian. The struggle between traders, however, was keen. Men of no credit, morally or financially, borrowed money to buy goods, carried them into the forest and, owing to the high price they had paid compared with the more substantial men, resorted to trickery to defraud the savage. Rum, dear to the Indian, was the curse of the entire trade. Again and again the more responsible savage leaders complained of the evils thus wrought and although the governments occasionally tried to improve conditions their attempts came to nothing. Traders would press in ahead of one another, far beyond the trading stations, so as to meet the young savages as they returned with their season's furs from still deeper in the wilderness, to make them drunk and to secure the skins before they reached the more reputable traders. In 1718 in Pennsylvania, a chief reiterated the frequent complaint that his young men had been so debauched before they reached home that they had even no clothes left and no guns with which to hunt again.[1] The character of the traders in general steadily declined until all accounts agree with that of one of themselves who said that they were almost wholly the "dregs and off-scourings of the colonies."[2] Here and there a man of superior ability and character continued to live the half-savage life of this frontier beyond the frontier and performed valuable service for native and colonist alike, but for the most part the men who spent their lives debauching the savages with drink, mating with their squaws, risking the chance of murder in many a drunken orgy, deteriorated rapidly in charac-

---

[1] *Minutes of Prov. Council of Pa.*, III, 47 and *passim*.
[2] James Adair, cited by Hanna, *Wilderness Trail*, II, 302. There is ample evidence for the other colonies.

ter, so that the trade which brought to the seaboard centers its annual tribute brought to the border the constant danger of massacre and savage war.

To return to the settlements, we have still to consider those there who ranked below the shopkeepers, small farmers and others who had achieved a certain amount of capital and independence. Although we now have available a dozen or more careful studies of the indented servant and slave in the colonial period, no thorough examination has yet been made of the position and numbers of the free whites of the wage-earning class, and it is therefore difficult to estimate their importance. In the aggregate, however, the group must have been fairly large. For one thing, few indented servants or slaves were employed as sailors, perhaps because the chance of escape was too great, and the sailors who manned the many hundreds of little vessels engaged even by 1713 in colonial commerce must have numbered many thousands. A contemporary estimate places those of the ports of Salem and Boston in 1717 at over thirty-five hundred. Closely allied to these were the fishermen who served on the New England fishing fleet. These, perhaps, were not strictly speaking wage-earners, but nevertheless they had no capital in the enterprise. A boat's crew usually consisted of three men and the master, the crew receiving the value of one-half the catch, amounting sometimes to £8 or £9 a man for the voyage, of which three were generally made in a season to the banks. The smaller boats for the nearby fishing, of course, made frequent trips, staying out until full in summer or only for the day in winter. Whether justly or not, the moral character of the fishermen of the time was considered very low, and most of the money they made was probably spent quickly.

On shore almost every observer agrees as to the scarcity of free white labor. Nevertheless in the older settled portions of the colonies there must have been a considerable number of those who had to work for wages and yet who did not wish to sell themselves as indented servants for a term of years.   In the town of Newbury, Massachusetts, for example, the interesting list of heads of families already referred to shows that, out of two hundred and sixty-nine, twenty-seven possessed no land, and of these one had only one cow, one had two cows and a third had a horse.   The remaining twenty-four had no property of any kind.   Ten per cent of the heads of families in that village must therefore have been wage-earners and to these may be added such younger members of their households as were not serving as apprentices.   Mere reference to artisans of various sorts means nothing in this connection for they may have been either indented servants or free, but other references indicate that however scarce such wage-earners may have been they, nevertheless, were everywhere present.

It may well have been that such a class was not recruited to any great extent from immigration at the opening of the century, but it must have received more or less constant accretions both from above and below in the colonial population.   Contemporary observers agree that there was comparatively little extreme poverty in any of the colonies at this time, but the occasional laws for the relief of debtors, the frequent ones regarding poor relief, and the constantly expressed fear lest the poor become heavy charges on the communities, all indicate that there was more or less poverty in spite of optimistic descriptions.   The obstacles thrown in the way of the poor taking up residence in a town, so that they might not become entitled to poor relief, must have tended to sink them lower where they had already begun to fall.   Certainly all poverty was not limited to the frontier, and as an example of what might be found even on the Boston Post Road we have a description by Madam Knight of a household near the Pawcatuck River. The building was made "with Clapboards, laid in Lengthways, and so much asunder, that the Light came throu' everywhere; the doors tyed with a cord in the place of hinges; the floar the bear earth; no windows but such as the thin covering afforded, nor any furniture but a Bedd . . . an earthen Cupp, a small pewter Bason, A bord with sticks to stand on, instead of a table and a block or two in the corner instead of chairs." Yet these were not shiftless people for she adds that "bothe the Hutt and its Inhabitants were very clean and tydee: to the crossing of the Old Proverb, that bare walls make giddy Howswifes." [1]

In a note that shows one phase of the possibilities attending emigration, a traveler in Pennsylvania writes that "well to do people and such as cannot perform manual labor, but have all their work done by paying for it, can easily become poor in a few years—yea even fall into the greatest misery. The reason for this is that the day's wages are so excessively high, and help is occasionally not even to be obtained for money. . . . We have here, as I am told by a trustworthy party, cases where people who came to this country with much money and wanted to establish large plantations, were forced to relinquish them to their day laborers to whom they were indebted, and go away themselves empty handed." [2] Under the conditions of life for those with little accumulated capital, the mere maintaining of a neat and comfortable home required unremitting work, no little ability, and strong character. America was no place for the idle, the weak or the sick.

If misfortune or lack of ability thus added recruits to the wage-earning class from above, it must also have

---

[1] Madam Knight, *Journal*, 24.
[2] *Diary of a Voyage from Rotterdam to Philadelphia*, 19. Such a case parallels quite closely an earlier one in New England noted by John Winthrop.

been receiving constant accretions from below. The nature of the indented servant has already been described in the preceding volume, and we need not here again discuss the terms and usefulness of that type of labor in the colonies.[1] The great servant-importing provinces were Pennsylvania, Maryland and Virginia, but the need and desire for such servants in the North were great, and in Massachusetts, in 1710, the legislature passed an act offering a bounty of forty shillings a head to any ship captain who would bring into the colony any male servants from eight to twenty-five years of age. In Maryland, the proportion of indented servants and convict laborers to the entire population seems to have remained fairly constant at about nine per cent, but as the figures for servants include practically no small children whereas these are included in the population figures, the proportion of servants to all adults in the colony would be much greater, perhaps twenty-five per cent.[2] As the average period of servitude was five years, one fifth of the servant class, or five per cent of the total adult population, was passing annually from that status to the one of free whites. Of these, some, for one reason or another, reëntered upon a new period of servitude, and others became land owners but a very large proportion must have become wage-earners. The fifty acres of land which in many of the colonies were given as a "head-right," that is, fifty acres for every servant brought into the colony, inhered in the person importing the servant and not in the servant himself. It is therefore a mis-

[1] T. J. Wertenbaker, *The First Americans* (*A History of American Life*, II), chap. ii.

[2] In such a brief discussion I have not attempted to differentiate between the different types of servants. There were three classes of those who became servants by indenture: convicts sentenced to transportation by British courts; servants who signed a contract in Europe, including several types; and the free-willers or redemptioners who sold their own services voluntarily for a term of years. There were also certain important legal distinctions between servants by indenture and those by "custom of the country."

take to think that on completion of his or her term of service the servant at once and automatically entered upon the status of freeholder. The indenture usually called only for clothes, a little ready money, and an ax or hoe. It was, however, not difficult for the new freedman to acquire the fifty acres upon application if he so desired. The instructions to the governors of North Carolina, for example, from 1667 to 1681, required them to grant to freed servants fifty acres, and this was occasionally done as late as 1737. The same instructions were issued to the governor of Virginia and probably complied with. In Maryland the old system of granting the importer of servants the fifty acres per head was abolished in 1683 and thereafter all land was sold, but there seems to have been no case in which the freed servant did not receive the fifty acres if he demanded them.

In several ways the position of the indented servant was altered during the period covered by this chapter. The change in the Maryland law just noted put an end to the connection between the importing of servants and the acquisition of land, and thereafter the servant became a mere article of traffic like the slave, imported by captain or merchant and sold to the planter. This did not alter his condition for the worse perhaps, for merchants and large land owners had thus imported them for some time, and they continued to form part of the stock in trade of such men as Colonel Byrd all through the colonial period. In a number of the colonies several laws, such as those of 1705 in Virginia, of 1715 in Maryland and that of the same year in North Carolina, were passed about this period tending materially to improve the legal position held by the servant and to ameliorate his social condition. Contemporary descriptions of what that may have been vary widely, and undoubtedly the real position varied just as widely in the individual households or plantations where the servant may have been employed. Examination of court records indicates that his rights were upheld with considerable fairness whenever they came up for judicial decision. This was rendered easier in Virginia by the law of 1705 which gave servants the right to bring complaints against their masters into court on petition only and without formal process of an action. By the same act any contract for further service between him and his master or any matter relating to his personal liberty could be entered into only in the presence of a county court. Laws were also passed limiting corporal punishment and to some extent placing it under court supervision, although in the early part of the century such punishment tended more and more to be replaced by fines.

Beginning with this period, however, although the servant was gaining in legal rights, he was, speaking broadly, losing in social position. Throughout all the colonies, the increase in wealth and the growing distinctions between those who possessed it and those who did not tended to lower the servant's position as compared with the previous century when all alike were more under the leveling influence of the frontier. In Maryland, the increase in the number of convicts shipped by the British government brought the indented class in general more and more into disrepute, a condition affecting all the colonies to a lesser degree. In those in the South, however, the factor which operated most to lower the position of the white servant, as well as of the white landless wage-earner, was the enormous increase in the number of Negro slaves in that section which began in this period. Up to about 1700 the great majority of the laboring class had undoubtedly been indented servants with a smaller number of free wage-earners on the one hand and Indian or Negro slaves on

the other.   From that time on the slave for life rapidly
tended to displace the indented servant and free white
wage-earner in the colonies from Maryland southward
and to differentiate that section economically and socially from the North.

With regard to enslaving the Indians, New England
had early taken the lead and throughout the colonial
period held more Indians in slavery than any of the
other colonies except South Carolina, where in 1708
there were fourteen hundred Indian slaves against forty-
one hundred Negroes.   As late as 1706 Massachusetts
provided for the sale of Indian children under twelve
years of age taken in war.   With the chartering of the
Royal African Company in 1672, however, the traffic in blacks had entered upon a more active stage.   The
greatest demand came from the sugar islands, where the
Negroes soon outnumbered the whites several times, and
it was probably the very close connection between
South Carolina and the West Indies, as well as the nature of its crop, which caused that colony early to become a leader in the use of Negro slave labor.   By 1715,
with a white population of sixty-two hundred, there
were over ten thousand black slaves there, a much more
rapid increase than in any other colony.   In the same
year it is estimated that there were twenty-three thousand Negroes in Virginia with a white population of a
little more than seventy-two thousand, and in Maryland, three years earlier, eight thousand Negroes against
thirty-eight thousand whites.   In succeeding years the
proportion of blacks rose rapidly and the type of agricultural labor under Southern conditions thus became
definitely determined.   Of the economic and social results of this movement we shall speak in a later chapter
and here will discuss only the position of the slave
himself.

Of the details of the trade, the capture of the blacks

in Africa, their purchase by the dealers, and the often described horrors of the passage overseas, there is no need to speak again. Once arrived in the colonies and sold to his new master, the slave found kind or harsh treatment depending more upon the character of the master than upon the laws of the colonies. From the beginning to the present day, and occasionally for the better as well as frequently for worse, it must be recognized that the Negro has never been treated upon a basis of strict legality but according to the dictates of white sentiment. In some respects his position was similar to that of the indented servant. As the colonial system of labor based upon indentures was a development of the apprentice system, so was the system of slavery, in a way, a development of the indenture system, in which servitude was for life instead of for a fixed number of years. Although from one aspect slavery at first differed from white servitude, mainly in the mere extension of its period, the results of this extension were so great as gradually to alter the whole conception of the system and to change fundamentally the legal status and social position of the slave.

This change was marked in the years covered by this chapter during which, in spite of many cross currents of opinion, slavery began definitely to crystallize into the system of later periods. Although there had been more or less legislation from 1660 onward tending to define and somewhat to alter the status of the Negroes, it was only after they became numerous in proportion to the whites that we can trace the beginnings of the Negro problem, and that was in the first decade of the eighteenth century. Even as late as 1698, although there were many slaves in all the colonies, they were not coming in more rapidly than white servants, and Governor Nicholson of Virginia advised the board of trade that six hundred servants had recently been imported and that four or five hundred Negroes only were expected during the summer. The colonists, however, desired slaves, in the North mainly for house servants, and in the South for field labor also. Moreover, the English government, at the prompting of the merchants, was doing everything possible to encourage the trade, which received an enormous impetus in 1713 by the signing of the Asiento with Spain, giving the English a monopoly of the Spanish colonial slave trade. The New England traders too had been quick to seize upon their opportunity and by the beginning of the eighteenth century the "Guinea trade" was already enriching the merchants of Boston, Newport and other places.

The rapid increase in numbers of the Negroes in the colonies, however, brought some of the disadvantages of the system clearly before the settlers, and there was in consequence more or less difference of opinion as to its desirability. Of most importance was the question of safety. It must be recalled that the Negroes of this period were far from being the good-natured, tractable, often devoted and loyal beings into which, in many cases, they developed after a generation or more of living in America. By 1700 there were many American-born Negroes but those constantly being brought over from Africa were still savages, unable to speak English and naturally rebellious at their new condition. As the numbers increased, the possibility of a general uprising against the whites or of the massacre of white families on isolated plantations was a real one. Even by 1712 in three of the southern counties of Virginia the black outnumbered the white population, and throughout the early eighteenth century there were a number of attempted insurrections in several of the colonies, which kept the whites in terror. Moreover, along the entire border, until the Peace of 1713, there was the menace and often the presence of warfare with the Indians. The various acts passed by one colony and another, in the South as well as the North, during this period, and which were aimed at restricting the importation of additional Negroes undoubtedly had their origin in the fear of their increased numbers. All these laws, however, were disallowed in England as interfering with a lucrative trade, the fostering of which was beginning to be one of the prime commercial concerns of the merchants of the mother country.

On the other hand, in spite of his dangers, the Negro unquestionably filled both an economic and social need of the colonists. The supply of domestic servants, either free or indented, was inadequate. In the South, white labor was not adapted to the cultivation of rice, which was rapidly becoming the leading source of wealth in Carolina. The development of large tobacco plantations depended upon the presence of a correspondingly large labor supply. So long as a planter was limited to tilling the soil himself with the help of only a few others, there was no possibility of rising above the grade of yeoman farmer. Although the economic development of America would have been impossible without the indented servant, nevertheless there were distinct drawbacks to that type. The first year was usually lost to the Southern employer while the newcomer was becoming acclimated. There was also the necessity of an annual turnover of a part of the labor owing to the fulfilling of the term contracted for and the impossibility of replacing the laborers thus lost except by a new importation from England. These conditions made the slave for life appear an attractive asset in spite of his drawbacks. The conflict of opinion on the part of employers is evidenced by the laws to hinder importation, which represented fear, and the continued purchase and demand, which represented economic necessity.

The former motive was also represented by domestic

laws regarding the Negro. Prior to 1692, for example, in Virginia, slaves accused of capital offenses had been entitled to the same procedure, including a jury, as whites, but by an act passed in that year the accused was to be tried immediately by persons designated by the sheriff, without jury, and the evidence of even one witness was held sufficient to convict. By the law of 1723 any number of Negroes over five found guilty of conspiring together for murder were to be punished by death. Many laws in different colonies could be cited to show the increasing severity of the slave code, but in spite of some horrible individual cases of cruelty the practice was much more humane than the legislation would indicate as a possibility. What is of more interest and importance than an occasional lurid picture is the steady change in status and social consideration.

In Virginia by the time of the codification of 1705, slavery had advanced sufficiently far from the conception of mere servitude to create the legal necessity for the fiction of considering the slave in some of his aspects not as a chattel but as real estate. Aside from the purely legal influences of this upon his condition, which were by no means wholly bad, the mental influence was distinctly inimical to consideration of him as a man. In the earlier decades evidence indicates that although the English always showed more racial consciousness and prejudice than the French or Spanish, nevertheless, neither on that score nor on that of type of labor was there then any such impassable gulf between the races as developed later, and which may be noted as forming and consolidating in this period. Not only in the house but in the fields, white servant and Negro slave worked side by side, and the law frequently took note of cases where they absconded in company from their master's service. Slavery was not a legal status recognized in England and in its development in the colonies the dis-

tinction between those who must be free and those who
might be enslaved was based upon that between Christian and heathen. As the seventeenth century drew to
a close, however, legislation brought out clearly the new
conception of racial inferiority rather than religious difference. By the Virginia act of 1682 Christianity was
held not to confer freedom upon Negroes, mulattoes and
such Indians as were sold by others as slaves. This was
made even more severe, as was punishment for intercourse between the races, in the codification of 1705.
That either the race prejudice against the Negro was becoming much stronger than against the Indian or the
economic factor more determining, is indicated by the
fact that in 1705 the term "mulatto" was legally held to
include not only the children of mixed unions between
whites and Indians but also the great-great-grandchildren
of such connections with Negroes. Miscegenation will be
considered again but we may here note, in connection
with the developing race prejudice, that it was legislated
against in all the colonies, always with severer penalties
for the Negro.

That the disabilities of the black were beginning to
be racial and not merely due to his status as a slave in
this period is also shown by the laws as to free Negroes.
In Maryland, for example, in 1717, it was enacted that
no Indian, slave, free Negro or mulatto servant could
testify in cases concerning a white person. In 1705, in
Virginia, Negroes, mulattoes and Indians were forbidden
to hold any civil, military or ecclesiastical office, and in
1723 even the suffrage was denied to free Negroes, mulattoes and Indians. In North Carolina, in 1715, the same
three classes were excluded from voting, and in the same
colony, the much later law of 1746 seems merely to have
put in statutory form what had been the custom in part
in this period of forbidding "negroes, mulattoes, bond
and free to the third generation, and Indian servants and

slaves" from testifying in cases involving white persons. To have continued to develop the fields of America by the use of white labor would have been a slow process. History is a matter too complex for us to remove one element and to picture what might have been the result. As a consequence, however, of attempting to exploit rapidly the illimitable resources of the American forests by the unlimited labor supply of the African jungles, we find already arising that "little cloud out of the sea, like a man's hand" that was later to overspread the heavens.

Having thus reviewed some of the main groups of colonial society in a rapidly descending scale, we may inquire what were the possibilities open to the colonist starting in any of these ranks to advance himself above it. The most hopeless position, of course, was that occupied by the slave. Following earlier laws passed in Maryland and Virginia, it was enacted by Massachusetts in 1698, Connecticut and New Jersey in 1704, Pennsylvania and New York in 1706, and South Carolina in 1712, that a child of a slave became himself a slave, thus apparently closing the avenue of escape for the future as well as the present. In the same period new laws were also passed which made manumission more difficult. Moreover, the slave could not legally own any property. Although in practice he was allowed to gather together some personal belongings and occasionally given a patch of ground which he might plant for himself, nevertheless, in spite of rare cases in which he made money enough to buy his freedom from a willing master or was manumitted for other reasons, the odds against this new recruit to civilization were too heavy, and there is no case during this period of a free Negro having achieved anything beyond the position of a wage-earner or the owner of a small farm with, very rarely, a slave of his own.

For the indented servant, the case was very different. He could look forward at the end of a few years to becoming free to work for himself, and practically no social disability seems to have been attached to his former period of servitude, which was merely a contractual relation entered into voluntarily by himself (with the exception of the convicts), usually as a means of defraying the cost of his emigration to America. When his contract time expired, he was therefore in the same position as any other freeman with little or no capital. For such there were ample opportunities depending upon ability and inclination. If he had the luck to have a good master who became interested in him, his progress might be made easy in many ways. In the South, he might often become an overseer and, if industrious and saving, could accumulate enough in a few years to start a small plantation of his own, though an observer in South Carolina said that few did so on account of their shiftlessness. For those with less administrative ability and only their trade or labor to offer, the wages were high and the demand for their services practically unlimited.

Many of the contemporary descriptions must not be taken too literally as they were written for the purpose of inducing immigration and were no more reliable than such literature in our own day. Against such it is well to set the less optimistic utterances of occasional homesick souls. "O these Liars," writes one of these, who says that they described the climate and country only to lure others over. "If I but had wings to fly, I would soon hie myself from hence to Europe, but I dread the tempestuous ocean and the pirates." "Whosoever is well off in Europe better remain there. Here is misery and distress, same as everywhere, and for certain persons and conditions incomparably more than in Europe." The cost of all manufactured articles is high, he says, and the administration of justice speedy and good, "otherwise we have the same old world as in Europe." [1]

[1] *Diary of a Voyage from Rotterdam to Philadelphia*, 23.

On the other hand, wages were three times as high as in England, wrote another, and although this was an exaggeration, the high wages did make the accumulation of a modest property possible for the skillful and industrious.[1] Letters from immigrants to their relatives picture the conditions. "It is a great deal better living here than in England for working people," wrote one. "Poor working people doth live as well here as landed men doth live with you thats worth £20 a year. I live a simple life and hath builded a shop, and doth follow weaving of linen cloth, but I have bought 450 acres of land in the woods."[2] Another, evidently under the influence of the new freedom, wrote that "the farmers or husbandmen live better than lords. If a workman only work for four or five days in a week, he can live grandly. The farmers here pay no tithes or contributions. Whatever they have is free for them alone. They eat the best and sell the worst."[3] Still another wrote that "here is no want of victuals or clothing. Here it is a good Country for you people to come into" and offered to take care of one of his young cousins should he be sent over.[4]

The high wages both for labor and all sorts of craftsmen and artisans, the fishing on shares, the possibilities for the adventurous in the fur trade, positions for the clerically minded in a shop or the office of a merchant, the welcome accorded the country peddler, the small scale on which foreign commerce might be begun—all these and many other ways of beginning modestly with large possibilities made America a land of opportunity for those with energy and industry. It was above all else, however, the chance to secure land that attracted the

[1] Gabriel Thomas, *An Account of Pennsylvania and West New Jersey, 1698* (reprinted, Cleveland, 1903), 28.
[2] "Early Letter from Pennsylvania," *Pa. Mag. of Hist. and Biog.*, XXXVII, 334.
[3] Quoted in Pa.-German Soc., *Proceeds.*, IX, 153.
[4] "Early Letter from Pennsylvania," *loc. cit.*, 338.

majority of the immigrants, as it became the ambition of most Americans themselves. This was, perhaps, particularly true of the Germans, and in one list of twenty-nine hundred and twenty-eight adult males passing through England on their way here in 1709, eighteen hundred and thirty-eight were farmers. In another list there were one thousand and eighty-three out of fifteen hundred and ninety-three. In this regard, however, in spite of ample land yet available here and there, the land accumulations of the very rich and the desire on the part of the well-to-do to keep as much in their own hands as possible, were beginning to have their effect on the opportunities for the small man. In local struggles against new methods of the rich engrossers or in the diversions of the streams of migration and settlement, we can trace the beginnings of such effects, although in the next period this struggle was to become sharper, more bitter and more vocal.

In New England the custom had been to grant lands to new groups of settlers who would establish a new town and church, divide among themselves without cost part of the land allotted and retain the remainder in common ownership. From time to time this might be divided again or from it allotments made to newcomers. We have already seen, however, how this system, so favorable to the small man without capital, was being altered by the new policy of granting or selling large tracts to individuals or companies who held them for speculation. In the case of the tract owned by John Reed we have also seen how he tried, and to some extent succeeded, in introducing the English system of long-term leases instead of sales, thus doing away with the freehold so dear to the heart of the New England pioneer. It would be a mistake, however, to give the impression that the very rich formed a separate predatory group attempting to loot the continent, as contrasted with generous or

public-spirited classes below them. In 1700, for example, when the little farming town of Hatfield in
Massachusetts decided to open more land for new home-
steaders, the older proprietors violently opposed giving
up any of the undivided commons according to former
usage, insisting that the new settlers or the young men
of the village who were growing up and starting households of their own, should be required to lease the land
and become permanent tenants of the older group of settlers. On this occasion the new men won after a two
years' struggle but the episode was symptomatic of more
general and bitter agrarian contests which we shall note
in the next period.

In New York, the engrossing of enormous tracts permanently retarded the settlement of the province. The
dislike of new settlers to becoming mere tenant farmers,
the terms on which the speculators offered the lands for
settlement, and the growing confusion with regard to
titles owing to the loose wording of overlapping grants,
all helped to divert to Pennsylvania immigration which
otherwise would have poured up the Valley of the Hudson. In Maryland the system which developed of
speculating in lands by means of taking out warrants for
tracts but not carrying the process so far as to get the
grants issued, thus saving the payment of quitrents, tied
up enormous amounts of uncultivated lands. Although
Charles Carroll, then agent in control of land affairs, was
instructed in 1712 to stop this speculation, the trade continued and reached very large proportions. Not only
was the actual amount of land thus covered by these warrants enormous but the committee of the assembly which
was appointed to examine into this grievance twenty
years later found that, owing to the indefiniteness of the
location of some of the warrants, three or four men held
options on all the vacant lands on the Potomac between
the Monocacy and Susquehanna and back of the Eastern

Shore settlements from the Pennsylvania line to Dorchester County.

In Virginia, Spotswood said that servants whose terms were finished and who became small farmers settled out on the frontier. About the same time, the council writing to the Board of Trade said that the chief cause why many of the families of older settlers, whose lands were worn out, "as well as great numbers of young people and servants just free," were crossing over to North Carolina was the lack of land to be had on fair terms in Virginia, though they also suggested it was to avoid creditors.[1] As we shall see later, the increase in slave labor was probably another cause, but the inability to get fresh lands well located and on easy terms was undoubtedly an important factor in the emigration. As the older portions of the colonies became more crowded and even the wilderness far beyond the range of settlement became preëmpted by those fortunate or astute enough to secure title, the small man without capital or influence began to feel himself more and more hemmed in and enmeshed in the power of those who had both. Little by little the resentment over the land situation, combined with other factors which one by one came into play as the century advanced, tended to bring classes and sections into sharp alignment, and to create a smouldering fire of resentment on the part of the frontiersmen and frequently the small farmer or landless man of the older settlement against the rich, which was to create a fertile field for propaganda in the days to come.

[1] Alexander Spotswood, *Official Letters* (Va. Hist. Soc., *Colls.* new ser., II), 227; *N. C. Colon. Records*, I, 691.

CHAPTER V

The Intellectual Outlook
1690-1713

In the history of the American mind, the period from 1690 to 1713 is a notable one. If we estimate it merely by production we may agree with most students who find it to be the nadir of the intellectual life of the colonies, but its most essential feature is that the pause thus indicated was not a mere halting of activity in one direction to be resumed later, but the hesitation which comes when one movement has spent its force and before a wholly different one has got under way. During all the earlier part of the seventeenth century, the culture of America, like most of the settlers themselves, had been merely transplanted from Europe, mainly from England. In 1643, of the eighty ministers in New England, one-half had been graduates of Cambridge or Oxford. Fifty years later, however, seventy-six out of eighty-seven in Massachusetts and thirty-one out of thirty-six in Connecticut were graduates of Harvard. "The Country consists now most of Natives, few of which have read much or been abroad in the world," wrote Governor Nicholson of Virginia in 1701, and again he says that the natives "begin to have a sort of aversion to others, calling them strangers." [1] From the days of settlement down to the end of the seventeenth century we have to note the slowing down of a cultural movement imported from the mother countries. From the beginning of the eighteenth

[1] *Cal. of State Paps., Colon., 1701*, 631; Byrd, *Writings*, xii.

113

onward we have to deal with the rise of a distinctly colonial culture. It is, perhaps, needless to add that this was constantly under the influence of the European.

The university-bred and other cultured men who had come from England and elsewhere had not realized the magnitude and absorptive power of the task of subduing the forest. By degrees they had found their energies diverted into new and more material channels. Many a one must have echoed Pastorius when even he said, in a moment of discouragement in his Philadelphia outpost in the wilderness, that "never have metaphysics and Aristotelian logic . . . earned a loaf of bread." Not only the work to be done but the rewards to be gained must have led many, as we have already noted in speaking of the clergy, to abandon the life of the spirit for that of active business.

If the earlier culture had withered it had by no means died, and the constant importations of books indicate a widespread taste for reading, confined to no one section. In the South, there were no bookshops because there were no towns and consequently no centers for distribution of books any more than of clothes or other articles, but this does not mean there were not constant importations. The rich imported them direct from their English agents, as they did everything else, whereas the smaller people could get them at the stores of the planter-merchants, as they did other things. "You know some of the newest books, if they be ingenious will be mighty acceptable," wrote William Fitzhugh from Virginia to his brother in England in 1690.[1] In Philadelphia, books were probably imported by the general merchants but by 1714, at least, there seems to have been a shop devoted particularly to them, for Colden wrote in that year that "our Bookseller tells me that there is not one Bible in Town to be

[1] *Va. Hist. Mag.*, III, 255.

sold." [1]   At least a dozen years earlier Abraham Delanoy
was selling books in New York and at the beginning of
the century we know the names of nine booksellers in
Boston.   In New England the dealers also used the
itinerant peddler as a selling agent, and although we do
not know what works may have been sold in that way
the business thus handled seems to have been considerable.   James Gray, for example, "that used to go up and
down the Country Selling of Books," as his obituary in
the *Boston News-Letter* says, left £700 in coin. [2]

In so far as we can judge by inventories of estates,
there was no very noticeable difference between the pro-
portionate number of households in the North and South
which possessed books or the number of volumes in
them.   In Virginia, Colonel Nicholson's library, of
which we have a catalogue in 1696, showed over two
hundred titles in religion, science, gardening, commerce,
travel and other departments, and the number of volumes, of course, was considerably greater.   Colonel John
Carter had an excellent medical library, by 1690, and
Captain Arthur Spicer in 1699 had many medical works,
a fine collection in law, and among other general works
a copy of *Macbeth*, Browne's *Religio Medici*, and
Bacon's *Advancement of Learning*.   Such moderate
sized libraries as these appear to have been fairly frequent
in the better Southern homes, and Ralph Wormeley, who
died in 1701, had a very much larger one, one of the
most notable in any of the colonies.

The largest in America at this period, however, was
that of Cotton Mather in Boston, which numbered about
three thousand volumes.   In the next generation, in spite
of the continued growth of the Mather collection, it may
have been outranked by that of Colonel Byrd of Vir-

---

[1] Cadwallader Colden, *Letters and Papers* (N. Y. Hist. Soc., *Colls.*,
1917), I, 14.
[2] Issue of April 9, 1705.

ginia who collected four thousand, but such unusually large libraries were due more to the chances of individual taste than to general conditions in any section. Whether or not there may already have been a somewhat wider distribution of books in New England than in the South, and for the accurate determination of this we have not sufficient data, the two sections were certainly less differentiated in this respect in 1700 than they were to become later. In the matter of subscription libraries the people of the South were temporarily better off at this time than those of the North. The largest single institutional collection was undoubtedly that of Harvard, although we have no catalogue of its contents until 1723 when it numbered thirty-two hundred titles. The Boston "public" library was almost wholly destroyed by fire in 1711 and we have little information as to its size either before or after. In 1698 a library had been sent over for King's Chapel by William III, which is now in the custody of the Athenæum, and there was another parochial library in Boston, as well as one at Newport. In Connecticut the only public collection of books in this period was the very small one at Yale. In all the Middle colonies of New York, the Jerseys and Pennsylvania there were only four small parochial libraries.

In Maryland there had been a small public library in the state house at Annapolis from 1697 and also a library in King William's School, presented by that monarch, and when the state house was burned in 1704, these were merged. In the former year, Governor Nicholson had suggested to the house of burgesses that they appropriate funds to buy books to be added to the royal gift to form a public library to which all persons wishing to study or read might have access. In Virginia there was a small library at the College of William and Mary from 1699, and it was probably within this period that Edward Mosely of North Carolina made a gift of volumes for the establishment of a provincial library at Edenton.

The most notable efforts to bring books to the people, however, were those of Doctor Thomas Bray of England who became commissary for the Anglican Church in Maryland in 1696. Finding that for the most part only poor men who could not afford books were willing to go to the colonies as clergy, he determined to establish a library in every parish, primarily for their benefit. Becoming much interested and wonderfully successful in this work, he broadened its scope so as to include circulating libraries for laymen as well. He recognized one of the main difficulties which the development of culture was to encounter in the South when he said that "Standing Libraries will signifie little in the Country, where persons must ride miles to look into a Book; such Journeys being too expensive of Time and Money: But Lending Libraries, which come home to 'em without Charge, may tolerably well supply the Vacancies in their own Studies." Anticipating a very recent view of most librarians, he said regarding the danger that borrowing would prevent people from finding the books that they might expect on the shelves, "I heartily wish the great Use and frequent Borrowing of Books out of these Libraries, may make it a real objection." [1] In addition to the parochial libraries already mentioned in the North, all of which were established by him and his associates, except that of King's Chapel in Boston, he placed one in nearly every one of the thirty parishes in Maryland. That at Annapolis contained one thousand and ninety-five volumes and was one of the largest public collections in America. The laymen's library at Nanjemoy held nine hundred and eighty-two volumes, and others were also placed in Virginia and the Carolinas. The parochial

[1] Quoted by B. C. Steiner, "Rev. Thos. Bray and his Libraries," *Am. Hist. Rev.*, II, 63.

one established at Bathtown, North Carolina, included eleven works of history and travel, five dictionaries, fifteen works on natural history, mathematics, heraldry, biography and law, two on sports, three of essays, and a volume each of poetry, medicine and mythology. With this parochial library went also one for laymen of eight hundred and seventy volumes and pamphlets. Outside of Boston there was no town in all New England which could then boast of such a collection as was freely open to the public in this little North Carolina village. In 1700, South Carolina, on receipt of two hundred and twenty-five volumes, established a provincial library and passed the earliest library law in the colonies, making the use of the library open to any "inhabitant" who would give his note for the value of the book drawn while in his possession and promise to return it. Unfortunately no arrangements were made to add new books to these libraries from time to time, and only in occasional instances did the colonists take sufficient interest to do so for themselves. After the death of Bray, therefore, the libraries established by him languished, and in many cases became lost and scattered. It was a noble effort of a noble man, but it fell in the very midst of that pause which I have noted as marking the interval between the decline of a purely imported culture and the rise of one of native growth. It has been estimated that Bray sent thirty-four thousand religious works alone to the colonies during his life, but the movement was one from without. Although it must have been of considerable influence at the time, it failed to take root, and when a generation later a genuine movement for circulating libraries and reading rooms did spring up it had the strength to live and develop because it came from the colonists themselves, filling a genuine need that they had by that time come to feel.

In 1700, however, it is evident from the standpoint

of both private and circulating libraries that the equipment of the people of the South was more nearly equal to that of the Northerners than it was to be some generations later.   Nor, on the whole, was the type of book which interested the readers of the two sections very different.   Religious works were exceedingly numerous in both of them, but in general the Southerner seems to have had a larger proportion of the classics and more particularly of recent *belles-lettres*, history, science and law.   His interests appear to have been wider, and, although there was much of the Puritan spirit in the South, as there had been from the beginning, it was not as antagonistic to the arts as it was in New England. In the North, art was judged almost as a department or expression of ethics.   In the South it was enjoyed merely for its own sake.   The planter's spirit seemed to unfold itself in the sunshine which flooded his fields, whereas the New Englander wrapped himself up in a somber earnestness of purpose against the ills of life and fortune as he did in his heavy coat against the bitterness of the bleak winters.

In the seventeenth century, the conception of the absolute in America had been dualistic; in the eighteenth it was to become monistic.   The intellectual colonist, closely linked as he was with the movement of thought in Europe through practically every book upon his shelves, was to duplicate in the movement of his own thought that rationalizing tendency which was to be characteristic of eighteenth-century Europe.   Whatever may have been the comparative numbers of books or their readers in New England and the rest of the colonies, there was a difference in spirit which is evident.   The New Englanders, although narrower, were more intense.   The Southerner read and pondered.   The New Englander wrestled with his ideas.   The things of the spirit for him had not simply reality but almost corporeality.   He was fairly scorched by the flames of hell—or rather, perhaps, he marveled why his neighbor was not. Whereas in the other colonies, therefore, the transition from the seventeenth-century viewpoint to the rationalism of the eighteenth was gradual, it is not a mere chance that we find the same change in New England marked by a spiritual crisis of the first magnitude.

It is not necessary to rehearse all the well-known details of the Salem witch trials of 1692, during the course of which one hundred and fifty accused persons were imprisoned, legal evidence being set aside, and twenty victims put to death, one by the horrible torture of being pressed for several days under heavy weights. The story of this blot on the history of Massachusetts has been related at length in the preceding volume.[1] Finally the reaction came. Sober sense asserted itself after the irreparable harm had been done. Courageous laymen like Thomas Brattle and Robert Calef exerted themselves to the utmost. In 1700 Mather's *Wonders of the Invisible World,* which had been published in 1684, was mockingly answered by Calef's *More Wonders of the Invisible World,* which was a rationalistic attack, and an effective one, upon the clergyman's attitude toward natural phenomena. After due reflection, Samuel Sewall as well as some minor actors in the tragedy made public acknowledgment of their transgression and asked for forgiveness. Even Cotton Mather confided to his diary doubts as to his own part, and later was on one occasion to do public battle for scientific enlightenment. That a merchant should worst one of the most noted clergymen in all New England and carry the minds of the people with him was surely a portent of coming change. His book, published in the first year of the new century, was a signal gun of a new struggle.

[1] T. J. Wertenbaker, *The First Americans* (*A History of American Life,* II), chap. vi.

Another controversy in which the Mathers engaged brought forth another contestant in the lists against them, and just as the success of the layman Brattle against the learned clergyman was a sign of the times, so was the fact that the Reverend John Wise, son of an indented servant, should boldly attack Cotton Mather, empurpled in the local glory of the third generation of distinguished New England divines. Although the controversy was a religious one, it is notable that the main interest of Wise's book lies in its political doctrines and that those show complete divorce from the religious and biblical sanctions which the earlier New England leaders had found so essential. Just as colonial interests were becoming economic rather than religious, so colonial thought was becoming political rather than theological. The works of Sidney, Locke, Cumberland, Puffendorf and other writers on government were beginning noticeably to influence the doctrines of Americans, the ground of the new country proving fertile soil for such seed. In Wise's book, which although written in this period was not published until 1717, we find a New Englander maintaining a nonreligious sanction for government and a belief in democracy, two immeasurable advances from the Puritan thought of a generation earlier. Government he asserted to be "the effect of human free-compacts and not of divine institution" and that it was solely "the product of man's reason." "All power is originally in the people," he also adds, and that the only end of government is to promote "the good of every man in all his rights, his life, liberty, estate, honor." And finally, he states, "it is as plain as day light, there is no species of government like a democracy to attain this end. There is but two steps from an aristocracy to a monarchy, and from thence but one to a tyranny." [1] Wise was ahead

---

[1] *Vindication of the Government of the New England Churches* (Boston, 1772, 2d edn.), *passim*.

of his time but what his virile mind was clearly thinking out and clothing in words of power was beginning also vaguely to possess the minds of others. To Brattle, the merchant pleading for common sense and rationalism, we have to add the village clergyman Wise, son of a laboring man, pleading for equality, democracy, and the people as the sole seat of power.

This change in the intellectual atmosphere is also well illustrated in the field of historical writing. In 1702 Mather published his *Magnalia Christi Americana*, an ecclesiastical history of New England from its founding to 1698. The book, as his biographer says, is "flung together." As a picture of the ideals of the Puritan ministers as depicted by one of them, it has high value but it is full of errors and thoroughly uncritical. Five years later young Thomas Prince graduated from Harvard but he had already begun to make his remarkable collection of books, documents and source material of all sorts on which he was later to base the first critical historical work produced in America, and, although his book was to be long delayed and not to appear until well into the next period, we may note the spirit with which he is already at work, as contrasted with Mather. "I would not take the least iota upon trust," he says. "Some may think me rather too critical. . . . I think a writer of facts cannot be too critical." "In short, I cite my vouchers to every passage; and I have done my utmost, first to find out the truth, and then to relate it in the clearest order." [1] Here indeed is the freshness of a new dawn illumined by the first glow of the rationalizing and scientific spirit.

The founding of the Royal Society in England in 1662 had been of marked influence in fostering scientific interest in America as well as at home, and Americans made many communications to it. In 1713 Cotton

[1] Thomas Prince, *Chronological History of New England, in the Form of Annals* (Boston, 1736).

Mather, who was a somewhat frequent contributor,[1] sent in his paper "Curiosa Americana" and soon after was elected a Fellow, as was William Brattle the next year, and in the following period a number of colonials, south as well as north, were thus honored. Science, however, was still in its infancy, and even in Europe natural history, for example, was yet in the stage of making collections of objects and discussing "their meaning in terms of the flood of Noah." Here and there colonists were busy in such work, and Paul Dudley, Cotton Mather and others in New England were sending specimens or accounts of strange phenomena to England. Absurdly unscientific as many of these were, such as Mather's description of a Triton, half man and half fish, which was supposed to have been seen on the shores of Connecticut, they were not considered unworthy of credence by European scientists, and undoubtedly stimulated American scientific interest. In South Carolina in 1705, a Mrs. Hannah Williams was collecting specimens of "some of Our Vipers and several sorts of Snakes, Scorpions and Lizzards in a Bottle" as well as "Other Insex," pressed plants, birds, a wild bees' nest and native clothing and utensils to send to England, apparently to Sir Hans Sloane.[2] In Philadelphia, a few years later, Christopher Witt, who joined the theosophical colonists upon the Wissahickon, probably founded the first botanical garden in America.

Astronomy had been making rather more rapid strides than natural history, and even as early as 1686 an observer reported that he conjectured the Copernican system was beginning to obtain in New England. As perhaps no other scientific hypothesis was more influential in breaking down medieval theology, it is interesting to find

[1] G. L. Kittredge, "Cotton Mather's Scientific Communications," Am. Antiq. Soc., *Proceeds.*, new ser., XXVI, 18-57.
[2] "Early Letters from South Carolina upon Natural History," *S. C. Hist. and Geneal. Mag.*, XXI, 5.

that by 1714 Mather was preaching the doctrine from his Boston pulpit. Not less so is the comment thereupon by that typical Puritan business man of the old school, Samuel Sewall. "Dr. C. Mather," he records in his diary for that year, "preaches excellently from Ps. 37. Trust in the Lord, &c., only spake of the Sun being in the centre of our System. I think it inconvenient to assert such Problems." [1] Sewall's was probably the more widely held opinion. Astronomical knowledge found its way to the people at large mostly through the almanacs, which in this period were still mere slender compilations of tables, with none of the literary embellishments which were to make them an element of popular culture a generation later.

Medicine at this time was far below even the condition of that science in Europe. There was no means of securing a medical education in the colonies except by apprenticeship to some practising physician. Boys of from fourteen to seventeen might be apprenticed for from four to seven years, and besides picking up such information from their master as they could, were obliged to perform all sorts of menial work, even those who came of good families. What constituted sufficient medical education to permit of being licensed by the legislature at this time may be learned from the petition of Samuel Higley of Connecticut who was licensed in 1717. He states that he had "more than common education" and that "being employed three years in keeping school, did improve all opportunities in the study of physick and chirurgery," and for two years had studied under Doctors Thomas Hooker and Samuel Mather. The library of the ordinary doctor must have been very scanty, for in the inventories of even successful practitioners we frequently find the books valued at only a pound or two. The centers of

[1] Samuel Sewall, *Diary, 1674-1729* (Mass. Hist. Soc., *Colls.*, ser. 5, VI), II, 31.

medical education of the time were Leyden, under the celebrated Hermann Boerhaave, and Paris for surgery, but in this period not a single American took his medical degree in Europe, the first to do so being William Bull of South Carolina in 1734.[1] As no provision was made for instruction at colonial colleges, the consequence is that no colonist of this period had a right to the use of the title.   There is indeed one sole exception.   In 1720, Daniel Turner was granted the degree of M.D. by Yale. He was an able surgeon in London, where his calling was by rigid custom joined to that of barber.   Desiring the respectability of a doctorate, he had applied to the colonial college, whose rector he had met.   But as he sent with his application a handsome gift of books, the honorary letters he obtained in return were said by certain wags of the time to stand for *multum donavit*.

Although lectures on the cadaver were being given regularly in Paris and Strassburg, dissections were very seldom performed in the colonies until after 1760, except by stealth.[2]   In 1690 owing to the suddenness of the death of Governor Slaughter in New York, an autopsy was performed on his body by six physicians to see if he had been poisoned, but these were not usually permitted unless suspicions of foul play had been aroused.   There were no hospitals until later and the apprentice's opportunities of studying diseases were limited to those which his master's patients might have the goodness to contract. Midwifery was wholly in the hands of women, obstetrics not usually forming part of the doctor's studies or practice until after the middle of the century.   It was not until its later decades that the duties of apothecary and

---

[1] At the close of this period some were going to Edinburgh; see list in *New England Genealogical and Historical Register*, XLI, 391-392.

[2] Two years before the English government placed the bodies of criminals at the disposal of doctors (1752), Dr. Peter Middleton and Dr. Samuel Bard gave a lecture on a cadaver cut from the gallows in New York; *Annals of Medical History*, March, 1926.

physician were divided, and the more lucrative branch of the doctor's work in our period was still the compounding of his innumerable "potions," "elixirs," "infusions" and "electuaries." What they may have contained, we do not know. Elder, wormwood, anise, nitre, antimony, iron, sulphur, calomel and sometimes opium in enormous doses were among those mentioned. It is probable that some of the fantastic compounds of the day were not in actual use, though in some of the household books of receipts we find remarkable remedies. Thus in William Penn's "Book of Phisick" he notes that to cure a pain in the eye, a white-shelled snail should be pricked and the liquid dropped into the eye several times daily. To draw out a thorn, a dried snakeskin was to be applied, and for bruises he advised a disgusting concoction of six pounds of butter, a bottle of black snails, rosemary, lavender, elder, "new Cow-dung as much as will go into a great oyster shell and half as much new hen dung," frankincense and other ingredients.[1] If these were the medical notions of an intelligent man such as Penn, we need not wonder at some of the country remedies then in vogue. The prescriptions were as vague as their contents were varied, and we find as doses "a pretty draught," "the bigth of a walnut" or "take a pretty quantity as often as you please."[2] The general credulity, the lack of any proper system of licensing, and the absence of degrees, all helped to make the field a fertile one for the quack, and in Europe as well as in America, the eighteenth century was quite as much the age of quackery as of common sense. The first American patent medicine seems to date from the period of this chapter, and from 1711 "Tuscarora Rice" became a favorite remedy for tuberculosis.

[1] "Extracts from the Book of Phisick of William Penn," *Pa. Mag. of Hist. and Biog.*, XL, 475, 478.
[2] Quoted by H. F. Long, "The Physicians of Topsfield," Topsfield Hist. Soc., *Colls.*, XVI, 13.

Although the period was, as we have pointed out, one of pause between two movements, it held promise of the great development in colonial science which was to come in the next few years. James Logan, Cadwallader Colden, Mark Catesby and John Mitchell all came to the colonies at this time. Of the native colonials, John Bartram was a lad in Philadelphia, Jared Eliot was already a young man in Connecticut, and Zabdiel Boylston had begun his practice of medicine in Boston.

In literature, the works which have most retained their vitality for modern readers were almost all written in the South, although published in England. In Maryland, an unknown author, who chose to call himself Ebenezer Cook, produced in 1708 in *The Sot-Weed Factor*, a satiric poem of genuine power. The picture which he gives of certain aspects of life in the colony may not be accurate and certainly is not flattering, but there was no poetry produced elsewhere in America at the time which has retained its interest as has this racy and vigorous satire by the unknown Marylander or English visitor. In Philadelphia, it is true, young Aquila Rose was considered a poet, and in Connecticut Richard Steere in 1713 was influenced by Milton and in one short poem showed a somewhat unusual appreciation of nature. Sewall and others in Boston handed about both Latin and English verses, but the entire Northern output of the period is negligible except as an indication of misdirected energy and lack of taste.

In Virginia, the rich planter, Robert Beverley, annoyed at the errors he had noted in the proof sheets of Oldmixon's *British Empire* which he had seen in London, undertook to write the history of his native colony himself and made a book that is still alive. It has some of the qualities which characterized the writings of the Virginian William Byrd in the next period—complete freedom from pedantry, an easy familiarity, a freshness of view and of phrase. It is the very antipode of Mather, who could never take up his pen without breaking out into a rash of classical quotations. From the study and the smell of the lamp, we pass into the fields with the breeze through the pines. Still farther south, in North Carolina, we find one of the only two good books of travel produced during this period. In 1700 a young Englishman, John Lawson, came over to Charleston and made a trip through the two Carolinas, finally settling in the northern one, which he found a "delicious country." His book, which contained an account of his journeyings, a long description of the Indians, and some chapters on the natural history, was an excellent bit of work, intelligent, vivid, amusing.

The other travel sketch, even more sprightly and entertaining, must be credited to a New England woman, the Madam Sarah Knight already quoted. But her keen observations, clothed in picturesque and racy phrases, did not find their way into print until a century and a quarter later, and her fellow New Englanders missed the chance to read what was by all odds the most entertaining bit of literature produced among them. This illustrates one handicap of the colonial writer of the day, the lack both of means of production and of a sympathetic public. For many decades there had been a printing plant in Boston and by 1715 there were five there. There was also one in Philadelphia, one in New York from 1693 and one in New London in 1709. These, however, were under censorship, and Bradford's imprisonment in Philadelphia in 1692 for having printed matter displeasing to the Quaker party was the cause of his removal to New York and the establishment of the press there.[1] The royal governors were instructed to license printed matter and in Boston not only did the local gov-

[1] I. Thomas, *History of Printing in America* (Am. Antiq. Soc., *Trans.*, V), 89-92, 95, 98-99, 104-105, 291-292.

ernment also maintain the right summarily to suppress any publication which displeased it but the clergy through their influence likewise held a fairly rigid, though unofficial, control. In 1690 the first attempt to publish a newspaper in America was tried in Boston but suffered from censorial infanticide and the journal, *Publick Occurrances,* was murdered in its first issue. Five years later, Thomas Maule, a Quaker of Salem, was proceeded against merely for circulating a book which he had had printed in New York, but escaped owing partly to the reaction following the witchcraft excitement.[1] In 1700 an answer to one of Cotton Mather's pamphlets was written by the Rev. Mr. Colman and others, who found it necessary to send it to New York to be printed, on account of the control of the Boston press by the clerical clique. For the same reason, Brattle had to send his book against Mather to London and when it arrived in the colony, Increase Mather, who was then president of Harvard, had it publicly burned in the college yard. The system was beginning to break down somewhat during this period but the few cases cited show the difficulties, and to some extent the risks, which an author ran who wished to publish matter displeasing to the official and clerical censors.

Throughout the whole period, the only journal of any sort published in any of the colonies was the *Boston News-Letter,* a pitifully small and dull weekly which was founded in 1704. It contained belated news from Europe, the clearings and entries at the Custom House, and other bits of one sort and another. It has an importance as the beginning of the periodical press in this country but did not afford the slightest opening for literary talent. An author of a book or pamphlet was thus limited to running the gauntlet of official censorship

[1] C. A. Duniway, *The Struggle for the Freedom of the Press in Mass.* (*Harvard Hist. Studies,* XII), 68-69, 70-73.

and religious prejudice attending publication by the few local presses in the North or sending his work to England, a lengthy and costly proceeding. For shorter productions, such as poems or brief essays, the only method of bringing them to the notice of others was the "broadside" or else circulation in manuscript.

Moreover, there was almost no public which an author could reach. The population of the colonies was so scattered that, in the absence of a periodical press, the problem of the distribution of ideas was almost as great as that of evolving them at all. The lack of postal facilities was another factor militating against the spread of ideas. In 1691 a postal service between Massachusetts, New York and Pennsylvania had been established and in 1711 this was extended to New Hampshire but the South was not included for another generation. At the opening of the century it was stated that practically the entire correspondence of Maryland and Virginia was with England and that they would exchange scarcely a hundred letters a year with the Northern colonies if a post were established, whereas the cost would be £500 annually. The cost of sending a letter between New York and Philadelphia was nine pence and between the latter town and Boston twenty-one pence. If it weighed over an ounce, the charge was quadrupled, and it must be remembered that the value of money was then several times what it is today.[1] There could thus be practically no common intercolonial intellectual life. With respect to the development of even a local culture, the South, owing to its lack of presses, was particularly handicapped. It is naturally in centers of population, where opportunities for intercourse and discussion are greatest, that the interest in intellectual matters is keenest. In this regard, South Carolina was the best off of the Southern colonies, and

[1] W. E. Rich, *The History of the United States Post Office to the Year 1829* (*Harvard Economic Studies*, XXVII), 12, 26.

in Charleston there did develop an intellectual and artistic life which was equal to that of the Northern towns. At this period, however, even the towns of the North were so small that the difference between that section and the South was less than was to be the case later.

The facilities for education of the people at large from Pennsylvania northward, although somewhat better than in the South, were not notably so in this period. The half-hearted attempt made by Penn's government to make education a function of the state was soon given up, and the only school in Philadelphia, an excellent one in which Pastorius was teacher, was a religious institution of the Quakers. It was by no means typical, however, in its high standard, of the educational facilities in the rest of the colony. In New York there were few schools and those of poor quality. All accounts agree as to the low intellectual level of the people, both rich and poor. Some of the best families sent their boys to England for schooling or occasionally to Boston, but "the City is so conveniently Situated for Trade and the Genius of the people are so inclined to merchandise, that they generally seek no other Education for their children than writing and Arithmetick. So that letters must be in a manner forced upon them" wrote one observer in 1713.[1] The people objected to any expenditure for educational purposes, and the poorer elements depended much, as everywhere in the colonies, on child labor. In the whole of Westchester County in New York in 1704 there were only six families who were able "to spare their children's time more than to learn to read and write."[2] In the town of New York itself there was considerable illiteracy, and in a petition to the king in 1701, of the six hundred and eighty-seven who were of

[1] Quoted by W. W. Kemp, *The Support of Schools in Colonial New York* (N. Y., 1913), 68.

[2] Kemp, *The Support of Schools in Colonial New York*, 67.

sufficient importance to sign such a document, sixty-one or nearly one in ten had to sign by mark. Early in the eighteenth century the Society for the Propagation of the Gospel opened a missionary school in the town but the people generally showed no inclination to help themselves.

Both Rhode Island and New Hampshire had a few schools, and the former particularly was not as backward as has often been thought, but in that entire section of the colony of Massachusetts which is now the state of Maine, there was not a single school until the first master made his appearance in 1701. In the other portion of Massachusetts and in Connecticut conditions were better, but there also the people were to a great extent opposed to the expenditure of public money for school purposes and the old picture of every village with its free school and a population athirst for learning is a pure figment of the imagination. Such schools as were operated under the laws and were called free, required the payment of tuition from all but those pupils whose parents were too poor to afford it, and consequently were quite different from our modern public schools. There was nothing democratic about them and it was not intended that there should be. As the population of the towns became more scattered owing to the filling up of the land, attendance at the town school became more and more difficult for those on the outskirts. These were opposed to contributing in taxes to the town schools and to paying for the support of a teacher in their own part of the town as well, when they did so. From this arose the demand that the town school be held in different sections of the town in the several quarters of the year, and there thus evolved at this time what has been known as the "moving school," which marked the first stage in the development of our modern school district. Even in such towns as maintained a school throughout the year, the children attended for only a quarter of the time.   It must be remembered that there was no compulsory school attendance, the ony theoretical requirement being that children should receive from some source a certain amount of education, the town school and the higher grammar grades being maintained merely to facilitate that process.

In spite of the excellent legislation to secure this, and which has already been described, it was far from being complied with.[1]   In Connecticut in 1690 the legislature stated that there were many people who were "unable to read the English tongue," and in 1701 that of Massachusetts declared that the law was "shamefully neglected in divers towns."   In the latter colony, Andover, Woburn, Watertown, Middleboro, Dedham, Haverhill, Groton, Framingham and other towns were indicted from time to time for having no schools, and in Middlesex County, although there were nine towns which should legally have had grammar schools, only four had them.   Natick was probably an exceptionally bad case, but in that town in 1698 only one child in seventy could read.   Of thirteen proprietors of Manchester in 1716 eight could not write, and in this period we constantly find many men and almost all women signing by mark.

Several factors had operated together to bring about this decline.   For one, there was the enlarging of the number of neighborhoods, of which we have just spoken, in the larger towns, which resulted in quarrels over payment for the schools and over their location.   Another was the unsettled condition due to the war and its attendant losses and poverty.   Deerfield, for example, apparently had no school from 1703 until 1720 when it had recovered from the effects of the massacre.   Still another was the development of the frontier where pov-

[1] T. J. Wertenbaker, *The First Americans* (*A History of American Life*, II), chap. iv.

erty and new conditions made schools difficult to maintain and where the intensified struggle for a mere subsistence emphasized a purely material outlook on the world and made education seem less necessary.   Moreover, New England society was in a state of disintegration.   The unity of religious spirit, which had never been complete, was rapidly declining.   The town school had never been intended to be purely a secular affair.   The educational aim of the earlier settlers had not been to make good citizens but to instruct the Christian youth sufficiently that they might search the Scriptures.   The civil and ecclesiastical functions had been inextricably mixed in the early church-town organization, and that organization, which was never conceived as merely secular, had happened to be the most convenient one for the administering of schools, which had thus somewhat accidentally become a function of the state.   Under the new Massachusetts charter of 1691 the control of the church over the state had been abolished and consequently the school administration, which remained in the hands of the town meeting, became a secular matter.   The old religious sanction for education passed away with the decline in religious zeal, and the newer ideal of an educated citizenry for the benefit of the state was only just beginning to take its place.   It may be noted that one of the factors which was greatly to help the development of this ideal was the placing of education in the control of a state wholly secular, a situation never contemplated by the New Englanders and which was forced upon the "die-hard" church party by the English government. This and the evolution of the school district were the two important contributions of New England in this period of transition, which marks both the lowest ebb in educational activity and also the turn for the better.

Renewed efforts as well as a more liberalizing tendency are found to be at work.   The fines for noncompliance with the school laws were increased and new laws were enacted intended to secure better teachers. Connecticut in the two Hopkins Grammar Schools of Hartford and New Haven had excellent institutions to work with, and in Boston the Latin School under Ezekiel Cheever from 1670 to 1708 was undoubtedly the best school in any of the colonies. The new tendencies struggling with the old appear clearly in the collegiate education of the section at this time. Harvard, which at the close of the century had an attendance of "forty or fifty children, few of them capable of edification by such exercises" according to Cotton Mather, had been intended from the beginning as a training school for the ministry, and of the total number of graduates from its founding one half had become clergymen. The course of study had been designed for that end and must have been unsatisfactory to those who aimed at a liberal education rather than a mere preparation for clerical life. In an effort to prevent the liberalizing of the institution desired by a party including John Leverett and the two Brattles, the old party, including the Mathers and Sewall, lost control and in 1708 Leverett became president. Meanwhile some of the church leaders in Connecticut who had long been anxious to found a college in that colony on exactly the lines of the unregenerate Harvard saw their opportunity, and interested the members of the losing party in Boston. These assisted the undertaking and in 1701 the "Collegiate School," as it was called, later to be known as Yale College, was founded. From that time on it replaced Harvard as the stronghold of the strict Calvinists, the older institution continuing in the path of liberalism. During all the period covered by this chapter, the new college had no buildings, almost no library, and a most uncertain habitat and organization. As its former president Arthur T. Hadley has said, "for many years it was difficult to say what it was and where it belonged."

New England girls were rarely taught more than reading and writing at most, although there was a girl's boarding school in Boston by 1706 and by 1714 a "finishing school" where various minor arts were taught in addition to arithmetic. In the homes, dame schools and town schools, boys learned reading, writing and arithmetic, although a good many learned none of these. A very few comparatively attended the higher grammar grades, and an occasional lad from New York went to England. The population of the colonies from Pennsylvania northward in 1700 may be estimated at about one hundred and forty-three thousand. Of this total the only boys receiving any education higher than that afforded by the grammar grades of a few schools were the "forty or fifty children" who were studying the narrow ecclesiastical curriculum at Harvard. Such in brief was the educational situation in the North at the opening of the new century.

Turning now to the South, we find different conditions resulting in somewhat different systems but without any great difference in the resultant level of general education in this period. The scattered nature of the population and the absence of towns and villages introduced an element of great difficulty. Facilities were best in Virginia where we find grammar schools, endowed free elementary schools, the "old Field Schools," (formed by several families in a neighborhood combining to hire a teacher), and private tutoring. The Symms Free School, founded in 1634, and the Eaton Free School, probably not long after, were the two oldest institutions in the colony and were in existence all through the eighteenth century. At its opening, we have the names of a number of other endowed schools, and there is ample evidence to show that the "old Field Schools" were numerous, although it is harder to trace the existence of these private institutions than those of New England which were matters of public record.   It is indicated that frequently the poorer children of the neighborhood were taught in these community schools as well as their richer neighbors, and we also have occasional record of schools maintained especially for the poor, such as the endowed parish school of St. Stephen's in Northumberland County where the children were not only taught at the expense of the school but lodged and clothed as well.   In the South as in the North, the laws governing apprenticeship, both of children learning trades and of poor children without homes, required that the master or guardian should see that the child was taught to read and write.   That the law was enforced in Virginia and also that there were facilities for learning is indicated by the records of Surrey County where we find between 1679 and 1684 fifty instances of guardians giving bonds to have their wards taught in schools.

There was some excellent legislation contemplating school systems in both Maryland and South Carolina in this period, but as we found in New England, passing laws and having them complied with were different matters.   Only one school is definitely known to us in this period for Maryland, King William's at Annapolis, which developed into the St. John's College of today. In North Carolina, although its total population did not probably exceed seven thousand, we know of several schools, such as those at Pasquatonk, Chowan and Sarum.   Of the children in the last a visitor wrote that they "can both read and write very distinctly and gave before me such an account of the grounds and principles of the Christian religion that strangely surprised me." [1] In South Carolina there were two schools at Charleston and we know of one or two in the country districts.

---

[1] Quoted by C. L. Smith, *History of Education in North Carolina* (Herbert B. Adams, ed., *Contributions to American Educational History*, no. 3), 17.

Probably in the other colonies as in Virginia, the richer planters had their children taught first in the "old Field Schools" or by private tutors. To a much greater extent than in the North, the older lads went to England for their higher education, and in this period, from Virginia, we find among others Bartholomew Yates receiving his B.A. from Oxford in 1698, John Span going there in 1705 as a boy of eighteen, and Mann Page there four years later at seventeen. In Maryland there was the same practice, and young Charles Carroll went to Europe for a number of years' study, returning in 1723. The same was true of the South Carolinians and the educational opportunities thus given to wealthy Southern lads were incomparably greater than those obtainable by New England boys at Harvard, practically none of whom went abroad. For those in the South who could not afford this training the door of opportunity was opened by the fulfillment of a long-cherished scheme in Virginia when William and Mary College was founded in 1693. Virginia seems to have led the South as Massachusetts and Connecticut did the North and, indeed, all the colonies, but if we consider the whole of the two sections there was apparently no startling difference in the level of general culture between them. This is also borne out by a comparative study of signed documents, those in the South showing no larger a percentage of signers by mark than in the North. In the South among the more highly educated there were no such men of encyclopedic learning as Mather and some of the other New England clergymen. On the other hand, among the greater number of Southerners who had had an Oxford training and European education there was a more humane attitude toward art and letters, a more cultivated savoring of life.

CHAPTER VI

THE LIFE OF THE SPIRIT
1690-1713

ONE cannot arbitrarily divide man's psychic life into intellectual and spiritual, and it is somewhat arbitrary to discuss literature in one chapter and the other arts in another. Yet in dealing with the matters to be discussed in this chapter—arts and crafts, painting, music, morals and those actions and reactions which we designate as humanitarian—we are looking at the life of the colonists from another angle than that from which we viewed it in the last chapter. We have entered, however, upon a part of human nature which defies sharpness of definition. What, for example, is art? What are the essential qualities which justify us in speaking of a people or of an age as artistic, and in the absence of which we may pronounce them inartistic? It is obvious that such questions cannot be discussed at length here, and yet it is necessary to raise them in order to approach that of the artistic life of the colonies in this period with understanding or at least with modesty. There were certain obvious shortcomings which strike us at once. Although, as we shall see later, there were some painters at work, they did not produce a single canvas of high quality. There were no museums or exhibitions. There was no musician of note and no concert. With one possible exception there was not a poem written which has now any interest other than antiquarian. And yet, although art produced fewer flowers at the top, it is by no means certain that it did

139

not strike its roots deeper in the soil and that America
was not then more artistic than now.

Granted that in every department of life it is to the
exceptional individual that we must look for the highest
achievement, nevertheless we may question the vitality
of any movement which has no roots in the life of the
common people.   In spite of the hordes who troop
through the museums what is the æsthetic taste of the
great bulk of that element today?   It may be studied in
the popular radio program, the pictures on the movie
screen, the colored supplements of the Sunday papers,
and the catalogue of any large mail-order house.   What,
moreover, is its artistic product?   The only answer is
that it is nonexistent.   Its craftsmanship finds expression
in changing the washers on the faucets or tinkering with
the Ford.   Art today, to a considerable extent, is like one
of those floating islands of roots and branches bound
together and covered with soil and vegetation but which
have no foundation and are sustained in insulation above
the earth.   This was not the case in the earlier colonial
period, and in tracing the development of art in America
we have to follow two distinct movements—on the one
hand, the continuous degradation of the art of the people,
and on the other, the temporary disintegration of the
artistic life of the upper classes, but which later with the
turn of the century entered upon a new period of growth.
It is notable, however, that this new growth was in the
development of an art for the rich, that it sprang only
from the demand of a small cultured class, that it was
largely a professional art to be bought and paid for by
those who could afford it, and that side by side with its
development the arts practised by the common people
and their æsthetic taste became steadily more degraded.

In many respects the increasing accumulation and concentration of wealth during the early eighteenth century
tended to widen that breach between the rich and poor

of which we have already spoken in other connections. This was true of art as well, but it is not altogether easy to see why it should necessarily have been so, for folk art is never dependent upon the possession of wealth. Puritanism partially accounts for it but, although the Puritan spirit was inimical to the artistic spirit, it did not banish all its forms or impulses. Such a Puritan of the Puritans as Samuel Sewall was one of the most constant versifiers of the period, and the sternest of them had their portraits painted, wore rich clothes and accumulated beautiful furniture and costly plate. Nor can we explain it wholly by the primitive existence of frontier life. One of the most vigorous of all arts is that of the half-naked Negro of the African jungle, who lives under conditions far more primitive, and with less resources, than any American frontiersman ever had to face.

No explanation of this more rapid degradation of the artistic impulse of the people in America as compared with Europe is wholly adequate. Perhaps we may find one as good as any in the fact that, unlike the savage, the colonists in America were trying, each in his own generation, to attain at once to a level of cultural equipment that was a product of many centuries of civilized effort and to do so in a new environment which was, in itself, adapted only to the level of savagery. The task was too great and the instrument—the human spirit itself—broke down and disintegrated. The qualities it lost were those which were least essential to the material struggle with the environment, as those which were strengthened were the ones most essential.

It was not wholly an unconscious process. "The Plow-man that raiseth Grain is more serviceable to Mankind, than the Painter who draws only to please the Eye," wrote a New Englander in 1719. "The Carpenter who builds a good House to defend us from the Wind and Weather, is more serviceable than the curious Carver,

who employs his Art to please the Fancy." [1]   Food and
shelter are indeed the primary requirements.   But after
securing these, the African and the American Indian had
time and energy left for art in the same environment
which was beginning to make it seem a superfluous
luxury to the white man.   The latter did not have it,
because of his insistence upon that higher standard of
material living to which he was accustomed and which
was beyond the ken of the savage.   In so far as outward
conditions were concerned it was not the frontier that
destroyed such arts as the people practised, but the effort
to maintain the only familiar standard of living, under
conditions which made it impossible except by a partial
exhaustion of energy.   It may be noted that the only
parts of the country where the folk songs and folk art
continued to live—such as the Carolina mountains—
were precisely those where the standard of living remained stationary at a primitive level from the
beginning.

This movement of degradation was to be retarded
from time to time by the infusion of new blood in
streams of fresh immigration from Europe, and in the
period covered by this chapter there was still much genuine artistic impulse among the people.   We have already
spoken of the self-sustaining nature of the ordinary
colonial home of the more modest type, and of the multiplicity of household industries.   It was in these that the
art of the people found its expression.   Of the household
utensils of one sort and another, a great number were
carved by the men in the long winter evenings and were
not only made serviceable but were ornamented with
designs, though this minor art was found rather more
often among the Dutch and Germans than the English.
By the opening of the eighteenth century, the latter had

[1] *An Addition to the Present Melancholy Circumstances of the Province Considered* (Boston, 1719), 7.

already lost much of the love of carving which they had brought with them in the seventeenth and we do not find later the carved beams, posts, studs or pendants which the earlier settlers had wrought into their houses. These expressions of the builder-owner's craftsmanship and taste were disappearing under a clapboarded exterior and a lathed and plastered interior. Moreover, although the great mass of the furniture used by the common people was of native, and, much of it, of household manufacture, the elaborate designs carved upon the flat surfaces were disappearing from the pieces made at home, which were becoming simpler and cruder from the standpoint of craftsmanship, at the same time that the furniture being made by the professional colonial cabinetmaker was rapidly improving. By 1713 few rural householders had either the desire or the ability to make such elaborate pieces as their fathers or grandfathers had made in the preceding century. The somewhat easier method of painting was being employed, though this also frequently gave scope for artistic impulse and ability, and was in vogue all through the colonies, the styles varying somewhat with the nationality of the craftsman. The art ran the gamut from a mere outlining of the panels to most elaborate patterns of leaves and flowers, sometimes combined with carving, sometimes replacing it entirely, and giving ample satisfaction to the strong colonial love of color. It must be remembered that we are now speaking of work done by the farmer or artisan for his own use and satisfaction and not by a professional for sale.[1]

Another of the minor arts of the household was the decorative weaving practised by the women from Maine to Carolina. We have already spoken of the importance of the bed in the household furniture, and most of this weaving was of bedspreads for those who could not

[1] H. D. Eberlein and Abbot McClure, *The Practical Book of Early American Arts and Crafts* (Phila., 1916), chap. ix.

afford the damask and silk coverings used by the rich. The handwoven coverlets were frequently wholly spun, dyed and woven in the same house, and the great variety of designs and the infinite opportunity for varying the color combinations gave unlimited scope to the artistic creativeness of the housewives, of which they took full advantage in their relish of the task.   In the realm of needlework there was also ample opportunity for self-expression, and it is interesting to note that the samplers which served as the basis of instruction exhibit in their modest sphere the same development which we find in nearly all other spheres of colonial life.   At first, we have nearly a century of mere imitation of English models, slowly degenerating until the lowest point of interest and excellence is reached about 1700.   By 1721 a distinct American type has become noticeable, the art improves, and by 1750 it shows a freedom and originality along an entirely different line of development from the contemporary English.   It thus epitomizes the whole trend of colonial life and we can see the fateful foreshadowing of the eventual rupture of the empire as we follow the designs wrought by childish fingers diverging more and more from those of their cousins overseas.

The art impulse lasted longer in some departments than in others and there was much excellent work done by professional craftsmen in America in the metals, although practically nothing in brass until the latter part of the eighteenth century.   Among other articles wrought in iron by the smith of any village or plantation were door hinges, knockers, weather vanes, andirons and all sorts of household gear.   In the vanes, for example, the initials of the owner or some design appropriate to the purpose of the building were wrought with an artistry and an individuality which lent a charm that is wholly submerged in the stock manufactured article of today.   Similarly our hinges have become so utterly uniform, utilitarian and ugly that they are hidden away in the crack of the door as far as possible. The early iron ones, on the contrary, in their many different designs and bold or charming lines lent a character and interest to the plank doors of the houses of our forefathers that are wholly lacking in the stock paneled door of practically every house today. In the andirons, these obscure local smiths, whose names are utterly unknown, achieved a grace in the modeling of foot or stock or finial that has been lost by their modern successors either in factory or at the village forge. Even the smaller utensils of the kitchen, such as the wafer irons, gridirons and others, received a decorative value in design or form which bespoke an appreciation of both which has become meaningless to the same class of people today. Moreover, the fact that the great bulk of household articles were made by the owner himself or especially for him by a near neighbor enabled him to give expression to his own personality, and the finished and furnished home thereby acquired a distinct individuality and character.

In the somewhat more differentiated craft of silversmithing this also held good as practically every article was made for the purchaser according to his general instructions. In this craft the workman of the period achieved notable distinction and his work was little if at all inferior to that of his best European competitors. In this, as in so many other things, however, the Southerner relied upon importation from England, and we know of no colonial-made silverware in that section until the latter part of the eighteenth century. In the North the craft showed a natural tendency to center in the larger towns where wealth was greatest.[1] In this period the best work was done in New York and Boston,

[1] C. L. Avery, *Colonial Silver in the Seventeenth and Eighteenth Centuries* (N. Y., 1920), liii.

although there were also many smiths scattered through the rural districts, such as Job Prince in Milford and René Grignon in Norwich, Connecticut. Indeed, within a few decades later we can name about seventy villages in that colony, Rhode Island and Massachusetts, in which we know such smiths were at work. A very large number of these craftsmen, out of all proportion to their comparative racial numbers, were Dutch and French, the former being by far the more important in their influence upon the development of colonial style. The great bulk of all work done in the colonies was for people of moderate means, and we find in almost all departments—architecture, furniture making, and others —a tendency toward simplicity, strength and vigor, in which perfection of line and form become the dominant characteristics.

In this period, the musical life of the colonies consisted almost wholly of instrumental or vocal music in private houses, taverns or occasional gatherings out of doors, such as impromptu dances or the country fairs. In New England, the first pipe organ was installed in King's Chapel in Boston in 1713, it having been given to that church by Thomas Brattle after having been refused by the Brattle Street Church. The congregational singing throughout New England was incredibly bad, and the first instruction book was published at Newbury in 1712. Nevertheless singing was popular even in Puritan Massachusetts, and Cotton Mather complained that the minds of the country people were being much corrupted by the "foolish songs and ballads" which the peddlers were carrying into all parts of the colony. As an "antidote" he proposed to distribute hymns. There were some instruments in New England, such as a virginal in Sewall's house, and by 1716 the organist of King's Chapel advertised that he taught music and dancing, mended virginals and spinets, and offered for sale a recent importation of flageolets, flutes, hautboys, bassviols and violins.

Evidently there was an increased interest in musical matters becoming apparent, but the influence of New England in colonial musical culture has been much over-rated, and the musical life of the Middle and Southern colonies was far richer. Pipe organs had been installed in Philadelphia and in Port Royal, Virginia, by about 1700, and all musical instruments were more numerous than in the North. The Swedes and early Germans had brought their fiddles and flutes with their folk songs,[1] and there were many violins among the English, and an occasional bagpipe wakened Scotch echoes. The spinets and virginals were found only in the richer households.

Nowhere in the colonies in this period, however, was there any organized musical life. The opera and, so far as we have record, concerts do not appear until a few decades later. At this time Charleston, South Carolina, and not Boston would seem to have been the musical center of the continent. Artistically her citizens were more cultured and the Southern port was that of entry for most of the artists who, in the van of the never ending European stream, were already beginning to come to "barbarous America" to sell their talent for a better price, oddly, than it would fetch at home. These went first, as a rule, to the rich islands of the West Indies, and thence naturally took the short route to America by way of the South.

In another art, that of the theater, New England influence was not simply negligible but openly hostile, and the development of the drama, one of the notable features in the later decades covered by this volume, has to be traced during the whole period in the Middle and

[1] R. R. Drummond, *Early German Music* (*Americana Germanica,* Univ. of Pennsylvania), part I.

Southern colonies only. Even there, however, it was not successful at the opening of the century, although a professional troupe appeared in Charleston in 1703 and in New York the following year.

Although the ownership of paintings among the well-to-do was fairly common both North and South, the two sections showing no difference in this regard, I have failed to find recorded the name of the artist of a single canvas during this period, except an occasional portrait painter. Besides paintings, prints of various sorts appear to have been moderately abundant, and houses containing forty or fifty may be found with considerable frequency in several of the colonies. However, these were usually described by their frames or values and, except for a few such as "Julius Caesar," "Scipio Africanus" or "A View of London," we are left to conjecture both as to their subjects and artists. Such descriptions as "one large horse battle," "one large picture with roots," or "a large picture of images, sheep and ships" offer considerable scope to the imagination.

Of paintings produced in the colonies in this period, we have no records except of portraits. In New England, it is believed that a Tom Child was painting in Boston from 1692 to 1706, Joseph Allen from 1684 to 1728 and that a Lawrence Brown was also there in 1701. In New York there was the interesting family of Duyckinck, of whom the first Evert seems to have been still painting portraits until his death in 1702. A grandson was painting on glass, and Evert 3d was also painting in this period, probably being the artist of the Beekman portraits. Gerret Van Randst was another New York artist of the time. John Watson made pencil drawings in Perth Amboy as early as 1715 and was said to have had a collection of European pictures, both originals and copies. In Philadelphia, Christopher Witt, whom we have already mentioned as starting the first botanical garden there, also painted portraits, at least one of which, that of Johannes Kelpius, has come down to us. In Delaware and Maryland, by 1711, Gustavus Hesselius, the Swede, was beginning his long career. It has been said that there was no painter in Virginia and that all the portraits of this period were done in England, but a letter from William Fitzhugh in 1698 in which he orders six frames, some colors and oils, "with half a doz. 3 quarter clothes to set up a painter," indicates that one was at work there, or at least expected. In Charleston we know that a portrait of Governor Johnson was painted as early as 1705 and a certain Henrietta Johnson was painting pastels there by 1708, at least fifteen examples of her work surviving. Both in the colonies named, and others, there may have been more obscure artists at work, and it must always be remembered that our knowledge of all such facts depends upon painstaking local research, much more of which has always been done in New England than in the South. The more that we learn of the life of the latter, the more does the similarity of conditions in the two sections appear, until the great social change brought about by the rapid development of slavery.[1]

This similarity, however, was least marked in the religious life and outlook of the Northern and Southern colonies. The citizens of both sections, speaking generally, were largely under the influence of certain ideas that we are wont to consider as being essentially Puritan in character but which in reality were but the outlook on life of the more sober elements of the English middle class of the period. In such matters as the observance of the Sabbath, for example, the laws of Virginia were quite similar to those of Massachusetts.[2] In both it was

[1] J. H. Morgan, *Early American Painters* (N. Y., 1921), 8-21.
[2] *Cf.* T. J. Wertenbaker, *The First Americans (A History of American Life*, II), chap. xi. By 1690 the degree of enforcement differed.

unlawful to fish on that day, to go on a journey, to transport goods or to do any other work, and trivial violations were punished with almost as much frequency in the Southern as in the Northern, colony, the attitude in the Southern one becoming rather stricter toward the end of the seventeenth century. In 1699 petitions were sent to the house of burgesses from three Virginia counties praying that every citizen should be forced to attend some place of worship, and such a law was passed in that year. The grant of a charter for William and Mary College had been requested by the assembly in words which might have been used for Harvard or Yale. It was desired, so the petition read, "to the end that the Church of Virginia may be furnished with a seminary of ministers of the gospel, and that the youth may be piously educated in good letters and manners, and that the Christian faith may be propagated among the Western Indians." [1] All this is merely to say that the sound elements of the English population of all the colonies were drawn originally from the same reservoir of sober, God-fearing people in the home country. The old belief of the New Englanders, carefully nursed by their later historians, that they alone formed such a strain in the colonial population was based only on prejudice, ignorance and abounding conceit. The pictures of Virginia and Maryland as settled almost exclusively by gay Cavaliers, so dearly cherished by certain local writers in the nineteenth century, is quite as far from fact.

It is true that what we may call the sectarian aspects of religion were different in the several colonies. The New England people had been dissenters from the start for the most part, those of New York a heterogeneous mixture, those of Pennsylvania Quakers and German sectarians, those of Maryland Catholic, Anglican and Puritan,

[1] H. B. Adams, *The College of William and Mary* (*Circular of Information of the Bureau of Education*, No. 1), 17.

and those of Virginia, Anglican, as were those of the Carolinas, with a large dissenting element. But to a certain extent all of these had had gradually to adapt themselves to the fact that the colonial churches were three thousand miles from Europe and were subject to different conditions. Although the Congregationalists in New England had proclaimed independency whereas the Anglicans of Virginia had not, nevertheless the Church of England in Virginia was a far more independent body than, say, the Church of England in the county of Kent at home. Just at the opening of the period of this chapter, the Bishop of London did, indeed, become represented in the colony by a commissary, but the colonial church had run its own affairs for so long that whenever the new commissary came into conflict with the colonial order he was practically powerless. In Virginia, for example, the right of presentation had passed to the parishioners and practically all power had centered in the vestries as against the governor, commissary and clergy. The central authority, although acknowledged in theory, was in fact so slight that the Anglican parish of the South was almost as independent and congregational as were the avowed ones of the New England colonies. There was thus through all the colonies and many of the sects a strong though unacknowledged undercurrent of independency.[1]

On the whole, the congregations of New England received the best ministrations. In Maryland there were a few devoted Roman priests to minister to the less than three thousand Catholics, and there were, of course, many clergymen of the several denominations in all the colonies who were serious and godly men, but there was a larger proportion of these in the Puritan colonies. The problem, however, was not wholly one of men but

---

[1] Cf. T. J. Wertenbaker, *The First Americans* (*A History of American Life*, II), chap. v.

of physical conditions also. In the colonies from Maryland southward, the scattered population, the long distances, the lack of roads, and the swamps and difficulties of the country affected the religious observance of the colonists as they did so many other aspects of their social and intellectual life.

In Maryland, for example, the Romanist, Father Mosely, had to preach to a congregation on the first Sunday of each month which was fifty miles from his house, another on the second, which was forty miles farther, taking him ninety miles from his congregation of the third Sunday. The Reverend James Blair gives a description of the situation in North Carolina in 1703. Suppose the clergyman, he says, "minister of one precinct . . . and this precinct, as they are all bounded with two rivers, and those rivers at least twenty miles distant, without any inhabitants on the road, for they plant only on the rivers, and they are planted in length upon these rivers at least twenty miles, and to give all those inhabitants an opportunity of hearing a sermon, or bringing their children to be baptized, which must be on the Sabbath, for they won't spare time of another day, and must be in every ten miles distant, for five miles is the furthest they will bring their children, or willingly come themselves; so that he must, to do his duty effectually, be ten or twelve weeks in making his progress through one precinct." [1]

Under such conditions, in an age when the missionary spirit was not strong in any denomination except the Roman Catholics and Quakers, it was almost impossible to secure men of ability and piety to go out to the colonies as ministers. With the new century, the Society for the Propagation of the Gospel did send out many missionaries who established Anglican congregations in

[1] Quoted by F. L. Hawks, *History of North Carolina* (Fayetteville, 1857), II, 297.

many of the colonies, including Massachusetts and Connecticut, but not a few of them were unfit. The most loquacious letter writer among them, John Urmiston, was in continual difficulties with his people, was fined for drunkenness, and on the other hand expressed his own opinion in a letter to the secretary of the Society when he wrote that he "would rather be vicar to the Bear Garden than Bishop of North Carolina." [1]

In the period under review, there were two conflicting tendencies at work, one toward a greater toleration and the other toward the setting up of established churches and even toward persecution. The former of these was most noticeable in the North, and the latter in the South. In Massachusetts a great step forward had been taken under the compulsion of the English government when the new charter of 1691 had done away with the Congregational Church test for the franchise. Moreover, both in that colony and Connecticut, partly owing to the drawing in of the frontier on account of the Indian wars, the population of the older towns had become greater, and just as we have noted how this affected an alteration in the school system, so it also affected the parishes. In many cases the town, in a word, had become too big for the single town church just as it had for the single town school, and the records are full of demands for a division of the church to suit the needs of new neighborhoods. So many exceptions had to be made from the old rule that the church rapidly tended to become divorced from the political town and to become rather an affair of the ecclesiastical parish. This occasioned many quarrels among the congregations, and occasionally that part of one which wished to, split off and reorganized as a different sect.

The numbers of these had been slowly but steadily in-

[1] *N. C. Colon. Records*, II, 374.

creasing, and due partly to the general decline in religious zeal and partly to better acquaintance, much of the old spirit of persecution was dying out among the Puritans. By 1700 there were nine Baptist churches in New England, a Baptist had been president of Harvard, and at the ordination of a Baptist minister in Boston in 1717, Cotton Mather preached the ordination sermon and deprecated the earlier persecutions. That the sectarian spirit was still very much alive, however, may be savored in a tart and amusing colloquy which has come down to us. Being in great danger crossing the ferry at Portsmouth, Rhode Island, the Anglican missionary George Keith was rescued by a former Quaker acquaintance, who refused to allow his men to receive any pay. "I thanked him very kindly for his help in our great Danger," wrote the Anglican in his journal, "and said to him, John, ye have been a means under God to save our natural Life, suffer me to be a means under God to save your Soul. . . . He replied, George, save thy own Soul, for I have no need of thy help; then said I, I will pray for your conversion; he replyed, the Prayers of the wicked are an abomination." [1]   Nevertheless, mutual toleration was growing, although both in Massachusetts and Connecticut all tax payers had still to contribute to the established Congregational Church, and, thus, if they belonged to some other, had to pay doubly for religious support. Connecticut, originally the more liberal of the two, had become the more narrow, and although in 1708 it passed an act permitting the establishing of Anglican churches, this was mainly due to a fear for the charter in view of the Anglicans' complaints of their treatment. Nevertheless, it was a step forward. In the same year the adoption in that colony of the Saybrook Platform, which gave jurisdiction over the town churches to a

[1] George Keith, *A Journal of Travels from New-Hampshire to Caratuck* (London, 1706), 36.

consociation of ministers, rather led the Connecticut Congregationalists away from those of Massachusetts and nearer to the Presbyterians, who were at this time just beginning to establish themselves in the Middle colonies.

For over twenty years Francis Makemie had been traveling up and down the coast from New York to South Carolina as an evangelist, and by 1705 a regular presbytery met at Philadelphia, choosing him as moderator and enrolling five other ministers. In another dozen years twelve more were added and these labored mainly among the poorer Scotch, Irish and Welsh of the Middle colonies. Pennsylvania maintained its liberal policy and not only were some of the earlier German arrivals adding materially to the number of sects in the neighborhood of Philadelphia but that city also became at this time an asylum for some of the persecuted Catholics from Maryland. It was a period of general persecution for the Romanists, and severe laws were passed against them in both Massachusetts and New York, at the instigation of the Earl of Bellomont, then governor of both colonies. Nowhere in America, however, did they meet with such harsh treatment as in Maryland. In 1691 that colony became a royal province, and in the same year the Church of England was established, and all citizens regardless of religious faith were taxed for its support. Laws passed during the next twenty years, aimed directly at the Catholics, forbade them to hold any political office, took away the franchise, denied them the right to hold religious services except in private houses, and in one act—which was partially disallowed by the English government owing to the extreme harshness of its terms even for that period—Catholics were forbidden to teach or to have their children sent out of the colony to be taught by others of their faith elsewhere, and all priests were forbidden to preach, hear confession, administer the sacraments or minister to the dying.[1]

In both North and South Carolina in this period, also, the Anglican Church was established and the payment of tithes made obligatory. It is notable, however, that in South Carolina the law establishing the church provided that the minister should be chosen by the majority of the inhabitants, as had been the custom if not the law in Virginia. To show the conflicting currents of the period, it may be noted that whereas in 1691 the English government had abolished the church test for the franchise in Massachusetts, in the Carolinas in 1704 conformity to the Church of England and receiving of the sacraments according to the rites of that church were made essentials for election to the assembly. Although taxation to maintain an established church was still the law in Connecticut and Massachusetts, early in the next period this was to be greatly modified in favor of the dissenter, the tendency now started in those colonies thus running counter to the new movement inaugurated in the South. The new Southern policy, indeed, was not wholly unopposed, and it is not unlikely that the two "rebellions" in North Carolina in the first decade of the eighteenth century were caused by dislike of the new establishment and by the uneasiness of the dissenters.

When we come to consider what effect the religion of a people has upon their moral life, or, indeed, what that life may have been, we enter upon peculiar difficulties. The deeper we are able to probe into the character of this period, however, the less reason we find for attributing any greatly superior virtue, save that of more frequent church attendance, to the type of life developed in general by New England Puritanism as contrasted with the life of the Middle colonies or of the South. The com-

[1] S. H. Cobb, *Rise of Religious Liberty in America* (N. Y., 1902), 397-398.

plaints of ministers are the same in every age and the
comments of travelers frequently biased, nevertheless
there is such a mass of indictments of the commercial dishonesty of the Puritan trading classes that, added to first-
hand evidence, it cannot be disregarded.   For example,
Ward, writing in 1682, said that "it is a proverb with
those that know them 'whosoever believes a New-England Saint, shall be sure to be cheated: And he that
knows how to deal with their Traders, may deal with
the Devil and fear no Craft.' " [1]   Somewhat later Byrd
noted that none could "slip through a penal statute"
like "the Saints of New England," [2] and this is the constant comment of others having to do with them.   Even
the leaders, in their dealings with the home government,
had occasionally resorted not simply to subterfuge but
to deliberate falsehood.   This lack of veracity is noted
many times by Cotton Mather, who says in one place
that strangers say "many of your People here are not
Men of their Word.   In other places when we have made
a mere Verbal Agreement about anything, we think ourselves bound in Honour and Conscience to stand unto it.
In this place, if what is Agreed, be not under Hand and
Seal, it signifies nothing." [3]   Although the eighteenth
century was the heyday of bribery, the smuggling constantly indulged in during the period covered by this
volume must have had a particularly deleterious influence upon New England character.   The West India
trade after 1733, which will be discussed later, occupied
a peculiar position, but as to most of the rest of the
smuggling there was always in New England a considerable number of "fair traders" who looked down upon
it, and it was not accepted on all sides as legitimate from
the standpoint of the colonial conscience.   In 1725 the

[1] A Trip to New England, 45.
[2] Letter of July 12, 1736, Am. Hist. Rev., I, 88.
[3] Quoted by Winship, New England in 1682 and 1692, xiv.

subject of one of the theses submitted at Harvard was, "Is it wrong to smuggle goods for the purpose of withholding revenue from the King?" and although it was decided affirmatively it shows that the question was by no means outside the sphere of debatable morals. Those who indulged in the practice, and they were many and of high position, were therefore compounding with their consciences, with the usual effect.

It is natural, perhaps, that commercial immorality should be more conspicuous in New England than in the South as commerce occupied a larger part in the lives of the "Saints." If, however, we investigate a department of the moral life which is based upon one of the fundamentals of human nature rather than molded by the accident of occupation, we find comparatively little difference between the two sections. Whether sexual immorality was greater or less in 1700 than in 1900 is a statistical question which it is impossible to answer, as is also its comparative frequency in the different colonies. Although we have no statistics, however, we have numerous comments, the court records, and, in New England, certain church records which serve to guide us. The increasing number and severity of the laws against miscegenation indicate that the Negroes were beginning to complicate the problem in all the colonies, and naturally to a greater extent in the South where they were more numerous, but slavery had not modified social custom as yet to the extent that it was to do later. The ownership of slaves involved certain temptations and there is ample evidence of moral laxity in the South, increasing toward the end of the seventeenth century.

Interest, however, rather centers on the inquiry as to whether the supposedly stricter religious principles inculcated in New England resulted in a morality superior in this respect to that of the other colonies. Evidence indicates that it did not, although the problem is complicated by the fact that a peculiar standard became common, more or less, among New Englanders of all social classes in the early part of the eighteenth century, according to which fornication if followed by marriage, no matter how long delayed, was considered a very venial sin if sin at all. Thus, in 1722, a society of some of the ablest Harvard students of the day, including Oliver Peabody, John Davenport and Charles Chauncy, debated the question "whether it be Fornication to lye with ones Sweetheart (after contraction) before Marriage?" [1] In 1728 the minister at Longmeadow offered for signing by his congregation a "covenant for reformation" in which among other things they were particularly to express their "abhorrence of that notion advanc'd by some of late" that the practice just named was no breach of the seventh commandment.[2] Jonathan Edwards was, in part, driven from his church because of his strict attitude toward this custom. In New York, in 1695 a traveler reported that antenuptial fornication was not at all considered as a sin, and his generally unflattering picture of the morals of that town is borne out by other evidence.

The church records which contain the public acknowledgments of such "faults," show that the practice was extremely prevalent. In one Massachusetts church, for which the record seems to be complete, the practice would seem to have been indulged in before practically every marriage in the congregation, and the fact that, a little later in the century, a church in Connecticut passed a rule that out of charity, seventh-month children should be considered legitimate shows the extent of the laxity. A church would hardly feel called upon to do this today. As marriage was entered into very early,

---

[1] See remarks by William C. Lane on a manuscript volume recently acquired by Harvard College, in Colon. Soc. Mass., *Publs.*, XII, 229.
[2] Broadside, Aug. 22, 1728 (Library of Congress).

usually under twenty for boys and frequently as early as sixteen and even fifteen for girls, the conditions are obvious. Such cases were dealt with very leniently by the churches and as a rule the parties were accepted into good standing immediately after their ordeal of public confession before the congregation.[1]

The main difference between the Southern colonies and the North, therefore, seems to have been that although indulgence may have been equally common in both, what was frankly regarded as a sin in the former was coming to be regarded in the latter very much as a mere peccadillo for young people, provided marriage followed, should there be a child. It is fair to say, however, that we have much fuller records for New England, and that silence may not of necessity mean innocence in the colonies to the south. From Pennsylvania north, "bundling" was a common practice among the lower classes, and although it may have arisen from the primitive sleeping arrangements, as has been suggested, the same custom is by no means uncommon among savage races, and is practically identical with the *viagagavu* or "bush sleeping" of the Melanesians. In the colonies it seems to have been mainly confined to the Germans, Dutch and the New England Puritans.[2] Divorces were rarely granted in the colonies, the English church not allowing them and the crown refusing to sanction any law permitting them. They were, however, occasionally obtained in the semi-independent Puritan colonies of Massachusetts and Connecticut, which led the way toward a more liberal divorce policy.

Throughout all the colonies drunkenness was a prevailing vice, as it was in England, and nearly every event, such as house raisings, harvestings, christenings,

[1] C. F. Adams, "Some Phases of Sexual Morality and Church Discipline," Mass. Hist. Soc., *Proceeds.*, ser. 2, VI, 477-516.
[2] H. R. Stiles, *Bundling, Its Origin, Progress and Decline* (Albany, 1869), chap. i.

college commencements, funerals and even the ordinations of New England ministers, was frequently made the occasion of scandalous intemperance. The vices of the period, however, were mainly those incidental to the characteristic coarseness of the times, and crimes of violence are rather notable for their comparative rarity. There were occasional cases of arson, rape, infanticide and murder, but in general, life and property would seem to have been far safer in the colonies than in England. This was probably due mainly to the better economic condition of the lower classes. In marked contrast to the plague of highwaymen in England, and in spite of the fact that the roads in the colonies led through long lonely stretches of woods, I have found only one case of a colonial traveler being robbed in the whole of the century preceding the Revolution. In the larger towns footpads were more common, notably in New York, and as the century advanced mob violence and disregard of law became more frequent everywhere.

The colonists, however, appear to have been somewhat remarkably averse to bloodshed in an age when blood flowed freely. War made no appeal to them whatever and it was difficult to raise the quota in almost all the frequent calls to arms throughout the century. In times of peace this was also notable in the extreme rarity of the duel in colonial life. That it was a subject not without interest is shown by the fact that the question "Are duels lawful?" was discussed in the Harvard theses for 1690, 1705 and 1709, being decided each time in the negative. There was also occasional legislation of a drastic character, but so far as I have found actual records, there were only ten duels fought in all of the colonies from 1624 to 1763, four on Boston Common, and the remainder in New York and the South.[1] In

[1] Cf. E. B. Greene, Col. Soc. of Mass., *Trans.*, March, 1926.

the more sentimental histories of the South, dueling is sometimes represented as frequent in order to give a romantic flavor to the narrative. It certainly was not, even though there may well have been occasional colonial duels which have escaped my observation. This absence of the duel in a dueling age was probably due to the middle and lower class origin in England of the vast majority of the colonists, which was as true of the "Cavalier" South as of the supposedly more plebeian North. There was, of course, no such difference in origins, and this matter of dueling is but one of the constant social indications of similarity at this period between the two sections.

Of the more humanitarian ideas of a later period or of any organized charities, there is as yet but little trace. Punishments for crimes and misdemeanors, if somewhat milder than in contemporary England, were still brutal and severe. In Quaker Philadelphia, for example, both men and women were lashed on the bare back while driven at the cart's tail, and the criminal code of all the colonies was inhumane.[1] As yet imprisonment played only a slight part in the punishment of offenders, and was employed, according to contemporary European practice, rather for vagabonds and debtors. Although the criminal received such punishments as death, mutilation, branding, whipping and the stocks, the idea still uppermost was restitution to the wronged individual and to society. The Quakers, in Pennsylvania and to some extent in New Jersey, because they were opposed to such severe and cruel punishments, tended to utilize the workhouse as the basis of a new penal system, substituting imprisonment and hard labor for the older methods. The establishment of county workhouses in Pennsylvania date from this period, and it is mainly to the

[1] See T. J. Wertenbaker, *The First Americans* (*A History of American Life*, II), chap. ix.

development of this penological system that we owe our later prison system, which was adopted in Europe from American practice.[1] The early jails, however, were atrocious and the prisoners were herded together without regard to age, sex or offense, little children under fourteen being mixed in with all sorts of older and degraded criminals. The prisoners were obliged to pay for their board during imprisonment and if unable to do so might be sold to reimburse the jailer. A woman in the Philadelphia jail, who bore a child during her imprisonment, stated in a petition that the man who was responsible for her condition was the one who had had her imprisoned, and that she had no bedding in winter but was obliged to lie on the bare boards, endangering her life and that of the child. The following year, on the expiration of her sentence, the court sold her to the highest bidder to pay for "her diet and sundry expenses."

The poor were cared for by the local administrative units, town or parish, but there was no special provision for the insane. It was not a period of institutions or organizations, and charity was almost wholly an affair of individual cases. Occasionally churches would take up collections for some particular victim of misfortune, but throughout all the colonies probably the only organized charitable society for the relief of the poor in the period of this chapter was the Scots' Charitable Society of Boston, first started in 1657, reorganized in 1684 and still in existence today.[2] From time to time, spasmodic efforts were made to do educational or missionary work among the Indians, and Governor Spotswood was particularly interested in such work at the beginning of the eighteenth century, but there was little

[1] See C. R. Fish, *The Rise of the Common Man* (*A History of American Life*, VI), chap. xii.

[2] *The Constitution and By-Laws of the Scots' Charitable Society of Boston* (Boston, 1896).

general interest and only rare efforts on the part of any of the colonial churches.

Slavery and the slave trade aroused few doubts in even the sternest of the Puritans, although Samuel Sewall wrote a tract called *The Selling of Joseph* in 1701, to influence the passage of a law designed to discourage the importation of Negroes. The pamphlet was wholly without effect and in fact was by no means as zealous in its advocacy of the cause of the blacks as the earlier protest of the Mennonites of Germantown in 1688 or the *Exhortation and Caution to Friends* published in Philadelphia by George Keith in 1693, although the older New England historians used to give it greater prominence. Both in this and the next period the most powerful advocates of antislavery were all to be found in Pennsylvania, New Jersey and New York rather than in New England, where the trade in slaves was already taking strong hold.[1] The utilization of slave labor was not generally profitable in New England but the capture and importing of slaves for use in the other colonies was greatly so, and the leading merchants of Boston and Newport became deeply engaged in it. Complaints, indeed, were heard from the Southerners that the New Englanders were ruining them by forcing so many blacks upon them for the sake of the double profit from Negroes and rum.

In Boston, Cotton Mather was interested in alleviating the condition of such slaves as were there, and organized a small society for their betterment. The most zealous worker for the welfare of the slaves in any section at this time, however, was the French merchant, Elias Neau of New York, who gave up his business and devoted his entire time to visiting and laboring among both Negro and Indian slaves in the face of violent op-

[1] M. S. Locke, *Anti-Slavery in America* . . . 1619-1808 (Radcliffe College, *Monographs*, Boston, 1901), chap. i.

position. Public opinion was against his efforts to educate them, and he even had to have them meet in his own house for religious service, as the churches would not allow them in their buildings.[1] In such work as was done by this French Huguenot, in the protests against slavery by the German Mennonites, in the organization of our first charitable society by the Scots, in the contributions of French, Dutch and Germans to the arts, and in the number of French and Scotch doctors, we can already see some of the many ways in which the new colonial America was to be indebted to sources other than English.

In the brief survey which we have made of some aspects of colonial life at the opening of the eighteenth century we have also seen that its culture was more or less uniform and evenly spread throughout the entire length of seaboard. This was due to the similarity of the sources of emigration in Europe and of economic and social influences first met in the New World rather than, as yet, to any development of a common consciousness or of intercolonial influences making for uniformity. In the remaining chapters we shall have to note how the increasing richness of colonial life and the complexity of social structure resulted in a greater differentiation between the several sections, and yet, on the other hand, how increased communication, the growth of the press and the pressure from outer dangers, tended to bring the colonists together intellectually as they diverged socially.

The new social structure which was rapidly to be built up in the colonies during the eighteenth century, although drawing heavily upon Europe for its intellectual and artistic sustenance, was to be American in ori-

[1] M. Dix, *History of the Parish of Trinity Church in the City of New York* (N. Y., 1898), I, 156-158; Hugh Hastings, ed., *Ecclesiastical Records, State of New York* (Albany, 1901-1916), III, 1949-1950.

gin.   Whether the original settlers had come, as in New
England, largely in neighborhood or church groups, or
singly or in family groups only as was the case in the
South, they had brought with them a conception of
society and of life woven together unconsciously by a
thousand subtle threads derived from the culture of the
mother lands.   Upon this conception, quite as unconsciously, the wilderness had acted as a powerful solvent.
The process of disintegration, of which we have spoken
above in connection with New England, had been increasingly rapid throughout all colonial life as the seventeenth century advanced.   In Europe the immigrant had
been surrounded and supported by a thousand influences
of which he was but dimly aware or not at all—established methods of earning a livelihood and of distribution of goods, endowed institutions, traditional beliefs
and customs, political institutions, organized arts, such
as the theater, all sorts of social conventions.   He did
indeed bring the consciousness of these things and was
deeply influenced by them in his new environment but in
their tangible forms they had been left far behind, and
the new colonial-born generation knew them not at all.
The period of disintegration, however, was now drawing to a close.   The wilderness was subdued in the older
settlements.   Wealth was accumulating.   A leisured and
cultivated class was demanding a fuller and richer life.
If the novel and exigent conditions of the wilderness had
for a time lowered the interest in things of the mind,
the minds themselves had been quickened by the necessity
of new adjustments and of building up social life afresh
from its foundations.   "The youth are very Ingenious,
Subtile and of quick Capacities," wrote one observer of
the lads of New York, and others comment in similar
strain of the other colonies.   The time had come for a
new integration of colonial life.

CHAPTER VII

NEW BLOOD

1713-1745

THE period from 1690 to 1713 had been one of almost constant hostilities with the French and Indians, and although the most serious disasters occurred within the territory of the New England colonies, the disturbed conditions along the entire frontier from Maine to the Carolinas had acted as a rigorous check upon any extension of settlement into the wilderness. Indeed, even the Southern coasts were not immune from fear of attack, and in 1706 a combined Spanish and French fleet landed forces and unsuccessfully attempted the reduction of Charleston. Meanwhile, however, the colonial population had been multiplying rapidly both by natural increase and by immigration. It has been estimated that a total of two hundred and thirteen thousand in 1690 had grown to three hundred and fifty-seven thousand by 1710. Although here and there civilization had been pushed a little farther into the woods, most of these newcomers had settled along the coast well within the safety line of the older settlements, thus greatly increasing the density of population. A comparison of the settled areas in New England, even as early as just before King Philip's War in 1675, and again at the Peace of Utrecht in 1713 shows that in the forty years intervening there had been practically no change in the line of frontier settlements, with the exception of the filling up of that area between Narragansett Bay and the Connecticut River, south of the Massachusetts line. The population of Maine had actually decreased and the settlements in New Hampshire were still confined to a radius of about fifteen miles around the Piscataqua River. The western two thirds of Massachusetts was still almost uninhabited save for the towns strung along the upper Connecticut, and in nearly a generation and a half only one village had been added to the northward in that rich valley. Nor had there been any marked encroachment upon the wilderness in the other provinces to the south.

A line could be drawn back of the colonies extending from the watershed of the St. Lawrence to the highlands of Carolina, on the one side of which was safety and on the other a thousand dangers; on the one, peace, comradeship, helpfulness; on the other, terror, midnight massacre, the ever expected war-whoop of the savage. The fact that in twenty-three years the colonial population had nearly doubled and yet had been confined within this shadowy boundary line could not fail to be of marked social influence. We have already spoken of the effects upon the school system and also upon the town church in New England, but it was also noticeable in other ways and in other colonies.

Increasing density of population meant increasing clashing of wills and thoughts, and a keener competition for subsistence or for wealth. Church quarrels, agrarian discontents, economic pressure, had caused colonists to emigrate from one section or one colony to another. By the opening of the new century, there were New England settlements in Westchester and on Long Island in New York, at Frankford, Hanover, Bloomfield, Newark, Elizabeth, Woodbridge, Shrewsbury, Greenwich and Cape May in New Jersey, and at Dorchester in South Carolina. The land situation in New York was beginning to divert a stream into Pennsylvania. The Quaker influence of Philadelphia was spreading, through emigration, over West Jersey. From Virginia, especially in the back country, large numbers were moving northward into Maryland or southward into North Carolina, which latter colony was also receiving accessions from its southern neighbor. In the aggregate, this intercolonial drift must have been of considerable dimensions and influence.

By the opening years of the second decade of the eighteenth century, colonial boundary lines were thus frequently crossed by this restless movement of the more mobile elements of a population becoming too dense for the territory occupied under the conditions of the time. These men who were moving from north to south or south to north were seeking larger opportunity of one sort or another, hemmed in by that shadowy line to the westward. When peace should be declared it could be foreseen that the waters thus being stirred would overflow their bounds and pour in a flood over the hitherto forbidden frontier.

The great majority of the population which was thus growing uneasy in its confinement was still English at the opening of the century, in spite of the foreign elements of which we spoke in an earlier chapter. Only in a few places were English institutions seriously threatened by the presence of a large admixture of other stocks. New York, of course, was largely Dutch and French, with the English in a minority, and one of the earliest petitions to the Bishop of London from the new missionaries was that those foreign languages be prohibited for preachers, or at least Anglicans, and that school-teachers be allowed to give instruction in English only, on account of the danger that the other tongues might supersede it. In South Carolina changed representation in the assembly, due to the admission of new counties with a large French population, had aroused great opposition among the English settlers, who angrily asked, "Shall the Frenchmen who cannot speak our lan-

guage make our laws?" [1]   The French immigration was
not sustained, however, and by 1713 the only large
foreign element retaining their own language and customs was the Dutch.   The Welsh of Pennsylvania were
gradually being absorbed, and the Swedes of Delaware
although still remaining alien were only of local importance, and did not threaten the institutional su-
premacy of the English.

Events in Europe, however, had been occurring that
were to be of deep influence upon the destinies of the
colonies, and the enormous immigration of non-English
stocks due to those events and the swarming out to the
frontier of the rapidly increasing population due to the
Peace of Utrecht were two of the most important elements in the colonial development of the next three
generations.   On the one hand, the tens of thousands
who were to enter America in this new movement were
either without allegiance and loyalty to the English
government or were openly hostile to it, and on the
other, the great growth of the frontier was to create
behind the more differentiated economic and social life
of the older seaboard sections, a fringe of outer settlements which had much more in common with one another than they had with the seaboard colonies through
which their settlers had passed to the lands beyond.

The two storm centers of the Old World which were
most vitally to affect the destinies of the settlers in the
New were Germany and Ireland, although the religious,
political and economic disturbances of other countries
were responsible also for a certain amount of immigration here of non-English stocks.   The Thirty Years'
War in Germany, which ended in 1648, had been far
more disastrous comparatively than the World War of

[1] The chief opposition was from the religious dissenters who saw with
dismay how readily the Huguenots affiliated with the High Churchmen;
E. McCrady, *History of South Carolina under the Proprietary Government* (N. Y., 1897), 374, 391, 407, 440.

recent years. It has been estimated that in this earlier
conflict one county of Germany lost eighty-five per cent
of its horses, eighty-two per cent of its cattle, and had
sixty-five per cent of its houses destroyed and seventy-
five per cent of its people killed. Other parts seem to
have fared little better, and the Palatinate, which had
been the most fertile province of all, became a desert, a
place of desperation where for a time cannibalism was
not unknown. Although its great fertility and the apt-
ness of its inhabitants for agriculture enabled it to make
slow recovery, this and other parts of Germany were
harried again and again by the French in the latter part of the century. The unfortunate peasants
planted crops only to have them carried off and themselves treated with barbarous cruelty by that nation
which has always boasted of being the leader of civilization in Europe. To this was added in the latter part
of the century religious persecution by the Electors of
the Palatinate themselves, and throughout all the tiny
principalities which then made up the Germany of today the peasant suffered political and economic tyranny
from his petty rulers which left him no chance to rise in
the scale or even to maintain life for himself and his
family without the fear of pauperism and starvation.
Until the possibility of a better and a fairer existence in
the almost fabulous lands over the great sea came to his
knowledge, life seemed utterly hopeless for him and his
children.

In the north of Ireland, at the beginning of the
eighteenth century, there was almost as much bitterness
and hopelessness as in Germany. Although it was the
least fertile section of the island, the Scots who had been
settled there for some generations had made it by far
the most prosperous. The events of the English Revolution of 1689, however, had left Ireland crushed, and
with the new rulers came a new policy which in the next

twenty years completed the utter ruin. The Act of 1699 prohibiting the woolen manufacture applied to the unhappy island as well as to the American colonies, but worked far greater havoc there than here. Although the linen industry was encouraged, it was wholly dependent upon the fluctuation of foreign trade, and periods of prosperity were followed by others of deep depression which the people were not economically fortified to face. In the second decade of the new century when long-term leases fell due, they were renewed only at double and even treble the old rents, to the ruin of the Scotch Protestants whose standard of living was higher than that of the Catholic Irish. Wholesale ejections, then and later, caused intense suffering. The years from 1714 to 1719 were notable as years of prolonged drought, with resultant injury to the crops. In 1716 the sheep were largely destroyed by the rot, and for some years after 1718 there were epidemics of smallpox and other diseases. To complete the misfortunes of the unfortunate Scotch Presbyterians, under the Test Act of 1704 they had been made almost outlaws. The validity of their marriages was questioned, their chapels were closed, they were forbidden to maintain schools, and they could hold no political office above that of constable. When these men, suffering from the trade laws, from famine, from disease and from religious persecution, were dispossessed by the owners of their lands and turned out with no hope save that of finding a new home beyond the seas, they left Ireland with bitter hatred of England in their hearts. The part that these ejected refugees were to play in the destinies of two hemispheres was dramatically summed up in the inscription on the tombstone of one of them in the Shenandoah Valley of Virginia: "Here lies the remains of John Lewis, who slew the Irish lord, settled Augusta County, located the town of Staunton, and furnished five sons to fight the battles of the American Revolution."[1]   One of the many strands in the tangled skein of the story of our period could not be picked out more deftly.

In Switzerland, at intervals early in the eighteenth century, there was also great economic distress, and one group of emigrants to America have recorded that, even working day and night in their native land, they could not then earn daily bread.   Nevertheless a number of the Swiss cantons took severe measures to prevent these distressed people from leaving, and edicts against emigration were passed in 1720, 1735, 1736, 1738 and in later years.   The sale of such property as they might dispose of to pay their way to America was hampered in every manner possible and in some cantons even those who bought it were deprived of citizenship and land rights forever.

It was from such sources as these that was derived the enormous immigration into the colonies during the first three quarters of the eighteenth century.   The Scotch and Celtic Irish hated England with a bitterness that was an abiding passion.   The Germans and the smaller number of Swiss and other nationalities had no thought of her, save as they came into contact with her colonial representatives who might in one way or another exploit them or hamper them in their desperate resolution to acquire and maintain property rights in the new land to which they had been driven and for gaining which they suffered untold pain and disillusion.   For many of these refugees the effort to reach America spelled only death by disease or the tortures of hunger and thirst; for others it meant slavery almost as evil—save that it was not lifelong—as that of the Negro, with the bitter breaking of family ties; for the happiest it meant long years of intense toil and the slow winning of a foothold.

[1] Given by J. A. Waddell, *Anns. of Augusta County* (Staunton, 1902), 112.

They had suffered all the ills that life could inflict, and when they reached America it was with the grim determination to wrest from what remained of the years some of the rights and happiness that had hitherto been denied to them.

If the conditions which made the enormous movement possible were thus European in origin, the movement itself was largely fostered in America. As we have already seen, the need for laborers and artisans of all sorts was constant and imperative in the colonies, and as the eighteenth century advanced there was added to this the demand for settlers to give value to the enormous tracts which the speculators had secured by various means. The earlier need merely for servants, farmhands, and workmen to assist in the households, small farms or estates, which were the homes of the owners themselves, enlarged rapidly into a competitive rush to secure human beings by the score, the hundred and the thousand, to people the outlying wilderness on a wholesale scale, so as to make fortunes for the speculators of the old settlements. In the seventeenth century, letters from emigrants to their friends or relatives at home had made the latter to some extent familiar with the thought of the New World. Kidnaping, the option of service in America as against hopeless years in a debtors' prison, or the sentence of transportation upon criminals had all swelled the movement westward, but with the beginning of the eighteenth century the business of fostering immigration became better organized. A large literature in several languages sprang up, designed to paint the possibilities of the New World in such glowing colors as to induce voluntary emigration on a large scale. Much of it had no more relation to the truth than has the emigrant literature or real-estate advertisement of the present day. America was described as a country where wages were high, food cheap, land to be had for little or nothing, where there were no taxes, where a servant by hiring himself for a short time could pay for his passage and save enough money to become independent, where the climate was perfect and where the farmer or workman could live like a lord with little labor. Scattered among the suffering masses described above, such words seemed like a message from a better world, and the trickling stream of emigration from Germany and Ireland which we have noted in an earlier chapter became a veritable torrent.[1]

In most cases bitter disillusionment awaited the immigrant. The conditions of life here were wholly different from what he had been led to believe. In many cases the horrors of the voyages in the heavily laden immigrant ships almost equaled those of the "middle passage" for the African slaves who were being brought by the southern route as the European immigrants were by the northern one to fill the insatiable demand for human beings to develop the land, in the great expansion following the ending of the war in 1713. In this traffic in immigrants the Germans, perhaps, suffered the worst. Toward the middle of the eighteenth century, conditions, so far from improving with larger ships, became, if possible, worse, but all through the period the story is much the same.

As the methods of capture or purchase applied to the savages of Africa could not be used, the people had to be decoyed, and agents called "newlanders" went among them trying by every possible means, using every deception, to induce them to emigrate. Many of the thousands who left their homes started with more or less money and with no intention of selling themselves but expecting to pay for their passage and to have a little capital to set up with when they reached America. But

[1] H. L. Osgood, *American Colonies in the Eighteenth Century* (N. Y., 1924-1925), II, chap. vi.

there seems to have been, both for the agents and for the brutal ship captains bred by the trade, more money in selling the immigrants to pay for their passage than in transporting them merely as paying passengers. Therefore the delays of many weeks away from home at the start of the trip, exorbitant charges, willful separation of the emigrants from their baggage, even downright stealing of their property, all were resorted to in order to deprive them of their resources and to reduce them to the necessity of selling themselves.

Crowded into the ships "like herrings" on the final lap of the voyage from England after many weeks en route from Germany, disease was rife and the mortality appalling. The food was inadequate and frequently so rotten as to be full of worms and other vermin and to be uneatable except in the famine conditions which often prevailed. A delay due to calms or contrary winds brought the overcrowded shiploads into immediate fear of death by starvation or thirst. There are many instances when passengers almost fought for the bodies of rats and mice, a number where cannibalism was threatened, and one, at least, when it was practiced. On a ship bringing Scotch-Irish, six dead human bodies were eaten and the maddened passengers were cutting up a seventh when another ship was sighted and help obtained.[1] It was said that children under seven rarely survived the voyage, and in cases of childbirth the mortality was so great that mother and child were usually thrown overboard together. The sanitary arrangements were indescribably bad. The filth bred lice and other parasites at such a rate that they could be scraped off the bodies of the passengers. Dysentery, smallpox and other diseases swept through whole companies. Such meager statistics as we have tell us that on one ship two

[1] Mass. Archives, 15A:20. Cf. Thomas Chalkley, Journal (N. Y., 1808), 77.

hundred and fifty passengers died out of three hundred
and twelve, on another one hundred out of a hundred
and fifty, on another two hundred and fifty out of four
hundred, and on another only fifty survived out of four
hundred. In 1711 the figures indicate that eight hundred and fifty-nine were lost out of the total for the
year of three thousand and eighty-six, or nearly one in
three for every ship. In 1738 another set of figures indicates that between sixteen hundred and two thousand
died on fifteen ships, or approximately the same percentage with reference to the total.[1]

Even for those who reached Philadelphia, the main
port of entry, their troubles were by no means over. No
one was permitted to land, who could not pay for his
passage. The excessive and unexpected costs of the long
and complicated journey and the losses of baggage reduced many to the necessity of allowing themselves to
be sold who had never anticipated such a contingency.
Adults were so disposed of for terms of from three to
six years depending upon how much they owed the captain on balance. Youngsters from ten to fifteen had to
serve until twenty-one, and the smaller children had to
be given away to whomever would take them. Passage had to be paid for on account of those who died as
well as for the survivors, and as only the well com-
manded a sale they frequently had to take on themselves
an extra period of service to pay for the sick. An infamous practice sprang up, perhaps owing to the great
numbers of the sick and dead, that the entire shipload
would be held collectively responsible for the passage
of all, and thus even persons who could pay their own
way found themselves sold into captivity to pay that of
others, dead and living. A sick husband would see his
wife sold to pay for him, old or unwell parents would

[1] C. A. Herrick, *White Servitude in Pennsylvania* (Phil., 1926),
chap. ix.

be forced to sell their children.   Families were broken
up just as in the Negro trade and never met again.   Even
those who finally escaped all these perils, and landed
with a little property and their freedom, were preyed
upon by all sorts of sharpers who took advantage of their
ignorance to defraud them by spurious sales of land or
fraudulent contracts.   It was said at one time that the
appearance of a new immigrant ship was the signal for
a new flood of counterfeit money.   When we consider
the conditions in Europe from which these poor people
were fleeing, the horrors they met with on the voyage
from the brutality and dishonesty of the agents and captains, the toil and sorrow to which they came in the
new land of their dreams, and the vast numbers in which
they came, it is evident that we have to do with a force
of the first magnitude in influencing social conditions
and the sentiment of a large percentage of the colonists
with regard to government and the exploiting social
classes.   When these Germans and Scotch and Irish did
finally gain their footholds and establish themselves on
their little farms, what room or reason would there be
for loyalty to the colonial aristocrats or to the government of England three thousand miles away?

We have already spoken of the beginning of the German immigration to Pennsylvania due to the personal
contact of Penn with some of the German religious leaders.   The movement which began in the eighteenth century, however, was of different type and origin, and the
fact that Pennsylvania continued to be the largest recip-
ient of the immigration was due only in part to the letters sent home by those happily located at Germantown,
and the books published by Pastorius and others, particularly the *Curieuse Nachricht* of Daniel Falckner published in 1702.[1]

---

[1] Daniel Falckner, *Curieuse Nachricht von Pennsylvania* (J. F. Sachse, ed., Phila., 1905).

Five years later a part of the Palatinate was again overrun with troops, and large numbers of those dwelling on the left bank of the Rhine were rendered homeless. The next year several of these families fled to England in great poverty, were generously treated by Queen Anne, and then shipped to New York, where it was thought they might prove useful in the making of naval stores. Arrived in the colony, they were assigned land on the Hudson and founded the town of Newburgh. The winter of 1708-9 in the Palatinate was extraordinarily severe, and this combined with all the other ills that the people there had suffered seemed to be the last impulsion needed to start a movement that carried the Palatines to England by thousands. By October of the latter year, it is said that there were thirteen thousand seeking refuge in and around London. These were as well treated as possible, except that the Catholics were shipped back to Germany, and the bulk of those remaining were settled in England or Ireland. A company of six hundred Swiss under De Graffenried sailed for North Carolina and there founded New Bern.[1]

The remainder, about three thousand, were sent to New York, most of them believing that they would be able to settle in the fertile Schoharie region of which they had knowledge. Instead, they were planted on a tract on the Hudson which the governor bought for the purpose from Robert Livingston who is said to have made a large sum both from this sale and from his subsequent profiteering at the expense of the Germans under his government contract to feed them. The plan to have them make tar, in what was almost a military encampment, proved unsuccessful, the governor sank a large amount of his private fortune, which it is doubtful if

---

[1] V. H. Todd, *Christoph Von Graffenried's Account of the Founding of New Bern* (Raleigh, 1920), 225 ff. The name is also spelled "De Graffenried."

the English government ever repaid to him, and in the autumn of 1712 the unfortunate Germans were suddenly told to shift for themselves, with winter approaching. Finally, some months later, in great suffering, they migrated to Schoharie where they bought land of the Indians, who received them kindly.

Here, however, they were not to remain in peace, for in spite of all difficulties they soon prospered. This served only to arouse the cupidity of the Dutch and English. Governor Robert Hunter granted the tract which they had settled and improved to seven partners in Albany, including Robert Livingston, Jr., John Schuyler and others, and these at once attempted to oust the Palatines, who defended themselves by force. Three agents whom they sent to England to plead their cause were taken by pirates and when they finally reached England were thrown into prison for debt. The new governor, Burnet, however, treated the settlers with more consideration and suggested that they move to the Mohawk, where they might have lands granted to them and be useful in defending the frontier. About three hundred families preferred to remain where they were and to submit to the impositions of the new landlords. Others moved to the Mohawk country in the present counties of Montgomery and Herkimer, but another portion of the settlers, under Conrad Weiser, refused to remain any longer in the unjust and profiteering colony and emigrated to Pennsylvania in two bodies, one moving in 1723 and the other five years later. From that time on no Germans who could possibly help it settled in New York and the great stream of immigration went almost wholly to swell the numbers of the Quaker colony, whereas if its earlier members had been better treated it would have helped to build up the great valleys of the Hudson and the Mohawk. This avoidance by immigrants, and the grasping land policy by the leading families kept down the population in New York so that that colony lagged behind almost all the others in proportional increase of numbers. With an unrivaled situation both for overseas commerce and for the fur trade, with rich fields and fertile valleys, its natural advantages went for nothing and it excelled the other colonies only in the short-sighted avarice of its aristocrats who were laying the foundations for family wealth at the expense of their colony's welfare.[1]

For the most part the German immigrants of the eighteenth century were quite poor though by no means uneducated or unintelligent, and the vast majority were tillers of the soil. As a result of these two facts the demand which they all made was for land, for the purchase of which they had little money. It was necessary, therefore, that they should proceed at once to the frontier where they might buy cheaply as compared with the already settled areas or where they might simply squat on the soil without purchasing title with the hope of remaining undisturbed. During what may be considered the first period of their immigration, from 1683 to 1710, this had not been the case to so great an extent as in the periods following, and moreover lands in the neighborhood of Philadelphia were then much cheaper than after the growth of population had senc them soaring. During the second period, until 1727, the numbers of newcomers had greatly increased and by that time it was said that they and the English and Irish had "filled all parts of the country" so that all desiring land "must go far into the wilderness."[2]

During both the first two periods of immigration the numbers of Germans in the colonies are even more uncertain than they are later, and are largely a matter of

[1] S. H. Cobb, *The Story of the Palatines* (N. Y., 1897), *passim*.
[2] Quoted by D. W. Nead, "Pennsylvania-German Settlement of Maryland," Pa.-German Soc., *Proceeds.*, XXII, 35.

guesswork from inadequate data. There were probably scattered individuals in all or most of the provinces, but outside of Pennsylvania, the only considerable number of compact settlements were those of the Palatines already spoken of in New York, some small groups in New Jersey, the Swiss settlement at New Bern in North Carolina and three settlements in Virginia. It is noteworthy that all settlements by immigrants in this period tended to send out offshoots, and were constantly planting others farther out in the wilderness, the cause of these continuous fissions being usually some trouble connected with the land question. For example, some of the Germans who were planted at Germanna in Virginia on the Rapidan River at intervals from 1714 to 1720 by Governor Spotswood to operate his iron furnaces there, became dissatisfied after a few years because the governor refused to sell them any of the land on which they had settled, and in 1721 a group removed to a new site about ten miles from the Little Fork of the Rappahannock. Others migrated to what is now Madison County for the same reason.[1]

It must never be lost to sight in dealing with the whole eighteenth century prior to the Revolution that the fundamental basis of colonial economic life was agricultural. It is true that without the more rapid accumulation of capital from other activities the culture of the colonists would have risen far more slowly, if at all, above the level of yeoman farmer or country gentleman, and also that without the overseas commerce the colonists would have been unable to pay for the innumerable imported necessities and luxuries. Nevertheless not only was agriculture the basic industry, but for one person engaged in other occupations and who was directly interested in the difficulties or legislation affecting them, there

[1] H. Schuricht, *History of the German Element in Virginia* (Balt., 1898), 66-71.

were probably nine whose main if not sole interest was in land and its problems. For this reason the land policies of the colonial governments or of the rich landlords were of more far-reaching influence as irritants than could have been the trade laws of England. As the interior country became more settled the inhabitants grew farther away from any care about British imperial legislation until many decades later, when that legislation began to affect the "Western" problem. The deep seated resentment that was felt was directed rather against the local governments, the governors and their sycophantic cliques, and the wealthy speculators who claimed titles to the wilderness lands which the settlers had improved.

From 1727 we can form a somewhat more accurate estimate of the number of arriving immigrants, as beginning with that date there is an official record of all entering through the port of Philadelphia, the number of foreigners then coming in having aroused the alarm of the English element. Although far higher figures have been named, it is probable that there were at that time from fifteen to twenty thousand Germans in Pennsylvania, and the record mentioned indicates that in the remaining years to 1745 approximately twenty-two thousand arrived by ships, to which should be added the large natural increase from those already settled. As new arrivals came they seem to have pushed out to the frontier, which thus slowly advanced into the wilderness, and by the third decade of the century the stream found its way into the valley of the Shenandoah in western Virginia and began to pour over its fertile fields. The valley, flanked on the east by the Blue Ridge Mountains and on the west by the Alleghanies, runs in a southwesterly direction from Pennsylvania, and owing to the nature of its mountain walls, was accessible only

[1] See list in Oscar Kuhns, *German and Swiss Elements of Colonial Pennsylvania* (N. Y., 1901), 57.

with much difficulty from the eastern parts of those colonies which it traverses.

As early as 1726 or 1727 a German, Adam Müller, who after living for several years in Lancaster County, Pennsylvania, had gone to Virginia, did indeed cross the mountains and settle near the present site of Elkton, but his course was in contrast to the whole tide of emigration and settlement which followed later. The earliest link between the great valley and the Pennsylvania settlements seems to have been the old "Packhorse Ford" through the Potomac, a short distance above Harper's Ferry, over which the Indian traders made their way. Possibly in the same year that Müller entered the valley by the far more difficult route from the east, other Pennsylvania Germans followed this Indian trail and crossing the traders' ford settled the village of New Mecklenburg about twelve miles above the present Harper's Ferry. In 1732 Joist Hite (he spelled his name in a variety of ways) entered the valley with sixteen families who settled at various places, all near the present Winchester.[1]

Meanwhile, a Dutchman, John Vanmeter, had been beforehand with the new settlers, and had secured a grant of forty thousand acres from Governor Gooch of Virginia, part of which he sold to the immigrants. Others had also gone into the valley to join Müller at his settlement near Massanutten. There they were merely squatters, but after buying a title from Jacob Stover, who although a later settler seems to have succeeded in getting a grant of the lands, they were called upon to defend them from a claim of the Virginian, William Beverley. Stover is said to have represented every one of his horses and cattle as the head of a family in order to swell the acreage of his grant, but however that may be, he seems to have been eminently capable of

[1] H. Schuricht, *German Element in Virginia*, I, 85-87.

looking after himself and secured large parts of three present counties. The way once found, the Germans kept coming and settling, and by 1745 there may have been four thousand in that part of the valley which drains northerly into the Potomac.

The eastward part of the packhorse route to Virginia from Lancaster County in Pennsylvania ran southwestward to the Monocacy River in Maryland, which it followed for a way, and then westward over the Blue Ridge at Crampton's Gap. This route, later widened and improved, became known as the Monocacy Road by the time of the French and Indian War. Although the stream of immigration from Pennsylvania tended to pass through Maryland without stopping, it coincided with a speculative land movement among the planters of the eastern portions of that colony which will be spoken of in the next chapter, and in order to halt this stream of desirable immigrants special inducements were offered to prospective settlers. Beginning with a little settlement called Monocacy in 1732, the German settlement of Maryland continued, in 1745 the town of Frederick was founded, and three years later the county was established, the numbers coming in after that completely altering the character of the province. The name of Whittier's heroine, Barbara Frietchie, recalls this Maryland German stock.

Meanwhile, although less important, there had also been groups of Germans established by assisted immigration at Waldoborough in Maine, and in South Carolina and Georgia, there being perhaps twelve hundred in the last named by 1741. The period from 1734 to 1744 was one of great immigration from Switzerland, and it is estimated that in that decade twelve thousand immigrants from the German cantons found their way to the colonies, mostly to South Carolina where they settled on the frontier. If we accept the figure of twenty-five hundred in New York in 1720, and of eighteen thousand in Pennsylvania before 1727, and add the numbers which came to the other colonies subsequently, and allow for the natural increase, according to the colonial birthrate of a doubled population every twenty-five years, we would arrive at a total of nearly eighty thousand German and Swiss by 1745, which, although guess work, would seem to be a fairly conservative figure.

We have now to consider the other great stream of non-English immigration which with that noted above did so much to alter the outlook and sentiment in the colonies during this period. Before 1720, besides many scattered individuals here and there, there were a few communities distinctively Scotch-Irish in several of the colonies, but it was not until about the third decade of the century that they began to come in large numbers. It is said that a few settlements had been made in Chester County, Pennsylvania, by 1710, and that by 1712 a few pioneers had even crossed the Susquehanna River as squatters from Lancaster County, but the latter were recalled by the authorities upon complaint by the Indians. Between 1714 and 1720 fifty-four ships, each carrying some immigrants, arrived from Ireland at the port of Boston; before the latter year a number had settled in Orange County, New York; there was a settlement in New Jersey; and in 1722 a group settled in a bend of the Roanoke River in Halifax County, North Carolina. A freshet having swept away everything which the last had planted and built, they removed to the Cape Fear country and were the forerunners of the later large Scotch element there. As in the case of the Germans, however, the largest numbers of this first period of immigration entered by the ports of Delaware and Pennsylvania.

Large numbers came through New Castle between 1718 and 1720, and in the half dozen years following, the numbers increased rapidly, although they did not attain the figures of later decades. By 1729 there were probably about six thousand in Pennsylvania alone, to which should be added those in the other colonies. In that year an additional six thousand arrived at Philadelphia. The movement alarmed the authorities in Ireland and the colonies alike. "Not less than six ministers have demitted their congregations, and great numbers of the people go with them" to America, wrote a minister in Ulster in 1718. In another Irish letter we read that "Parliament is destroying the little Trade that is left among us. These and other Discouragements are driving away the few Protestants that are among us; insomuch that last year some Thousands of Families are gone to the West Indies [America]." In still another letter, in 1728, we read that "the humour has spread like a contagious distemper; and the worst is that it affects only Protestants, and reigns chiefly in the North." Another states that "the humour of going to America still continues, and the scarcity of provisions certainly makes many quit us: there are now seven ships at Belfast that are carrying off about 1,000 passengers thither: and if we knew how to stop them, as most of them can get neither victuals nor work at home, it would be cruel to do it." [1]

On the other hand, Cotton Mather wrote from Boston of the immigrants there, "I wish their coming over do not prove fatal in the end," [2] and Logan in Philadelphia was even more worried. In 1729 he wrote that "it looks as if Ireland is to send all her inhabitants hither; for last week no less than six ships arrived, and every day two or three arrive also." [3]

[1] Quoted in Scotch-Irish Soc. of America, *Proceeds., 1889*, I, 143; C. K. Bolton, *Scotch-Irish Pioneers* (Boston, 1910), 57, 67.
[2] S. P. Orth, *Our Foreigners* (Allen Johnson, ed., *The Chronicles of America Series*, XXXV, New Haven, 1920), 63.
[3] Quoted by C. A. Hanna, *The Scotch-Irish* (N. Y., 1902), II, 63.

Everywhere there was a strong prejudice against them, partly from the mistaken notion that they were Celtic Irish, who seem to have been unpopular apart from their religion. That this was not so is proved by the letters cited above from Ireland, from the fact that those in Massachusetts presented a petition to the assembly stating that they were Scotch and should not be considered as Irish, and from other facts. Those coming to Pennsylvania, however, became and remained unpopular because of their determination to wrest from the wilderness a new home and a living with little regard to the rights of others. Logan claimed that five families of them made more trouble than fifty of any other nationality, that they were very harsh in their treatment of the Indians, and that they had no regard for land titles, quoting them as saying that "it was against the laws of God and nature that so much land should be idle while so many Christians wanted it to labor on and to raise bread." [1] This was an expression of the genuine frontier spirit, and strikes a note that we hear more and more insistently in American history from the beginning of the eighteenth century. Up to this time there had been comparatively little occasion for this spirit to be hardened by coming into conflict with overseas authority or colonial class privileges. Until the Peace of Utrecht the frontier lay, as we have said, almost at the backdoor of the older settlements. There had been little differentiation between the inhabitants of the two sections. Moreover, the land policy of the New England colonies and the conditions in the others had not made a burning question of the amount of available land for the prospective settler until the alteration in New England policy, the absorption of great areas in other colonies and the great increase of population brought about an ominous change. All these factors working

[1] Hanna, *Scotch-Irish*, II, 63.

together with the opening of the back country after the peace and the inauguration of closer supervision by the British government in such matters as the laws regulating the "king's woods" developed after that period both a genuine frontier section and the frontier spirit.

Locally in Pennsylvania there was a complication in the fact that the land office was practically closed from the death of Penn in 1718 until 1731. The newly arrived Scotch swarmed over Conestoga Manor, which the Penns had reserved for themselves, and Logan was alarmed at the little respect shown for vested interests by them and the Germans. "We have many thousands of foreigners," he wrote in 1727, "mostly Palatines . . . of whom fifteen hundred came in last summer, many of them surly people, divers papists among them, and the men generally well armed. We have from the north of Ireland great numbers yearly. Eight or nine ships this last fall discharged at New Castle. Both these sets frequently sit down on any spot of vacant land they can find, without asking question. . . . Both they and the Palatines pretend they will buy, but not one in twenty has anything to pay with." [1]

In every colony which they entered they at once sought out the frontier, mainly because that was the only place where they could find land not already preëmpted either by settler or speculator. They quickly spread westward and by 1722 some had settled beyond the Susquehanna, by 1730 Chambersburg was founded, by 1735 a road was ordered laid out from Philadelphia to the Susquehanna at Harris's, and in the following year the Indian title was bought to the land between the North and South Mountains, and the tide that had been running up both sides of the Susquehanna then began rapidly to fill the Cumberland Valley. From there it

[1] Quoted in Scotch-Irish Soc. of America, *Proceeds.*, *1890*, II, 248-249.

continued on over unpurchased lands of the red men across the mountains and up the Juniata.

Likewise there had been other streams of immigration toward the south. Logan had complained early that the newcomers were settling along the lands in dispute between Baltimore and Penn on the borders of Maryland where it was impossible for either to give a valid title. The opening of the Shenandoah Valley in Virginia was immediately followed by an influx of Scotch as it had been by Germans. The title which Joist Hite had secured was being questioned by Lord Fairfax, so that many Scotch who had come to settle on these lands pressed on beyond them still deeper into the valley, where they felt themselves safe from any attack upon their titles or squatters' rights. John Lewis was the leader, but was followed by large numbers during the next few years. By 1738 the Virginia general assembly set off two new counties, Frederick and Augusta, both in the valley. Seven years later James Patton, a Scotch-Irishman, was made first county lieutenant of Augusta County, and so far to the westward was the influence of the new settlements already extending that in the same year he obtained a grant from the crown of twelve thousand acres, all to the west of the Alleghanies.[1]

Meanwhile, settlement continued in the other colonies, although to a lesser extent. Considerable numbers reached Georgia, South and North Carolina, and some families were brought in to develop lands in Maine. Wherever they came, they soon spread out, owing to land quarrels, squabbles with their neighbors, or the lure of the wilderness felt to the full by this genuine pioneer race. This process is well exemplified in Massachusetts. In 1718 Worcester was a frontier

---

[1] J. L. Peyton, *History of Augusta County, Virginia* (Staunton, 1882), 32.

town on the edge of the wilderness, inhabited by about fifty families of English. Apparently about the same number of families of the Scotch who arrived that year at Boston proceeded direct to the small settlement. At first, common danger from the Indians, in which the Scotch acted as sentries, seems to have kept the two elements fairly friendly, but after the danger passed factions broke out, the ostensible cause being a church dispute. The Puritans attempted to carry all things their own way and did so for some years. Finally, the Scotch made an appeal to the town that they be relieved from taxation for the Congregational minister and allowed to have a Presbyterian one of their own. This was refused. The following year, 1736, a considerable number of the Scotch sold their farms, went fifty miles farther into the wilderness and settled the Presbyterian town of Colerain on the Vermont line. Two years later another group left Worcester and settled a town about thirty miles west at Pelham. Those who still remained determined to build a church edifice of their own and did so but the Puritans, as lawless as they were cowardly, burned it down in the night. The result was another exodus of Scotch, and the founding the following year of two new frontier towns, Western (now Warren) in Worcester County, and Blandford in Hampden County, the latter far to the westward of the Connecticut River. As time went on, the younger men of these new towns continued to emigrate still farther, and similar distributions may be traced from the original settlements of the Scotch at Londonderry in New Hampshire and at Wiscasset in Maine.[1] It was from such stock that men like Horace Greeley were to come.

Although this Scotch element in the colonial population was to be very greatly added to in later periods,

[1] Charles K. Bolton, *Scotch-Irish Pioneers in Ulster and America,* chap. x.

particularly after the Battle of Culloden in 1746, and in the years immediately preceding the American Revolution, and to be mixed with a considerable proportion of Highland Scotch directly from Scotland, it is evident that they were already becoming a distinct factor to be reckoned with in the period covered by this chapter. Besides the nationalities already spoken of there were other additions, such as Jews in Newport and other centers, and some mere shifting of racial groups, such as the emigration in 1737 of a very considerable number of Welsh from Pennsylvania to a tract of ten thousand acres on the Great Peedee River in South Carolina. The Celtic Irish had also come in some numbers though it is impossible to estimate them even roughly. These all have their interest as indicating the growing complexity of colonial life and the restless inter-colonial movements of the times, but were of small importance as compared with the enormous addition of the Scotch and Germans, and of the great development of the frontier region.

This region, it should be noted, was no longer a part of the tidewater section or in close contact with it. When the Germans and Scots and other pioneers passed beyond the headwaters of navigation, and the leaves of the forest paths closed behind them, it was as though a green curtain had fallen, which was to separate them from the busy half-mercantile life of seaboard town and farm. Their eyes and thoughts no longer turned eastward to follow the wake of seaborne ventures, but westward to vast tracts of untilled soil and endless forest, where in cabined clearings or the meadows of mountain valleys, an American life divorced from the Old World was to be born. It was as though hitherto men had to some extent been walking backwards, still looking over-seas so long as they did not pass beyond the limits of tidewater bay or river stretches. It was when they definitely abandoned these, and the long line of pioneers plunged into the wilderness beyond, that the great renunciation of Europe took place, not less dramatic in retrospect because then only partially realized.

CHAPTER VIII

THE CHANGING SOUTH
1713-1745

AT the opening of the eighteenth century, as we have attempted to show, the main interest of all colonists, north and south, was in agriculture. In the North, there were diversified crops and a marked tendency for the inhabitants to settle together in fairly compact groups. In the South, on the other hand, there were the great staple crops of rice and tobacco, and the people were scattered over the country to a far greater extent than their Northern neighbors. In both sections, however, the great mass of the population were small yeoman farmers. The lands were seldom held on lease, and the labor was performed by the farmers themselves or by the help of white labor or a few slaves, the latter only slightly more numerous in the South than in the North. In Maryland, exclusive of a few great landholders, it is probable that the average farm or plantation was from one to two hundred acres, and in Virginia the large majority of the population tilled lands not much greater in extent. As North Carolina was largely settled by poor immigrants from other colonies, the holdings there must also have been small.

Throughout the South there were conflicting influences at work, some tending to break up the larger landholdings of the great proprietors and others to increase them. Occasionally the government interfered, as when the board of trade called attention in 1728 to the fact that Governor Burrington of North Carolina was making grants of five thousand acres each when the legal limit was six hundred and forty. Usually, however, the provincial governments were on the side of the large grantees, and the forces tending to reduce holdings were more economic than political. It was all very well to own thousands of acres of wilderness but the absentee proprietor in England, or the planter in the colonies, was likely to need money. In the absence of an adequate labor supply the amount of land that was actually under cultivation even of the largest estates was small, and at the opening of the century, the tenant class was so slight as to be negligible. Owing to these two facts, the only way to realize money on surplus lands was to sell them. As an example of this tendency we may cite the case of the holdings of the Earl of Shaftesbury in South Carolina. In 1712 he sold his barony of twelve thousand acres to Samuel Wragg. Three years later Wragg sold three thousand acres to Alexander Skene and three thousand to Jacob Satur. The following year Satur sold his portion which was then rapidly broken up into small holdings, completing the process of disintegration.[1]

Before the period of an ample labor supply and of a leasehold tenantry, it is interesting to note the sources of income of even such a large landholder as William Fitzhugh of Virginia. Although he was nominally a planter and owned twenty-four thousand acres, he derived a larger net income from his inland trade than from his plantation. Both yielded the same amount of sixty thousand pounds of tobacco a year, but in the case of his plantation this was subject to deduction for feeding and clothing his slaves.[2] In those localities or periods in which quitrents were collected these also tended to disperse large holdings or at least to discourage them. For example, in Maryland in the five years preceding

[1] S. C. Hist. and Gen. Mag., XI, 86, 91.
[2] "Letters of William Fitzhugh," Va. Mag. of History, II.

1733, warrants were taken out at the land office for an average total of over twenty-eight thousand acres annually. In that year the quitrent was raised from four shillings to ten a year, and during the next five years the amount of land annually taken up decreased about ninety per cent. In the next five years, when the rent was put again at the old figure, the amounts taken out increased fivefold even although the purchase price had been considerably advanced.

Such factors as these, however, were merely brakes retarding here and there a movement which others tended successfully to bring into full play. Probably the most important of these favorable factors was the illimitable labor supply produced by the development of the slave trade, combined with the better position of the tobacco market in Europe following the Peace of Utrecht in 1713. In the seventeenth century there had, of course, been large estates and a difference between rich and poor, but the impetus now given so emphasized certain existing tendencies as to make this difference far more striking and to create a new social structure, differentiated both from that of the preceding century and from that of the North.

Even allowing that slave labor was less efficient than that of the white indentured servants, its cost was perhaps only from one quarter to one half as great, and the supply ample. A white servant cost from £2 to £4 a year for the period of service, at the end of which he could, and usually did, leave his master just when his training had made him most valuable. On the other hand, a slave for life could be bought for from £18 to £30, which would average about £1 a year provided he lived for from eighteen to thirty years. Then, too, unlike the case with servants the children bred from the slaves added to the master's wealth just as did the increase of his herds. It was obvious therefore that the landowner who had sufficient capital to invest in slaves would be at a great advantage as compared with the farmer who had to till his lands himself or even as compared with one who had to depend wholly upon the use of servants.

Thus, when through the rapid increase of slavery the amount of land which the rich man could bring under cultivation was limited only by the number of slaves whom he could buy, the advantage of capital became overwhelming.   Not only was the economic surplus vastly increased by additional acreage and labor but there accrued also all the advantages attending any large-scale production, for the large plantation became nearly self-sustaining through slaves trained for the various tasks.   Moreover, the large merchant-planter had advantages both in shipping his crop and in marketing it in England, and in purchasing such goods and supplies as came thence, which in turn he sold at a profit to his poorer neighbor.   In addition, by the use of the overseer system he could multiply the number of his plantations, depending only on the amount of capital at his disposal. By 1749, for example, Richard Bennet had a dozen or fifteen plantations all the way from Accomac in Virginia to Cecil County in Maryland.

It is true that slaves were not owned solely by the rich. Indeed, perhaps the majority of all slaves in Virginia were owned by planters who had five or less.[1] Numerically these small slave owners continued to form the bulk of the population, but as is always the case when there is a field for its profitable employment, large wealth multiplied faster in proportion than the gains of the small man.   At the bottom of the economic scale there was the poor man who tilled his few acres with little or no help.   During the years of the wars the

[1] T. J. Wertenbaker, *The Planters of Colonial Virginia* (Princeton, 1922), 153.

demoralization in prices had brought him to the brink of destruction, and the soil from which he drew his exhausting crop was yearly wearing out. He had no money with which to buy new lands or slaves, and was fortunate if the year's end did not leave him in debt to the merchant-planters. Above him was the class of small farmers who had the advantages of larger lands and sufficient capital to buy a few slaves, and who thus maintained themselves in moderate comfort but without accumulating fortunes. At the top were those whose credit, capital or influence sped them rapidly along the new road opened up.

At first the small planter who tilled his own land had been able to raise better tobacco than the newly imported slaves. As late as 1731 Governor Gooch wrote to the lords of trade that "the common people make the best," but as the slaves became more efficient this countervailing weight grew less, and, in any case, as the governor added, "the rich Man's trash will always damp the Market and spoil the poor Man's good Tobacco which has been carefully managed." [1] The margin of profit was small, and although when planted on a large scale, the profits for the large planter were correspondingly great, the small man had a hard time to make both ends meet. After 1700 we do not find the freed servant easily accumulating enough surplus to enable him in turn to become a landowner; less than five per cent of those who arrived in the colony near the end of the seventeenth century, in certain test districts, appeared on the rent roll of later years.

All these conditions brought about the marked emigration from Virginia to North Carolina and other colonies which we have already noted. Among English people in whom the instinct to own land is strong, a

[1] Quoted by T. J. Wertenbaker from Gooch to the Lords of Trade, Brit. Pub. Rec. Off., CO 5/1321, 1322.

tenant class can be built up only where land cannot be bought, either because it is not for sale or because the would-be purchaser cannot afford to pay the price. Both these factors were now coming into operation together. The new conditions of labor and markets were making land more valuable and the wealthy planters were engrossing more and more of it for cultivation and for speculation. The very conditions that were in part enabling them to do so and making it worth their while, were at the same time preventing large numbers of the poor from being able as in the past, to acquire their few acres for a little farm. From the facts that the large estates were self-sustaining economic units based on slavery and that there was little or no town and general commercial life, there was not much for the white free laborer to do but to till the soil, inadequate as the return might be. Thus he was to a great extent forced to leave the tobacco colonies altogether, as many did, or to remain as a struggling tenant farmer. A supply of tenants, however, was just what the large land speculators wanted, so that the necessity of the poorer elements thus inured to the benefit of the rich. When the tide of German immigration set into Maryland a little later, the Germans not having the same desire for ownership in fee characteristic of the English and being willing to take land on leasehold, the advantage of the large landlords became that much greater. Hampered by poverty, by ignorance and by certain legal restrictions, these newcomers formed an ideal source for the building up of a tenant class.

The working out of all these elements may best be studied, perhaps, in Maryland. There the new methods of developing wilderness lands by the methods of overseers and tenants grew steadily from about 1720, the use of tenantry becoming important from about 1730. Four years after the later date the vast tracts owned by

Charles Carroll were not bringing in a pound of rent, but thirty years later they were returning over fifty thousand pounds of tobacco a year from leases. It is true that the rent would not in itself have made the owner wealthy. The advantage derived was that the income carried the cost of holding the lands which, owing to their being cleared by the tenants and to the growth of population, were steadily advancing in value. Instead of great tracts of uninhabited wilderness, the carrying cost of which had been so severe a drain on the owners' resources as in many cases to have forced them to sell, the owners now found themselves in the position of having tenants carry the land for them while it was being transformed from a forest into well-cultivated fields in the midst of a growing population. The tenantry were thus enabling the rich to absorb more and more land and adding to its value for them. The decreased land supply and rising price in turn made it increasingly difficult for the man with little money to become anything but a tenant and he was thus forced to swell the class which was contributing to this very result.[1]

The movement thus turned in a circle, with all the advantages on the side of those who possessed capital, influence or unusual ability, for this method of land development required all three. Buildings had to be erected for the tenants and this ran into a great deal of money when done on a large scale. Moreover the biggest operators had to spend much money in securing satisfactory tenants for their constantly enlarging operations, the demand exceeding even the steadily increasing supply. Carroll expended money in the Northern colonies, in Ireland and in Germany in order to secure his settlers; and some of the other large operators, such as Daniel

[1] C. P. Gould, *The Land System in Maryland, 1720-1765* (John Hopkins Univ., *Studies*, XXXI, no. 1).

Dulany, were similarly engaged in reaching after the supplies of tenants at their European sources. Carroll, as a result of his efforts, his capital and the favoritism originally shown his family in the grants, was building up improved tracts of from five to ten thousand acres each in the rich lands in the forks of the Patuxent. In 1731 Thomas Brerewood, on account of his relationship to the proprietor, secured a grant of ten thousand acres in Baltimore County, and soon built up a closely settled estate. Dulany took up great tracts in Frederick County and the development of that section, which in 1730 had been practically an unbroken wilderness, was so rapid that by 1745 he laid out the new town of Frederick, and within a decade the new county was second in numbers in the colony.[1]

Such operations as these, however, involved much money and were beyond the reach of those who had not capital, influence to secure large grants or credits, or sources of income other than such as could be made from a small plantation. Carroll, for example, inherited enormous holdings of land and other wealth from his father who had been close to the proprietor under the royal government; Dulany rose not simply by natural ability but by three successive marriages into wealthy and politically influential families; Edward Lloyd was receiver-general, an immensely convenient office in charge of the collection of quitrents; Richard Bennet was a large merchant; and so the list of those rapidly growing rich might be extended. In Virginia we have already noted that more than one half of Fitzhugh's income was from "inland trade," and Byrd and other great planters and landowners were also merchants trading with England. In addition, Byrd, as his father had been before

---

[1] For an account of Daniel Dulany, see St. G. L. Sioussat, *Economics and Politics in Maryland, 1720-1750* . . . (John Hopkins Univ., Studies, XXI, nos. 6-7), chap. iii.

him, was receiver-general.   In these respects, however,
the average man was at a permanent disadvantage.
Without a voice in the councils, which were composed
of those of wealth and position, without influence with
the proprietors or crown officials, large land grants did
not fall to his share because of a handsome face, charming manners, chinking coffers or family relationships
Agriculture alone, as we have seen, did not leave sufficient surplus when pursued on a modest or, indeed, a
large scale to permit profitable speculation in developing
great landholdings, and the character of commercial life
in the South was such that it did not afford alternative
opportunities for the small trader or petty merchant as
did conditions in the North.

With the exception of Charleston there was scarcely
anything that deserved the name of a town during this
period.   In Maryland the largest center was Oxford on
the Eastern Shore, with the small village of Annapolis
second.   Baltimore had not yet really come into being.
In Virginia, Norfolk was the most promising but was
still scarcely more than a hamlet with the beginnings
of a fair trade.   North Carolina had Wilmington which
was said to have a hundred houses in 1745, and Edenton
with fifty by 1728.   Charleston, with between five and
six hundred about 1730, was the metropolis of the
South, and that center alone offered opportunity for the
various occupations of the ordinary townsman. Georgia,
which was founded as a new colony in 1732, was unimportant in this period save as a frontier outpost and
for the fur trade.

Although in the founding of that colony the usual
economic motives had been stressed, and the military
function, which most appealed to the crown, the main
object among some of the projectors, notably James
Oglethorpe, had been to provide an asylum for the poor
and debtors in England who had fallen into their con-

dition through misfortune of one sort or another and
who belonged to a fairly reputable grade in society.
Both in the motive which thus led to its establishment
and in the unique form of government given to it, the
last of the thirteen colonies differed materially from the
others. It alone received a direct financial grant from
Parliament. We may note in passing that the first prohibition law in what is now the United States was passed
for this province in 1735, it then being made unlawful
to bring any strong liquors into the colony under any
name and any brought in had to be publicly destroyed
under pain of heavy fine. Land grants were limited by
law, though not strictly in practice, to five hundred
acres, and estates, even down to fifty acres, were to be
held in tail male, not only that in a military colony each
holding should have a male defender, according to old
feudal usage, but that unthrifty colonists, who in a
colony so founded were expected to be numerous, would
not be able to alienate their land and thus make possible
great inequality in property. Another evidence of the
idealistic character of the project was the ban against
slavery. But these provisions did not represent the sen-
timents of the settlers; they fell into disrespect, and by
the time Georgia became a royal province in the middle
of the century, had largely been abrogated.[1]

When town conditions were present in the South,
as in Charleston, the petty capitalist had the same
opportunities as in the North. The career of the first
Manigault, for example, is instructive as to the possibilities for the man starting with only a small capital.
Having come to Carolina late in the seventeenth century
with his brother as a Huguenot refugee, he started farming, found it unprofitable, and moved into town. Beginning by running a boarding house, the savings soon

[1] For a brief account see H. L. Osgood, *American Colonies in the
Eighteenth Century*, III, chap. ix.

enabled Gabriel to buy a small brandy distillery. To this he added cooperage for the products of the still, and soon was able to build another plant. With the profits derived from the two distilleries, he became a shipping merchant and when he died in 1729 left two store-houses, his distilleries and other property. His son, Gabriel, extended the shipping business, and by 1754 was able to retire from that and devote himself to the banking which came in with the later period, becoming extremely wealthy.[1] The tendency even in that colony, however, although less marked than in the other South-ern ones, was for commercial business to fall into the hands either of the large colonial planter or of the Eng-lish merchant firms.

The large planters shipped their tobacco direct to England, and with the proceeds or credit derived from the shipments imported goods for their stores. The small farmer, who had only the produce of a few acres to dispose of, could not afford to ship it abroad and had to sell to the local buyers. On the other hand, instead of getting his English goods at English prices he had to buy them either from the local merchant or the repre-sentatives of English houses. In Maryland this business tended more and more to fall into the hands of the big English concerns, such as the Cunliffes, Hydes, Hunts, Gildarts and others. Foster, Cunliffe and Sons of Liver-pool, for example, had their Maryland headquarters and chief factor at Oxford, another large store on the Chester River, and a smaller one halfway between, and other firms were equally well located strategically. Against such competition as that or of the large landowning politically influential Virginia planter and storekeeper, the small merchant who might attempt to set up for

---

[1] He was thought to be the richest man in the American colonies; E. McCrady, *History of South Carolina under the Royal Government* (N. Y., 1901), 402.

himself was helpless, and the absence of town life precluded the necessity for a multiplicity of small retail shops. The only intruder who seems to have annoyed the larger and well-intrenched merchants was the little, huckstering New England trader who sailed in his own small boat into the creeks and rivers of the plantation colonies and chaffered with the smallest planters and even with the servants and slaves. "Some of these Banditti," wrote Byrd to a friend in Salem, Massachusetts, "anchor near my estate, for the advantage of traffiquing with my slaves, from whom they are sure to have good Pennyworths. I am now prosecuting one of them whose name is Grant, for this crime, and have evidence sufficient to convict him. I wish you would be so kind as to hang up all your Felons at home, and not send them abroad to discredit their country." [1]

The greater part of Southern trade was, of course, in the shipping of tobacco and rice and the importing of English manufactured goods, and the new rule of 1730 that rice could be shipped direct from Carolina to European ports south of Cape Finisterre temporarily enlarged the circle of their commerce. But if tobacco and rice were the great staples, they by no means formed the only exports even to England. The *Virginia Gazette,* established in 1736, in its custom-house news gives us the cargoes carried by the vessels in the overseas trade and we are thus enabled to picture the commerce carried on by that colony. In the shipments to England the products of the forest, particularly staves, form an important element and nearly every vessel carried these in addition to the ever present tobacco. A few typical examples will suffice to indicate the extent of these other commodities. Thus one small vessel was loaded with one hundred and fifty-six hogsheads of tobacco, and ten

---

[1] Letter from William Byrd to Benjamin Lynde, *Va. Hist. Mag.,* **IX.** 243.

thousand staves; another three hundred and eighty hogsheads and twelve thousand staves.   Another carried six hundred and thirty-five hogsheads, eight thousand staves and fifty-three tons of iron; another four hundred and twelve hogsheads, six thousand staves and thirty tons of iron.   Yet another held three hundred and four hogsheads of tobacco, ninety-six hundred staves, twelve hundred feet of plank and twenty-one hogsheads of deerskins.   In Virginia furs had taken a subordinate place, but many vessels carried small consignments.[1]

In the export trade to the West Indies there was a large business in foodstuffs and we find such cargoes as seven hundred and sixty-four bushels of corn, sixty barrels of pork, ten barrels of beef, seven of tallow and three of lard; or fourteen hundred bushels of corn, eleven thousand shingles and a hundred bushels of peas.   Another of these provision vessels carried fifty barrels of pork, fifty barrels of beef, thirty of bread, a thousand bushels of peas, ten boxes of candles, five hundred pounds of butter and ten thousand shingles.[2]   Wheat was beginning to be an important crop also, and in Maryland at the end of the period of this chapter there was a sharp line of political cleavage between the wheat-growing Eastern Shore and the other counties, over the export duties on grain and tobacco respectively.   When Richmond was laid out in lots in 1737 one of the inducements offered to prospective purchasers was that the new town was "in the midst of great Quantities of Grain."[3]

The colonies to the southward seem to have been sharply differentiated from one another in their foreign commerce.   That of North Carolina has not yet received the attention it deserves but from many indica-

[1] See Va. Gazette, June 17, July 8, Sept. 2, 23, 1737; Aug. 3, 1739.
[2] Va. Gazette, June 10, July 8, Aug. 12, 1737.
[3] Va. Gazette, April 15, 1737.

tions it would seem that its direct trade with England was small. Byrd stated that the trade was "engrost by the Saints of New England, who carry off a great deal of Tobacco, without troubling themselves with paying that Impertinent Duty of a Penny a Pound." [1] It is true that the colonel was healthily stocked with hearty prejudices and lost no love on either the "Saints" or the Carolinians, but other evidence bears out his statement as to how the neighboring tobacco crop was marketed. The clearances from Boston for the year 1732 show eighty-seven vessels arriving from North Carolina and an equally large number sailing thence. These figures must be compared with only ten Boston entries from South Carolina, sixteen from Virginia and twenty from Maryland. [2] In other words, North Carolina with a population of approximately thirty thousand as against the combined total of two hundred and sixty-five thousand for the other colonies was sending eighty-seven vessels to Boston against their combined total of forty-six. Evidently, even after making all allowance for the known heavy trade in naval stores, there was some remarkably close tie, presumably not religious, between Boston Bay and the innumerable coves—a little earlier much infested with pirates—of North Carolina. At the same time that this heavy trade was being carried on with Boston, only twelve vessels from North Carolina arrived at New York and three at Philadelphia as compared with the eighty-seven at Boston. [3] Another evidence of the lack of direct trade with England is found in the statement of a contemporary traveler that in the Cape Fear country "the cheapest Goods imported are 50% dearer than at Philadelphia, and most things

[1] Byrd, *Writings*, 32.
[2] *Boston News-Letter*, 1732, *passim*. The entries in the same journal a decade later, 1743, show the figures as sixty-one from North Carolina, six South Carolina, fourteen Virginia and eighteen Maryland.
[3] *N. Y. Gazette*, 1733; *Pa. Gazette*, 1734.

100%." [1]   The New England farmers, before they turned to commerce, had already acquired the reputation of being "hard milkers."

If the intercolonial and ocean trade of North Carolina was thus largely in the hands of the Bostonians, this was far from being the case with the large commerce centering only a little farther south at Charleston.   Pitch and turpentine found their way northward, and cattle were driven overland as far as Philadelphia, but most of the colony's trade went overseas to the West Indies, the wine islands and Europe.   The town's great importance even compared with the Northern mercantile centers is shown by the fact that whereas one hundred and seventy-three vessels arrived at Philadelphia in 1733 and one hundred and ninety-six the year before at New York, three hundred and seventeen were loaded at Charleston in 1735.   Although this was the high point, the annual Charleston loadings average about two hundred and twenty ships or considerably more than any other colonial port except Boston.   In 1737 the merchants organized their own marine insurance company.

Both in South Carolina and Georgia the fur trade retained a more important position than elsewhere in the South.   Douglass, indeed, set the figure for Charleston at from £25,000 to £30,000 a year, and though this figure may be too high, the trade was an important one, centering at the new village of Augusta, laid out in 1736. It was said that five years later a hundred thousand pounds' weight of skins was brought thence.   About six hundred horses were used in the pack trains, the skins coming in from the Creeks whose chief town lay about two hundred miles to the west.   Even beyond their country, in that of the Choctaws there were traders from the new colony of Georgia busy in detaching the natives

---

[1] Hugh Meredith, *An Account of the Cape Fear Country 1731* (Perth Amboy, 1922), 29.

from their alliance with the French.[1]   It was only at the very end of this period, in 1745, that indigo was first introduced into Carolina and opened a new road to wealth. In that year also a traveler reports that the Carolinians had begun to raise oranges in astounding quantities, stating that one ship alone had then recently carried over one hundred and fifty thousand to London.[2]   It would be ungenerous in this brief account of the economics of the period to forget the ubiquitous and obscure, but by no means humble, hog.   Governor George Burrington in a speech in 1733 said that North Carolina sent fifty thousand fat ones into Virginia in good years, and Governor Gooch of the latter colony reported to the lords of trade that this animal was one of the principal supports of the colony.[3]   He was certainly one of the mainstays of the poor all through the South.

Throughout all this period, Southern economic life was seriously hampered by the lack of a satisfactory currency.   As was pointed out in the preceding volume, tobacco had early become the medium of exchange, but the wide fluctuations in its price made it a most unsatisfactory one, and entailed much hardship as well as ill feeling between debtors and creditors.   Barter was necessarily resorted to for many transactions, and in North Carolina by 1720 as many as twenty commodities other than tobacco had also been made legal tender, but the fluctuations in their several prices naturally enabled the shrewd and unscrupulous to pay their debts in the least valuable.   In 1712 that colony resorted to paper money with the usual results of depreciation through succeeding decades until, by 1731, £100 sterling was

[1] William Douglass, *A Summary, Historical and Political* (Boston, 1749), I, 176; [B. Martyn], *An Impartial Inquiry into the State and Utility of the Province of Georgia* (1741), Ga. Hist. Soc., *Colls.*, I, 179.
[2] "William Logan's Journal, 1745," *Pa. Mag. of Hist. and Biog.*, XXXVI, 163.
[3] *N. C. Colon. Records*, III, 621; *Va. Hist. Mag.*, III, 118.

worth £800 in provincial currency. Maryland also tried the same experiment, with somewhat better success during the period of this chapter, but the lack of specie and the wide fluctuations in the purchasing power of the various media used were a severe handicap for the honest and less shrewd portion of the Southern people, as well as for trade in general.

As a result of the intricate interplay of all these economic factors, a new social structure was arising in the Southern colonies, some of the more striking aspects of which are those which have usually been abstracted and mingled together to form the popular picture of the "Old South." The intercourse between the rich Southerner and England was far closer, as we have seen, than was that of the inhabitants of the Northern colonies. Such men already mentioned in this chapter, as Carroll, Dulany and Byrd, had all studied in the mother country. Men and women on the large plantations did their shopping, not in such shops as those of Philadelphia or Boston but direct from London, and the ships which brought the goods came as it were to their very doors, or at least to the foot of their lawns and gardens which sloped to the river's edge.

Their ideals of social life were to a great extent those of the English country gentry with whom they mingled when in England, with whom they corresponded and whom they imitated as far as possible. Both the conditions of the wilderness and the lack of the proper economic base had permitted this only to a very moderate extent during the seventeenth century, but as frontier conditions disappeared in the tidewater sections and as the factors outlined in this chapter permitted the rise of a conspicuously wealthy class, its members began to utilize this new wealth in spacious and comely living. It is from this period that we can date the rise of the great places, such as "Shirley," "Rosewell" and "Westover," though many of the large mansions like "Mt. Airy" date from about the middle of the century. The rapid advance in the scale of living of the upper classes is well exemplified in the case of the Byrds, father and son. The father, who belongs to the period of our earlier chapters, was content to dwell in the first "Westover," a large but comparatively modest house. At his death he left about twenty-six thousand acres.[1] His son who died in 1744 left nearly a hundred and eighty thousand acres and built the beautiful house, which, somewhat marred by changes, is still one of the show places of Virginia.

When the newly acquired wealth of the period both permitted and seemed to require new homes befitting its owners, they turned naturally to the new style then beginning to prevail in England, as did the builders in all the colonies. The earlier colonial architecture had been largely medieval in its affinities, informal and picturesque, and had embodied much of the genuine folk spirit of England, Holland, Wales, Sweden or Germany, depending upon the nationality of the colonists. There had been both diversity and individuality, but the new builders, consciously striving for dignity, spaciousness and beauty, adopted the new Georgian style which after about 1720 spread very rapidly throughout the country. The books of such English builders as William Half-penny, Robert Morris and Batty Langley, all beginning to write between 1720 and 1730, quickly found their way to America and the greater architectural uniformity which now becomes apparent, was due to the fact that, in the absence of professional architects, the builders all followed somewhat closely the same texts.

There were, however, not only local differences in treatment between the North and the South but even between colony and colony. From this time the finer

[1] See J. S. Bassett's introduction to his edition of William Byrd II, *History of the Dividing Line* (N. Y., 1901).

Southern houses, almost without exception, were built of brick, generally made near by, although there were occasional importations, such as eighty thousand bricks brought in one London-owned ship entered from New England, and fifty thousand brought direct from old England in another vessel, to Virginia.[1]   Occasionally characteristics were extremely local, as the beautiful brickwork of the town houses in Annapolis where the bricks were somewhat larger than the modern ones, of a remarkably fine and smooth texture and of a lovely dull salmon color.   The jointing used there was also unusually thin and struck with a fine tool so as to give a crisp and delicate effect.   In Maryland generally the detail of the wooden trim was also rather more finely wrought than in Virginia where the interior was apt to be a trifle heavy although always vigorous and fresh.   In South Carolina, the demands of the climate made the coolness of the house a prime requirement, and this factor introduced certain local characteristics, so that, for example, piazzas and balconies developed there much more than farther North.

Without pursuing these details, we may say that the plan of these new Southern mansions was a composition in five parts, the large central mass and two smaller ones at each end, usually but not always connected with the center by passages.[2]   The ceilings were extraordinarily high, and the proportions of the rooms of striking charm and dignity.   The great hall frequently ran through the entire building and was sometimes open for two stories in height with the graceful staircase forming a notable

[1] *Va. Gazette*, June 10, 1737; May 25, 1739.   The list of English goods exported to Virginia and Maryland, 1698-1699 shows 26,000 bricks.   M. S. Morriss, *Colonial Trade of Maryland* (Johns Hopkins Univ., *Studies*, XXXII, no. 3), 139.   That three such lots should be found in the comparatively few lists of published cargoes would indicate that more complete returns would disclose many more.

[2] See pictures in T. F. Hamlin, *The American Spirit in Architecture* (R. H. Gabriel, editor, *The Pageant of America*, XIII).

feature.   The main part of the building contained from eight to a dozen or more rooms, and the placing of the kitchens and other offices in one of the wings added a number more to the total.   The treatment of the grounds and gardens became much more elaborate also, the house usually standing far back from the entrance and approached under an avenue of trees, though these shaded approaches, seventy to a hundred feet wide, were rather more common in Maryland than in Virginia.

As almost all the large places of this period in all the Southern colonies were on rivers, the lawns and gardens sloped down to the banks of the streams on one side, and on the other, as roads became more common, there was also an approach.   In South Carolina the most important place of this period was still "Drayton Hall" on the Ashley, an imposing three-story mansion, with columns of Portland marble, brought like much else of the material from England.   The charming Eliza Lucas, who came with her family from Antigua about 1737 to settle in Carolina, and who had been educated in England, visited at this house but unfortunately has left no description of the place as it then was.   In one of her letters, however, she describes another and smaller one and gives us some idea of the extent and treatment of the grounds then surrounding such mansions.   "Mr. Middleton's 'Crowfield,' " she says, "stands a mile from, but in sight of, the road and makes a very handsome appearance; as you draw near it new beauties discover themselves . . . a spacious Basin in the midst of a large Green presents itself as you enter the gate that leads to the House. . . . From the back door is a spacious walk a thousand feet long; each side of which nearest the house is a grass plat ornamented in a Serpentine manner with Flowers; next to that on the right hand is what immediately struck my rural taste, a thicket of young, tall live oaks. . . . Opposite on the left hand is a large square boling green, sunk a little below the level of the rest of the garden, with a walk quite round composed of fine, large flowering Laurel and Catalpas . . . at the bottom of this charming spot there is a large fish pond with a mount rising out of the middle the top of which is level with the dwelling House, and upon it is a Roman temple, on each side of this are other large fish ponds properly disposed which form a fine Prospect of water from the house." [1]

The life lived by the fortunate dwellers on these great estates has often been described, albeit a bit too romantically, and is probably the main feature in the popular view of the South. It was a life, as we have said, as far as might be on the lines of the smaller country gentry of England. "The eleven of Prince George's County" in Maryland, and "the eleven South River Gentlemen" contended at cricket. Where, two generations before, their ancestors carried their guns through the tangled wilderness in fear of the savages, the young bloods now pursued on horseback the equally wily but distinctly less dangerous fox, and one of the earliest "leading articles" of the newly established *Virginia Gazette* was on hunting to hounds. [2] What some have claimed to be the earliest Jockey Club in the world appears to have been founded at Charleston in 1734, and the Maryland Jockey Club, founded at Annapolis in 1745, included in its membership men from several different colonies. From that time on, although more notable a decade later, began the importation of blooded stallions from England, and racing stables began to be a costly item in a gentleman's estate. Of more practical use was the first breeding in this period of that substantial Southern product, the mule. As early as 1728, Byrd recommended their use for wilderness work but advised employing asses until

[1] H. H. Ravenel, *Eliza Pinckney* (N. Y., 1902), 53.
[2] Issue Dec. 3, 1736.

mules could be bred. This was being done in another two decades, and certain asses, such as the oddly named Maryland "Tickle Pitcher," were advertised for breeding.[1]

Of the intellectual and artistic aspects of this new Southern society we shall speak in a later chapter, and here merely stress the emergence of a new class distinctly set apart from the rest of the inhabitants. The eighteenth century did not inaugurate the distinction in the South between rich and poor, or even mark the introduction of slavery, but in its earlier decades it did witness the establishment of a class so wealthy, so powerful, its members so bound to one another by marriage and other ties, and so intrenched in influence with the various authorities as to set them apart in quite a different way from that in which the moderate distinctions of wealth had operated earlier. These new leaders, indeed, were true empire builders and if they were absorbing to themselves princely estates by means and influences denied to the hard-working farmer, nevertheless they were developing the country at a rate which might otherwise not have been possible. It may well be, as Governor Gooch asserted in 1728, that the concentration of vast areas of frontier lands in the hands of a few had not hindered settlement but on the contrary had hastened it by such methods as we have noted employed by Dulany, Carroll and others. He claimed that the Spotsylvania country, which was one of large land grants, had filled up more rapidly than Brunswick, where the grants were limited, though there may have been other and less obvious reasons for this. Moreover, we must not forget that when development was undertaken on a large scale, the risk of the large outlays corresponding to the profits was not small, and Dulany himself was thought to be involving himself in ruin in the early stages of his

[1] *Md. Gazette*, June 24, 1756.

operations in Frederick County. The many and frequently devious ways by which these great estates were acquired and the question whether the social rewards that fell to the share of certain members of the community were in excess of their social services do not concern us here. What interests us is that, in the new social order thus forming, certain stratifications were becoming so fixed as definitely to determine the status of the great majority of the Southern population in a fashion which had not been characteristic of the more mobile society of a few decades earlier.

The great cleavage, of course, was that between bond and free, and it has been claimed that this fundamental distinction tended to obliterate the lesser ones of differing wealth and social position among the free whites. It may be true that the slave owners did form a class which had a certain solidarity of feeling and of interest, but it must not be forgotten that the stigma brought upon physical labor by associating it with slavery became so great, as the number of slaves increased, as to react upon the white laborer, and to create a gulf between the white who owned even one or two slaves to toil for him, and the farmer or mechanic who labored for himself. Aside from its effect upon the black, it was probably this influence upon the whites which was one of the most evil effects of the "peculiar institution."

Although economic conditions varied to some extent in the several colonies at different times, on the whole the less than half a century between the dates of the building of the two "Westovers," with all the change that those two dwellings connote in the life of the wealthy class, had not been years of prosperity for the people at large. Most of them had witnessed the constant stream of immigration from Virginia already noted. In Maryland the war years to 1713 had brought great poverty and distress, owing partly to the low price

of tobacco, the high cost of shipping it to England under
war risks, and the fact that it also served as the colony's
medium of exchange. The period from 1720 to 1745
was also one of poverty and the accumulation of debt by
the poorer classes. The legislation against the clergy in
that colony in the period used to be considered as directed
particularly against the church, but the fact that the
attacks extended to the lawyers and official classes as well,
now makes this movement appear rather as the exhibition of "the jealousy of a debt-ridden agricultural
population toward salaried creditor classes." [1] At the
opening of the eighteenth century, it has been estimated
that over sixty per cent of the whites in Virginia had
neither slaves nor indented servants but tilled their own
soil. In the years immediately following, there was
little if any chance for these to rise in the scale. In the
whole tidewater section along the coast of the several
colonies, the creation and consolidating of the great
estates we have mentioned was then going on. Land
was increasing in value and the amount available
diminishing. In Maryland, for example, from about
1730 to 1760 plantation land tripled in price, and by
1754, except in Frederick County, there was not enough
vacant land left to erect a new manor. The freed
servant could not afford to buy even a few acres. The
farmer who had tilled his own found himself not only
struggling against economic conditions but becoming
more and more despised by every neighbor who was
sufficiently better off to be able to buy a slave or two
and live in any sort of shiftless way, provided that he
did not labor in the fields himself. Even if the figure of
sixty per cent be too large, it is nevertheless evident that
these conditions must have adversely affected a large proportion of the population, who had the options only of

[1] St. G. L. Sioussat, *Economics and Politics in Maryland, 1720-50*
(Johns Hopkins Univ., *Studies*, XXI, no. 6), 27.

sinking to the level of the "poor whites," of emigrating to other colonies or to the frontier and starting afresh in a new environment. The type of social structure on the seaboard had become fixed in a new form within a few decades, and as a result of this rapid economic transformation, there was no longer any place in it for large numbers who had survived, even if they had not flourished, under the conditions of a generation earlier.

Out on the frontier the air cleared. From western Maryland to the backlands of the new colony of Georgia, Germans, Swiss, Scotch, new immigrants from Europe and the poor from the older tidewater regions poured in to hew clearings, till new fields and build homes. There slavery brought neither wealth to the few nor blight to the many. It was a hard life but a man's. "When we came to the Bluff," wrote one of the Scotch immigrants who penetrated into South Carolina in 1734, "my mother and we children were still in expectation that we were coming to an agreeable place. But when we arrived and saw nothing but a wilderness, and instead of a fine timbered house, nothing but a mean dirt house, our spirits quite sank," and here their guide left them unexpectedly. The father encouraged them by manly words, but while they were beginning to make their clearing the fire which they had brought with them went out, and with no means of kindling a new one, the father had to try to find his way through the wilderness to another settler's to renew it. "We watched him as far as the trees would let him see, and then returned to our dolorous hut, expecting never to see him or any human being more. . . . Evening coming on, the wolves began to howl on all sides." They had been led to expect that houses would be prepared for them, and that transportation would be provided, but instead there was only the wilderness and they were forced to carry all their goods, including their beds and mattresses, on their backs through the thick forests and across swamps to the place appointed for their new abode.[1] Beyond them were no white men but trappers and hunters, the cow drivers herding their wild cattle here and there into pens in natural clearings in the forests, and the Indian traders and pack-horse men, with the young lads who led a half-civilized, half-Indian existence connected with the pack trains.

It was a lawless life at first, and the endorsements on the Augusta County sheriff's writs of execution in the Shenandoah Valley of Virginia are illuminating. "Not executed by stress of water," we read on one, "and def[endan]t swore if I did get across he would shoot me if I touched any of his estates; also he is gone out of the country." A whole cinema drama in three clauses! On others we find endorsed, "not executed by reason there is no road to the place where he lives," "not executed by reason of a gun," "not executed by reason of an axx," and "kept from Miller with a club." [2] There were religious Germans in the valley who had not been able to hear a sermon in five years. Nevertheless, the frontier prospered and as the mountain slopes and valleys to the westward of all the Southern colonies slowly filled up there came into being a new sectional alignment, and tidewater and frontier divided the South into two contrasted types of culture.

This contrast came to exist in all the colonies, north as well as south. In the North also, as we shall see, the rich likewise drew much further away from the mass of the people in this same period, but there were two points in which the two sections were sharply contrasted. In the North, although slavery was well established it did not develop sufficiently as to have the effects just noted in

[1] Witherspoon's account, quoted by Hanna, *The Scotch-Irish*, II, 27.
[2] Quoted by J. A. Waddell, *Anns. of Augusta County* (Staunton, 1902), 77.

the South, and the problems that the increasing complexity of society brought did not include the crucial one of the difference between the white artisan, laborer or farmer and the slave owner. If to that extent, at least, there may have been a greater solidarity of interest and sentiment among all classes of whites at the north, there was an influence at work in another respect which later tended to divide the wealthiest class in the North from the people at large as was not the case in the South.

The important relationship of debtor and creditor did not differ very materially between the tidewater and frontier sections or between the rich and poor in the North and the South. In the South, however, the position of the rich was by no means as independent as was that of the same class in the North. The great planter had, indeed, his tens of thousands of acres, his hundreds, possibly, of slaves, and his mortgages on the farms of his poorer neighbors, but there was a flaw in his imposing economic position. It seems to be the nature of the large planter, anywhere and everywhere, to run into debt to his agents. Whether it is due to the extravagance engendered by the traditions of open-handed hospitality on great estates, whether to the fact that a considerable time elapses between the drawing against his bankers for the proceeds of his crop and the sale of it, whether because these drawings are apt to be optimistically large and an unexpected drop in price starts the planter irremediably wrong, or whatever else it may be due to, the fact remains, and was as true of the West Indian as of the continental planters. The Southerner who was growing richer seemed to need ever more and more money to sustain the equally rapidly advancing scale of his living, the need of capital for the development of his plantations, the purchase of slaves, or the vast speculation in frontier lands. In the North, the divorce between the agriculturist and the merchant had become fairly complete, and the mercantile, money-lending speculating class was not involved in large agricultural operations as was the Southern merchant-planter. The fact that such a differentiation had not taken place in the South and that there the merchant class and the planter were to a great extent identical is the clue to certain later events.

As the century advanced, the Southern planter and the London merchant exchanged sharp letters over their mutual affairs, and complaints became more bitter on both sides. It was true that the mercantile nabobs of the North were also in debt to their English correspondents, but there was the great difference between the two cases, that whereas the Northerner was in debt for merchandise which could, more or less readily, be liquidated, the Southerner had spent the money represented by his debts either for living expenses or in such ways as did not permit of a speedy realization.[1] There were, of course, some in the South as well as in the North, who had handsome free balances, but for the most part the planters seem to have had one subtle bond in common with the poor frontiersman who had borrowed money to set himself up—they both alike owed that which they could not pay, and the feelings which the poor debtor entertained for his rich creditor of the seaboard, the opulent planter in turn entertained for the still richer London merchant upon whose advances he depended to a large extent for the conspicuous luxury in which he lived.

[1] J. S. Bassett, "The Virginia Planter and the London Merchant," Am. Hist. Assoc., *Rep. for 1901*, 553-575.

CHAPTER IX

THE COMMERCIALIZATION OF
THE NORTH
1713-1745

THE period immediately following the Peace of Utrecht was one of very considerable expansion in the North, both of trade and of the frontier. As in the South, those with business acumen, capital and influence took advantage of the new conditions to build fortunes rapidly. Whereas in the South, however, the new class which came into being was that of wealthy planters, in the North it was made up in the main of merchants and a very few manufacturers, and the new Northern "aristocrats" became sharply differentiated by occupation as well as by wealth, from the tillers of the soil. The development of commerce and the change from an agricultural to a commercial community are well illustrated in Rhode Island. In 1680 it had been reported to the board of trade that there was not a single merchant in the colony, but that the people lived comfortably "by improving the wilderness." In 1708 there were twenty-nine vessels owned by its citizens. By 1739 the little fleet had increased to one hundred, and by the middle of the century the number even of those over sixty tons had grown to three hundred. By 1720 Providence had embarked on its career as a seaport, and such families as the Tillinghasts, Powerses and Browns were turning from farming to trading. In 1721 James Brown and four others ventured on building a sloop of seventy-three tons and sending her to the West Indies.

The venture was successful, and the following year the young farmer, twenty-four years old, was confident enough of the new business to marry and to go himself as captain to the Leeward Islands. From that time the farm knew him no more, while his store and shipping business rapidly increased his wealth.

As we noted in an earlier chapter, the little trading vessels which sailed from the Northern colonies set out from almost every village on seacoast or navigable stream. In the years immediately following the war, however, a stricter and apparently unnecessarily harsh and nagging enforcement of the laws by port officers made very difficult the carrying on of trade from any except the ports of entry. A memorial issued at Hartford in 1716 states that the surveyor-general was trying to close up all Connecticut ports save one or two, in an apparent endeavor to force all vessels to clear from New London only.[1] In New York, two years earlier, Samuel Mulford in a speech to the assembly, called attention to the abuses practised in that colony by the naval officers even at the port of New York where so annoying were the conditions that, as he said, "not any man was fit to be Master of a Vessel . . . except he were a Lawyer; and then they should not escape, except it was by favour." [2] Among the examples he gave of the pernicious activities of the officials was that of a young man who sailed from the Connecticut shore to Long Island to be married and to carry over his wife's goods. The boat was seized, taken to New York and confiscated, the unfortunate bridegroom having to pay the owner £30 damages. To have sailed to New York to get his clearance papers would have added about a hundred and fifty miles to his twenty-mile trip. Although wheat was sell-

[1] Conn. Archives, Trade and Maritime Affairs, I, 72.
[2] Samuel Mulford, *Speech to the Assembly at New York* (N. Y., April 2, 1714), 1.

ing in Boston for nearly twice what it would bring in New York, the people at the east end of Long Island, a hundred miles east of New York, were not allowed to carry their produce to Massachusetts unless they took it to New York first and cleared thence.

Commerce, indeed, continued from the smaller places, but such obstructive tactics on the part of royal officials must have helped the natural tendency to concentrate trade in the larger centers. The increasing size of the vessels also forced shipping from creeks and coves into larger harbors. Moreover, in several respects business was becoming better organized, and shipping could be more advantageously carried on from those places where there was a certain amount of accumulated wealth and more frequent foreign news. For example, the risks of the sea were still great but these could be minimized by several persons taking shares in several ventures instead of each placing his capital all in one, and also by insurance. Both of these safeguards were easier in places where shipping interests were concentrated, and the number of persons interested in such business greater. Although insurance had long been effected by individuals this period saw the rise of corporations which made it their sole business—a change indicative of the new methods coming into vogue. In England the first two companies in the field, the London Assurance Corporation and the Royal Assurance Corporation, were both incorporated in 1720, and the regular registry of shipping began about six years later. In the colonies we have our first record of an insurance broker and the effort to organize the business in 1721, in an advertisement by John Copson in Philadelphia that "Assurances from Losses happening at Sea &c. being found to be very much for the Ease and Benefit of the Merchants" and that, whereas they had hitherto "been obliged to send to London for such Assurances, which has not only been tedious and troublesome but even very precarious," he would open an office where insurance could be secured locally from persons of wealth and standing.[1]

If commerce was thus becoming somewhat safer in some ways and organized on modern lines, it had by no means lost its flavor of romance, and even in the inter-mittent times of peace the merchants ran risks and used methods which today would be expected only in times of war. In the period of this chapter, piracy, privateer-ing and smuggling all helped to render commerce both highly speculative and highly adventurous. With re-spect to the first, a distinct improvement in public morals is discernible in that the merchants have now become the victims and not the partners of the piratical gentry, or perhaps the determined stand of the British government had made the risks for established firms too great. "Pri-vateers in Time of War are a Nursery for Pyrates against a Peace," wrote one of the earliest historians of the black flag at this time, and pointed out that with the Peace of Utrecht the sudden cessation of hostilities had led to so much unemployment among seamen that he had not "known a Man of War commissin'd for several Years past, but three times her complement of Men have offer'd themselves in 24 hours." [2] A noteworthy feature of the trade was the extreme youthfulness of most of the pirates, nearly one half of the fifty-two of Roberts's crew who were executed in 1722 being between nine-teen and twenty-five years of age. At that time the pages of the *American Weekly Mercury* of Philadelphia were filled with accounts of the depredations of such buccaneers, many of them Spanish, who infested the seas and not only preyed upon the West Indian com-merce in southern waters but even chased unlucky cap-

---

[1] *Am. Wkly. Mercury*, May 18/25, 1721.
[2] Charles Johnson, *A General History of Pyrates* . . . (London, 1726, 3d edn.), I, preface.

tains into the very harbors of Philadelphia, New York, Boston and Newport. In March one account noted eight Boston vessels burned at Honduras, and in May six were reported captured off Barbados. Many single captures were also noted, some in home waters. Although piracy remained one of the chances that the merchant had to take into consideration, nevertheless better employment conditions and the constant capture of pirates by the navy, sometimes with colonial aid as in the case of Blackbeard, gradually reduced the danger.

The causes noted as tending to concentrate commerce at those larger centers having good harbor facilities, and such other factors as the extent of the back farming country and the development of roads, not only increased the urban population of certain towns but shifted the comparative importance of these as the century advanced.

At its opening, Boston was far in advance of any other port on the continent, with New York second. By the beginning of the third decade, although Boston's shipping had increased so that the entries at the customs house numbered five hundred and seventy-eight, that of other ports had been increasing at an even more rapid rate, so that the figures were one hundred and seventy-three for Philadelphia, one hundred and ninety-six for New York, and about two hundred and twenty a year for Charleston, South Carolina. By the middle of the century Boston had fallen considerably behind Philadelphia, which became the center of both commerce and culture but which, in turn, was beginning to find a new, though less important, rival in Baltimore. That town developed rapidly because of three factors: first, the ease of floating the produce of the back country down the Susquehanna; second, unlike Philadelphia, the access to its wharves in winter; and third, the greater foresight of the Baltimoreans in building good roads to tap the hinterland. In population, the New England metropolis became steadily less important in comparison to the others. Her rivals New York and Philadelphia, originally far behind her, gradually overtook her, and then forged ahead. Later, her commerce was to decline both relatively and actually, but up to the middle of the period of this chapter, she was still the leading town on the continent and the richest commercial port.

This rivalry of towns, however, was a new phase in colonial life, and brought new motives and forces into play. The way to riches in the North did not to any extent lie in agriculture, and mere speculation in land could be carried on quite as advantageously, if not more so, by living in town than in the country. The opportunities for trade and commerce were greater and the amenities of life far pleasanter there than on the frontier or in the rural districts. To this general statement there was one notable exception in the case of the large land-owners in southern Rhode Island who have come to be known historically as the "Narragansett Planters." They were, however, not so much planters as large dairy farmers and stockmen. The particular part of the colony where they were located was admirably, almost uniquely, adapted for stock farming on a large scale, owing both to the fertility of its soil and the salt-water lagoons, which were more effective than fences as bounds. Here a society grew up which was an anomaly in New England and which was much more akin, in its creation of large landed estates with troops of Negro slaves, to the planter type of the South. Here also the Episcopal Church flourished under the inspiration of James McSparran, a missionary of the Society for the Propagation of the Gospel, and added its influence in setting the district apart from the rest of New England.[1] With

---

[1] Edward Channing, *The Narragansett Planters* (Johns Hopkins Univ., *Studies*, IV, nos. 3-4).

the exception of such peculiar cases as this "South County" of Rhode Island or the Valley of the Hudson, however, the country in the North became more and more given over to the small farmer of English or Dutch stock or, as in Pennsylvania, to the thousands of Germans and Scotch-Irish whose coming has already been described. The rich Northerners, therefore, for the most part, set themselves to enjoying life in the comfortable seaboard towns, and to discovering the means by which they might as rapidly as possible accumulate wealth in town ways.

The chief of these was commerce, both between the several continental colonies and with ports overseas. The intercolonial trade, with respect to the number of vessels employed, seems to have kept pace with the growth of that with the West Indies and the Old World. Indeed, between 1705 and 1732, the number of vessels entering Boston from other continental ports showed an increase of two hundred and thirty-one per cent, whereas that of vessels from overseas was only two hundred and twenty-one per cent. This intercolonial trade must have been of very considerable importance both from the standpoint of trade profits and from that of increasing the acquaintance of one colony with another. The fact that on an average one vessel was entering Boston from some other colony every day in the year, and that this same intercommunication, on a lesser scale, was going on between dozens of smaller places must have been a silent factor of great moment in bringing together the inhabitants of sections far remote from one another; although sometimes, as we noted in speaking of Colonel Byrd and the small traders, it was only to secure a round cursing if not the threat of a competent hanging.

The more important increase, however, was probably in the West India and foreign trade. Many of the voyages were circuitous, and a vessel reported as entering from another colony might well have been to Europe first. Moreover, even though the increase in the number of vessels in the two trades was practically the same, the tonnage of those in the overseas traffic was increasing more rapidly than that of the many small coasters. With the close of the war in 1713, trade with the French West Indies was no longer with an enemy, although it was for many years considered illegal under the terms of the old Treaty of 1686. For many reasons, however, it was profitable and in time became essential to New England. There it not only served to take off the surplus agricultural and other products suitable for the West India market and which could not be wholly absorbed by the English islands, but also served as the basis for a triangular trade of great importance. We spoke in an earlier chapter of the absolute necessity of an overseas trade of some sort if New England and the other colonies were to secure an adequate supply of specie or bills with which to pay for their English imports, and the need for the merchants to seek every possible outlet in order to accomplish this ceaseless and always difficult task. As a writer in the *Boston News-Letter* in 1734 said, after noting that the great trade increase had been in that with Europe, "this losing Trade, Sir, is a Monster, that can't be supported upon the natural Produce and Industry of our Colonies, but must be fed with Silver and gold." [1]

One of the new sources of trade which became highly profitable was opened by the steadily increasing demand for slaves in the sugar islands and the South. Although Rhode Island took the lead in this commerce it was shared in by the merchants of Boston and other ports, and fitted in remarkably well with other sources of profit. Vessels would leave for the coast of Africa, loaded with rum—the main currency used in the traffic—take on

[1] Issue of Feb. 28-March 7, 1734.

slaves, and sail for the islands or the South. Those which went to the West Indies were there loaded with the produce of the islands, particularly molasses. This was brought North to be distilled into the rum which in turn served as the basis of a new voyage to Africa, and the distilling of which, both for the slave trade and the ever increasing domestic consumption, became a considerable source of manufacturing profits. James Brown, whom we have noted as turning from farming to commerce, soon entered upon this new field. In 1736 he sent a sloop under his brother to the Guinea Coast but in that season the trade seems to have been overdone, for on reaching Africa the latter wrote home that he had come to a bad market. "There never was so much Rum on the Coast at one time before. . . . Slaves is very scarce: we have had nineteen sails of us at one time in the Rhoad, so that those ships that used to carry pryme slaves off is now forced to take any that comes." [1] Nevertheless, when the vessel had made its voyage and returned from the Indies, its cargo was sold at Brown's wharf for over £2600.

With the steady development of the continental hinterland, and the need for ever enlarging outlets for its products, the comparatively stationary markets of the English islands became less and less adequate, but with the rise of the French trade there arose also the opposition of the English islanders and of the absentee proprietors who lived in England. The latter wielded considerable parliamentary influence. After many years of effort, they finally secured in 1733 the passage of the so-called "Molasses Act" which placed a prohibitive duty on the import of foreign molasses and aimed to prevent all trade with the French West Indies. Had the act been complied with, it would have disastrously decreased the mar-

[1] Quoted by G. S. Kimball, *Providence in Colonial Times* (Providence, 1912), 248.

kets for Northern produce and also prevented the Northerners from securing the necessary funds for remittances to England. As a matter of fact it was neither enforced nor observed, and trade with the French and other foreigners continued and increased through the neutral islands and by smuggling. If, however, its financial and commercial effects were not important, the same cannot be said of its political and moral. The colonists felt that their legitimate trade and future expansion had both been sacrificed in favor of other portions of the empire, and the need of evading the law was so plain that it made smuggling respectable, with a corresponding lowering of moral tone.

The great increase in population and the extension of the frontier and the area under cultivation were irresistible forces steadily increasing the total produce of the colonies, and consequently the need for enlarging markets, swelling the volume of commerce, and the opportunities for profit. As always, there were fluctuations and occasionally crises. One of these began about 1730 and lasted for a number of years. In September, 1731, a correspondent wrote to the *Boston News-Letter* from New York that there "is little or no News in this Place, nothing but the melancholy scene of little Business and less Money, the Markets grow very thin." [1] Two years later a versifier inquires:

> Pray tell me the Cause of Trade being so dead,
> Why Shops are shut up, Goods and Owners are fled,
> And industrious Families cannot get Bread? [2]

In a few years the annual tax raised in that town for the poor had to be doubled, and a writer to the papers spoke of "the many Beggarly People daily suffered to wander about the Streets." [3]

[1] Issue of Sept. 2/9, 1731. [2] *N. Y. Gazette*, Aug. 13/20, 1733.
[3] *N. Y. Gazette*, Feb. 11/18, 1733.

In spite of these ups and downs, however, the volume of business grew decade by decade and capital accumulated. This naturally sought profitable employment and it is in this period that we have to note the beginning of manufactures on a commercial scale as contrasted with the home industries of an earlier day. In New England the chief manufacturing industry became that of rum which, as we have just noted, formed the basis of the slave trade, and, with the decline in the general taste for beer, became the popular drink among the lower classes. Moreover, it was one of the mainstays of the fishing industry which advanced rapidly in the third quarter of the century. Marblehead, which at the opening of the century had scarcely ventured into fishing, was sending out annually one hundred and twenty schooners by 1732 and owned one hundred and sixty a decade later.

In the Middle colonies, the capitalists seeking investment in manufactures turned to iron, and many companies, most of them successful, were formed to engage in the industry. Until about 1720 Massachusetts had been the chief manufacturer of iron but from that time forward the center of the industry shifted to Pennsylvania, and was one of the many indications that leadership was passing from the Puritan colony. The number of plants in Massachusetts, Connecticut, New Jersey and Maryland increased but the primacy in the industry passed to the capitalists of Philadelphia. So far behind did New England fall that by the middle of the century the people of New Hampshire were paying "a most Intolerable price" for the iron which they imported chiefly from Pennsylvania, Maryland and Virginia.[1]

It was characteristic of the growing influence of companies in business that these plants were owned and oper-

---

[1] James Birket, *Some Cursory Remarks Made by James Birket on his Voyage to North America, 1750-51* (New Haven, 1916), 12.

ated by groups of shareholders rather than by individuals or small partnerships. The highly successful bloomery forge known as "Pool," near the present Pottstown, for example, was owned in sixteenth shares by a group of men who were then advancing to prominence and wealth along this new road, particularly the Rutters and the Potts who became preëminent in the development of the industry. Germans, Welsh and Scotch were all prominent in it, and through intermarriage and intricate business relations a powerful group of ironmasters was built up much as the planters in sections of the South were consolidating their interests. Thomas Potts, Thomas Rutter, Anthony Morris, George McCall and others were among these new leaders who were laying the foundations for the industrial life of the colony.

Practically none of the capital which went into the upbuilding of manufactures seems to have come from agriculture. Morris, for example, was the son of a well-to-do brewer, and increased the family fortune in the same business before investing his surplus with Rutter and Potts in iron works. He became one of the owners of Colebrookdale Furnace, one of the fourteen founders of Durham Furnace, a shareholder in Pool and in a number of other enterprises under control of the same group. McCall was a merchant and storekeeper in Philadelphia, and an operator in town real estate before becoming interested in iron. Of the fourteen owners of the Durham plant one is described as a "gentleman," one as a brewer and seven as merchants. The old daybooks and ledgers of such plants as Pine, Pool, Colebrookdale, Warwick and others show that the interrelations of their business affairs was extremely intricate and that the owners of practically all of them were identical.[1] In most cases, moreover, the children of the orig-

[1] See especially J. M. Swank, *History of . . . Iron in All Ages,* chap. xiv.

inal pioneers in the industry appear to have continued and extended the operations of their fathers. On the other hand, that there was opportunity for able and enterprising individuals is shown by such a career as that of William Bird who was a laborer cutting wood for use at Pine Forge in 1733. Ten years later he had accumulated enough money, or gained enough credit, to rent an eighth interest in the furnace for £40 a year, and later became an important figure in the industry. When he died at fifty-five years of age he left a furnace, three forges and forty-four hundred acres of land. The tendency of the newly developed capitalists to work together in groups is also shown in the development of the industry in Maryland where such large land operators as Dulany and several of the Carrolls organized the Baltimore Company to build a furnace in 1733.

With the growth of the domestic iron trade came that of other manufactures based upon it. The first steel was probably made in Connecticut in 1727, and in the immediately succeeding years we find such articles as scythes and other edged tools being made, and finding a ready market—Boston exporting colonial-made axes to South Carolina as early as 1722.

New York distinctly lagged behind both her Southern and Northern neighbors in manufactures as well as commerce, but wealth was accumulating there also. Among the most important of the occupations in its effects was the illicit trade in Indian goods with the French of Canada by way of Albany and devious woodpaths, of which we have already spoken. Governor Burnet, Cadwallader Colden and other honest officials and colonials realized the extreme danger of this trade in detaching the Indians from the all-important alliance with the English and immensely strengthening the French influence among them. The danger to the colony, and in fact to the entire structure of the English empire in

America, weighed nothing with the merchant group who were becoming rich from this easy and lucrative business, and intrigue followed intrigue to outwit the governor and deceive the government in England. In fact, the merchants of New York early in the eighteenth century have the unenviable record of having been allied with the pirates, engaging in the most unsavory land scandals of any of the colonies, and risking the safety of all by the Canadian trade. Of land speculation in the North with reference to the accumulation of wealth, we have already spoken and shall again in the present chapter. We may note here, however, that such speculative enterprise was almost entirely commercial. The Northern speculator dealt in land as he would in any other commodity and with no idea, for the most part, of building up large agricultural estates for himself or his heirs. At this stage, for example, such extremely active business men as Samuel Waldo of Boston, who was engaging himself in the development of lands in Maine, were much more interested in buying and selling and in timber operations than in securing leasehold tenants.

One of the notable features of this period was the rise of new men. Such names as we have mentioned in one connection and another with the wealthy groups of the several colonies, Brown, Faneuil, Waldo, Morris, Rutter, McCall, Potts and others, mark a distinct break with the seventeenth century. These were not the descendants of the early leaders and founders but men of a new type, and their emergence from obscurity represents both new ideals for the upper classes and new relationships with the lower. Many of them were men of keen business ability, often only slightly troubled by ethical scruples, and bent upon carving out for themselves positions of prominence in the new world. Leadership in the North was becoming essentially a business affair. We have already noted the characteristic decline in the

ministry as a road to social or political influence, typi-
fied in such a case as that of John Reed, and this tendency is further emphasized by the turning aside in this
period into active civil life of such men as Stoughton,
Gridley and Stephen Sewall in Massachusetts and Gurdon Saltonstall, Jr., and Jonathan Trumbull in Connecticut, all of whom had originally intended to become ministers.

As in the South, so in the North, the growing wealth
of the few was utilized in a more luxurious mode of
living and in the erection of commodious mansions
which mark a great advance upon the preceding period,
the introduction of the Georgian style everywhere mod-
ifying the earlier type of house. Dignified dwellings,
of wood in New England, and of brick in New York,
New Jersey and Pennsylvania, replaced the simple homes
of the close of the preceding century. As contrasted
with the South, however, these were for the most part
town houses and must be looked for in Portsmouth,
Boston, Newport, New York, Philadelphia or other
towns and their near neighborhoods. Moreover, especially in New England, they were almost without
exception the homes of merchants, such as those of
Faneuil or Hancock in Boston or that of Captain Godfrey Malbone in Newport, which latter in spite of its
bad style that entertaining and observant traveler from
Maryland, Alexander Hamilton, found to be "the largest and most magnificent dwellinghouse" he had seen in
all America.[1] This divorce from the soil and from
agricultural interests of the main body of the wealthy
and aristocratic class in the North, and their gathering
into towns, were to have marked political and social
effects, but before touching upon those we must turn to
the country districts and to a very different economic

[1] Dr. Alexander Hamilton, *Itinerarium* (A. B. Hart, ed., St. Louis,
1907), 125.

class to see what their condition was in the new period.

The situation varied in the several Northern colonies, which from the standpoint of the agrarian question may be divided into three groups—New England, New York, and the two colonies of Pennsylvania and New Jersey. On account of lack of space it is impossible to consider in detail the development in each of the three sections, and we shall therefore confine the discussion mainly to New England. The soil there available for farming was neither very abundant nor very fertile, and the pressure upon it had become great by the end of the French war in 1713. As we have already noted, there had been only a slight extension of the frontier in the forty years from 1673, owing to the constant danger from the savages, whereas the population had increased from approximately fifty thousand to one hundred and twenty-five thousand. The unscientific methods of farming and the need for supporting a population which was becoming too great for the lands as thus tilled were rapidly wearing them out.

It was to this problem, of the wearing out of the soil, that the Reverend Jared Eliot of Connecticut, one of the most notable men in the social history of the North in this period, was devoting himself in the early part of the eighteenth century. His *Essays on Field Husbandry* were not published until 1747, after which they went through several editions, being reprinted entire in the *New-York Gazette* in 1754, but they were written from a journal covering the experiments of the preceding thirty years. A friend and correspondent of Benjamin Franklin and other leaders of colonial thought, and a member of the Royal Society, he devoted himself from the Peace of Utrecht onward to the improvement of colonial agriculture. A close follower of farming development in England, he wrote that in the old country poor land was recovered by sowing it with turnips and wintering sheep upon it, but that "our poor land is so poor that it will not bear turnips larger than buttons." [1] He also spoke of "our old land which we have worn out" and which cannot be recovered at all without dung "which cannot be had for love or money." He noted that ashes are an excellent fertilizer "but the misery is, we can get but little." From time to time he experiments and writes of improved types of implements, such as drills. Finding that planting in rows was advantageous but slow, he tries the wheat drill, turnip drill and others which had recently been invented by Jethro Tull in England.

His account of the development and adaptation of these new instruments is interesting as marking the beginning of an industry in which America was to take the lead. He finds Tull's wheat drill "a wonderful instrument," but as the first of its kind unnecessarily intricate, so with Yankee ingenuity he goes to work to improve upon it. I "applied myself," he writes, "to the Reverend Mr. Clap, President of Yale College, and desired him for the regard which he had to the public and to me, that he would apply his mathematical learning and mechanical genius, in that affair; which he did to so good purpose, that this new modelled drill can be made with a fourth part of what Mr. Tull's will cost." "The next thing I wanted," he continues, "in order to compass my design, was a dung drill; this was an invention entirely new, for which there was no precedent or model. For this I applied to Benoni Hylliard, a very ingenious man of this town, a wheelwright by trade. . . . At first we could think of no way but to make it a distinct instrument: but at length his ingenuity led him to set this and the wheat drill upon one frame, so that it became one instrument." These

[1] *Essays* reprinted in Mass. Soc. for Promoting Agric., *Papers, 1811,* 19

drills he found could do more in one day than a hundred men by hand. Nevertheless, in spite of all efforts to reclaim land and to utilize the new improvements, the wearing out of the land and the "thinking that we live too thick," he finds, are causing constant emigrations from the old settlements and removal of men to new places "that they may raise wheat." So early in New England history appear abandoned farms.

With the coming of peace and the removal of the Indian terror, there was indeed a vast swarming out of the long confined population into the wilderness to seek fresh soil and to carve homes for themselves and their children. A notable feature of this extension, as in the South, was that it no longer confined itself to the coast, tidewater streams or the near neighborhood of the old settlements. The general improvement of roads which marked this period everywhere in the colonies greatly helped in the settlement of the back country, and to a considerable extent nullified the necessity of water transport. The sudden development of the town of Rutland, almost in the exact center of Massachusetts and remote from access except by road, illustrates the new tendencies at work and the possibilities of a wider geographical distribution of population. A letter from that place in 1720 said that "this Town, which not two years since, seemed buryed in forgetfulness, and neglected, was without either Housing, or more than one Family inhabiting here; has now Fifty eight Houses." Ten more families were expected immediately, and the future of the town felt to be assured because "the distance from Hadley (through this Town) to Boston is said to be above 20 miles less than any other road yet known." [1] The centers of population are always strung on the highways of commerce and communication, and the fact that the character of these was

[1] *Boston News-Letter*, July 18/25, 1720.

beginning to alter presaged a correspondingly great alteration in the lines of colonial settlement.

Considering both the old land system of New England —according to which the original settlers of a town had been allotted their specific portions and in addition a share in the undeveloped lands—and the newer forms of land speculation, it is evident that the increasing pressure upon the soil and expansion into the wilderness could be counted upon to bring out a conflict of interests between those who were trying to exploit the land and those who were coming more and more to feel themselves cramped within their old limits. Such conflicts, in fact, did develop in a great many sections and were so numerous and serious as to engender all the bitter feelings of class conflict.

As an example of one type of controversy, that between the town inhabitants at large and those residents who had originally been allotted or in some way acquired an interest in the undivided portions of the township, we may take the case of Haverhill. In 1720 at a town meeting, the inhabitants unanimously voted to propose to the proprietors that a large portion of the undivided lands should be divided among all the inhabitants who had paid taxes from 1694 to 1714. Legally the title to all the undivided lands, including the "cow common" in the middle of the village, was indubitably vested in the proprietors, as in practically all New England towns. On the other hand, the increasing pressure on the land was beginning to make the noncommoners look with covetous eyes upon the large holdings of those who had been fortunate enough to secure grants of the commons in the early days of each town, or who had inherited or otherwise acquired them later.

To the request of the inhabitants of Haverhill, the proprietors returned answer that they saw no reason why they should part with their property. The noncommoners then voted, without the shadow of legal right, to "sell some common land to pay the Towns debts or charges," and further that a considerable portion of the undivided land should be laid out and given to those who should settle upon it speedily.[1] A little later they decided that every person should be entitled to land at the rate of an acre for every £1 which he had paid in taxes between 1692 and 1712. The proprietors attempted to forestall this plain confiscation by laying out the land themselves but the noncommoners then resorted to violence and theft, and stole and mutilated the books of record. The conflict dragged along until in 1723 the proprietors tried to divide among themselves the village cow common. The violent hubbub at once produced led the proprietors to invite some of the inhabitants to meet them with the intention of securing their assistance against the rest of the town by individual concessions. In other words, there was revolution in this quiet village, and the proprietors, in order to protect their property, felt it necessary to part with some of it as bribes to the leaders in order to insure their own retention of the rest. The records of the meeting enable us to follow the proceedings intimately and to watch one after another of the inhabitants dickering to secure what he had no right to but was extorting by force.

The parochial scale of the whole affair should not be allowed to mislead us as to its extreme significance. When the leaders of the noncommoners were asked for terms, William Johnson avowed that he "would not be easy unless they would fling up the cow common" altogether. "Mathew Harriman Junr declared that hee would be uneasy unless all the fences erected on the cow common were demolished & itt lay according to the vote of the ancient fathers & the proprietors rec-

[1] G. W. Chase, *History of Haverhill* (Haverhill, 1861), 252.

ords Burnt." Others agreed to make no further trouble if each secured a coveted bit of land. One asked two acres by his house, part of which he had already fenced in; another asked for six acres; whereas, among others, one of the deacons would be content with two. Finally the proprietors granted the less grasping ones what they demanded with the promise from them that "They appeare in all Town meetings, unless hindered by extraordinary Casualty & due oppose by Voate & argument, all such persons & voates as any way disturbe or hinder the proprietors in their peaceable Injoyments of Their lands divided and undivided."[1] This was agreed to but the lack of success in bribing the leaders was shown a year later when the proprietors started to lay off the common. Trouble immediately began again and the opposing factions set up rival town meetings and elected two sets of town officers. Finally, the legislature had to intervene on behalf of the proprietors, whom they confirmed in possession of their property and thereafter the townsmen had to buy it from them.

As the older towns filled up and the inhabitants became more and more pressed for room, such contests as this became frequent, and in nearly every town gave rise to physical conflict, legal squabbles or merely extreme ill feeling between the poorer inhabitants or newcomers and the older or richer families whose extensive ownership of the coveted common lands became steadily more valuable. Only those who know intimately the possibilities of passionate feeling in narrow rural communities can appreciate the intensity of the bitterness which such long-continued contests can arouse. The feeling would naturally be deepest in those cases in which the proprietors had originally been lenient in allowing the noncommoners to pasture cattle or cut wood on the waste land. Extended over many years,

[1] Chase, *History of Haverhill*, 270.

such permission would have seemed in the eyes of the poorer people to have established a sort of prescriptive right, and when their woods and grazing fields began to be forbidden to them, fenced off or sold, such conflicts as that in Haverhill were bound to ensue.

Sometimes in the newer towns which had been sold by the legislatures to groups of speculators and resold by them, such rights had been made part of a contract which was later repudiated. For example, Colonel Jacob Wendell of Boston bought at auction the rights to a new township in western Massachusetts and received a deed for twenty-four thousand and forty acres, less a thousand acres which had already been granted to John Stoddard. Philip Livingston of New York joined in the speculation and settlers were induced to start a settlement with the agreement that they should have free right to cut wood and dig stone, for fires, fences and building, in any part of the town. Later the heirs of Wendell and Stoddard repudiated the contract owing to the increased value of the undivided land, and started a contest that ended only with the abandonment of the settlement and the emigration of the embittered settlers.

Frequently the speculators offered lands to which they had no titles and sold them to unsuspecting pioneers who found themselves ruined by the cost of their purchase and removal, and without redress. Occasionally, there were official warnings of such practices, but it was not an age of paternalism, and the legislatures were all too often on the side of the capitalists. For example, in 1727, a group of such men, basing an extremely tenuous claim upon an old illegal Indian purchase of forty years previously, petitioned the legislature of Massachusetts for a confirmation. This was refused, and the deed was considered by the legislature, as indeed it was, of no validity. In spite of this, the company went ahead with their meetings and voted to warn off all squatters and to agree with such as had settled to become their tenants on lease. The next year they sent out a surveyor to lay off six miles square and to settle fifty families. Deeds were given to about forty-eight already settled there. The persistent efforts of the company, consisting of Joshua Lamb, Timothy Ruggles, Ebenezer Pierrepoint and others, to secure a confirmation of their doings from the legislature failed, but finally they secured in 1732 a large grant of another tract altogether, apparently simply because of their political influence and pertinacity.

This left the settlers on their old claim without any title. Fifty-six of these poor people petitioned the legislature, saying that they had been induced to settle by Lamb & Co. who had promised a valid title, that they had nothing of their own to subsist upon, and asked to be granted the lands which they had cleared, which petition cost them over £16. The general court then appointed an investigating committee which reported that there were about eighty families settled, of whom forty-eight had been placed by the company and thirty-one had squatted, but that they all had "expended the chief of their Small Fortunes," that they were law abiding, had had a minister for three years, and that to remove them would reduce them to extreme poverty.[1] The legislature finally voted that they be granted one hundred acres each but not rights of commons, and that they be required to pay for this very limited privilege the sum of £500 and in addition over £67 more for the expense of the committee. Each of the committee, it may be noted, were voted one hundred acres by the harassed settlers, who were soon ordered to raise £771 more by the court. By extraordinary efforts they raised all but £500, but that they

[1] J. H. Temple, *History of the Town of Palmer* (Palmer, 1889), 69.

seem never to have paid. In spite of repeated petitions they were not allowed to become a town until 1776. It appears not to have occurred to anyone that the fraudulent capitalists might be brought to justice. We can well imagine the feelings of this community, first deceived by the speculators, then forced by the legislature to pay over £1300, denied the rights of commons and the privilege of town government, with the titles to their lands—which were their sole property—in dispute for years, whereas they saw the men who had brought them into all this deep trouble go free and receive a grant from the legislature of six square miles.

It must be noted, in attempting to ascertain the social feelings of a considerable part of the population, that the above was not an isolated case but that such contrasts were only too frequently evident. For example, Colonel Samuel Partridge was a noted man in Hampshire County. He was a member of the colonial council, and undoubtedly his close affiliations in consequence with the ruling powers at Boston were useful both to himself and his neighbors in the west. As we follow his successful career we find him in one way and another turning up in possession of very choice bits of land acquired by other means than purchase. To cite a few instances, in 1720 the town of Northfield granted him one hundred and fifty acres; about the same time Brookfield gave him one hundred and sixty; and in 1725 the provincial legislature granted him five hundred. In fact, in one way and another, the great speculation in land was bringing wealth and commanding influence to such men as the above and to Colonel Oliver Partridge of Hatfield, Colonel Israel Williams of the same village, Colonel John Stoddard of Northampton and Colonel John Worthington of Springfield. Popularly known as the "River Gods" or "Lords of the

Valley," all of them became immense landholders, Williams's holdings extending through twelve towns.[1]

Let us now contrast this pleasing picture of rapidly accumulating wealth with the land position of some of the less fortunate neighbors of these shrewd colonial magnates, whose figures hitherto have loomed so much larger than those of the poor men at their gates. In 1733 five of these "simple men," whom we may take as examples, and who had settled on a largely barren tract of about fourteen hundred acres in that section of the colony, petitioned the legislature. They stated that they were dwelling there where "we have lived some of us three years, where we have spent the most of that little substance we have. . . . It was not the extraordinary quality of the lands that induced us to go upon it, for a considerable part of it is Ledges of Rocks, so as to render it unprofitable, but what induced us to settle upon it was our necessity, our principal dependence for support of ourselves in husbandry, and we had not a foot of land to imploy our selves and families upon, were exposed to idleness and pinching want, and being then unsensible how highly the Court resented such a way of settling, and apprehending that the principle thing they insisted on was that there should be no trading or stock jobbing [biting but unintentional irony, this] but an actual settlement and improvement in husbandry by the Grantees themselves with which we were ready to comply,—wherefore being thus unhappily entangled on said land" they humbly prayed for a grant, based on charity and pity. Charity and pity, however, were not the proper appeals for legislative grants, the prayer was refused, and only after four years did the legislature, which was quite ready to grant fraudulent speculators six miles

[1] D. W. and R. F. Wells, *History of Hatfield* (Springfield, Mass.), chap. xiii.

square *gratis,* agree to allow these few poor men to remain on the rocky acres they had cleared—that is, after they should have paid an adequate purchase price.

The new method of settling towns by granting them to speculators brought another grievance of which we have already spoken and of which we will now give a typical instance. In the earlier days most of the grantees of a town became its actual settlers and bore its hardships and burdens in common, all contributing to its upbuilding. Under the new system, however, the men who had the needful influence with the legislatures to receive grants or the necessary amount of capital to be able to buy at auction the enormous tracts which the legislatures sold only in single blocks were not pioneers but the capitalists of the settled towns. To them, as we have said, land was a mere commodity and their shares in the new towns mere counters in the game of money making, as stock certificates are today for the active trader. To the actual pioneer and settler, however, his land was his all. His acres and the sweat and the back-breaking toil which went to their clearing and cultivation were all that lay between his family and starvation. As he and his equally hard-working neighbors felled the forest, laid out roads, built together the rude meetinghouse and pinched their bellies to pay the minister's salary, the growth of their little town was of more significance to them than the whole of the empire; and the questions of taxation, of land tenure and of local government were the most important in the world.[1]

But in case after case that might be cited, they found that although they were doing all the work of establishing the new settlement, a large number, often a majority and occasionally the entire body, of grantees

---

[1] J. T. Adams, *Revolutionary New England, 1691-1776* (Boston, 1923), chap. vii.

remained behind in the comfortable old towns and from
them controlled absolutely all matters of taxation and
government, the settlers on the spot not being grantees
but mere purchasers without the rights of townsmen.
In Westminster, for example, in 1739 the proprietors
met in the town itself for the first and last time for
many years. With the exception of a very few, who
became actual settlers, they were all nonresidents living
in towns from forty to fifty miles away and refused to
travel through the wilderness that distance to attend
meetings. They voted themselves exemption from
taxes and declined to assist in building a meetinghouse
and making certain needed improvements, while they
at the same time voted to themselves some of the taxes
for dinners and other expenses. In 1743 the few resident proprietors journeyed to Cambridge, where the
meetings were held, but they were ignored and returned
to the town, unsuccessful in all their efforts and deeply
aggrieved. The next year twenty-four families petitioned the legislature, complaining that the meetings
were held fifty miles away from the town, that the clerk
and treasurer resided at that distance, and that when the
resident proprietors made the arduous journey to cast
their vote in the town's affairs, they were "outvoted by
a Majority of the Proprietors present who living so far
distant from the Spot cannot be supposed to know so
well as the Settlers what is necessary to be done." They
added that when the nonresident proprietors are prevailed upon to vote any money at all for highways they
spend most of it in sending up committees to look them
over, and that "they are so free and generous when they
assemble together at their meetings that a very great
part of what they vote to be raised for the Settlement
is generally expended to pay Tavern expenses." [1] The
proprietors continued to hold their meetings in the

[1] W. S. Heywood, *History of Westminster* (Lowell, 1893), 76.

vicinity of Boston and not a single settler was made a member of their standing committee. In 1749 the settlers again appealed to the deaf legislature for relief. After two years more a legislative committee finally appeared at the town, but it was not until 1759, when the maddening situation had already lasted for over twenty years, that their prayer to be incorporated as a town was only so far granted that they were set off as a district without representation in the legislature. This was just what they had begged should not be done.

It is not difficult to realize how, as these very real grievances against the capitalists and the colonial government were borne in upon the poor, hard-working pioneers of Westminster and of many other such communities, their attitude would become one of extreme resentment against those capitalists who were reaping unearned increment upon their landholdings, while at the same time refusing to bear their share of the burdens and treating the settlers very much like a colony of slaves who were to toil for their masters rather than for themselves. When some years later the word "slave" assumed an extreme prominence in the propagandist literature of the Revolutionary period it carried a meaning, though not as related to the British government, to innumerable settlers who had spent the best years of their lives in just such toil, and in embittering contests with the capitalists and with just such vain appeals for justice to the local government, as we have described. We have not as yet made a sufficiently detailed survey of the geographical distribution of radicalism, but it is significant that for a generation at least before the Revolution such districts as the northern frontier, western Massachusetts or eastern Connecticut where radicalism was much in evidence, were exactly those districts where disputed land titles, difficulties with speculators, absenteeism and other agrarian troubles were most in evidence.

In New Jersey, in the latter part of the period covered by this chapter and for some years thereafter, serious riots occurred owing to disputes between the proprietors of the colony and those landowners who had not acquired titles as legally required. Ejectment suits were brought wholesale, and frequently against those who honestly believed they had valid title by purchase or long possession. Throughout all the colonies, land titles were uncertain and even in Massachusetts, at the time of the Andros administration, there were few titles which could stand a rigid technical investigation. The efforts of the New Jersey proprietors, which became notable after 1743, irritated the people and kept the province in a turmoil for a decade. "Persons who had long holden under the proprietors were forcibly ejected; others compelled to take leases from landlords whom they were not disposed to acknowledge; while those who had courage to stand out, were threatened with, and in many instances, received personal violence." [1]

It is in this period that we note clearly the rising tide of this radicalism, the beginning of a distinct class conflict, the birth of the modern politician as a colonial type, and some of the evolving characteristics of our political machinery. The more than doubling of a population which had been largely confined within its old borders, had naturally greatly increased the keenness of competition between individuals and between social groups. Although this added to the opportunities for those who could avail themselves of them, it at the same time forced into lower economic rank, even if not into abject poverty, large numbers of those who proved less well able to take care of themselves under the harder test.

[1] Quoted from R. H. Morris Papers, by E. J. Fisher, *New Jersey as a Royal Province* (Columbia Univ., *Studies*, XLI), 193.

In addition to the conditions and results already briefly outlined, we have also to consider that the issues of paper money, which had rapidly increased in amount since the first which had been put out in connection with the finances of the wars from 1691 to 1713, had caused a vast inflation of the currency with its attendant result in raising prices. Although depreciation of the currency and an advance in commodity prices worked temporarily to the benefit of the debtor class and of those who were astute enough to take advantage of the speculative profits to be made, on the other hand, they worked great hardship to a large part of the population. By 1720 practically all coin had been driven out of circulation in Massachusetts and the prices in paper had doubled in twenty years. "Although this raising on one another in Trade, helps some, yet it hurts more," wrote a pamphleteer from the country, and added that "Salary Men, Ministers, School-Masters, Judges of the Circuit, President & Tutors at College, Widows and Orphans, &c are pincht and hurt more than any," as their salaries or incomes had not been increased in proportion to the rise in the cost of living.[1] But although the farmers had raised their prices to a considerable extent, they also, the writer complains, had by no means been able to keep pace with the prices extorted by the merchants. "We formerly," he continues, "sold Butter, Six Pence a Pound. That Six Pence would buy Two Pounds of Sugar and if we now have Nine Pence a Pound for Butter, that Nine Pence will buy but a Pound of Sugar or thereabouts. So that when we receive so great a Price as we do, yet we find it hard enough to rub along." [2]

From time to time attacks were made in print upon

[1] *The Present Melancholy Circumstances of the Province* (Boston, 1719), 13.
[2] *Idem.*

the capitalistic groups, and the rising tide of discontent combined with ignorance of commercial and financial matters began to presage trouble. The writer just quoted above strongly advocated taxing the waste lands held by the proprietors in the various towns so heavily as to force their sale to those who would improve them. Some years later a writer in the *Boston News-Letter* advocated the destruction of the merchants' overseas commerce, and by 1739 the growing economic distress brought about a crisis which threatened armed revolt. By that time, exchange with London stood at 525 as expressed in Massachusetts paper, and the ignorant and debtor classes were clamoring for larger additions to the circulating medium in the hopes of curing those ills of which the inflation already existing was one of the prime causes. An exceedingly crude scheme was put forward to organize a "Land Bank" which was to issue another £150,000 of paper money of wholly indeterminate value, and in 1740 over one half of the assembly elected that year were abetters of the plan.[1]

The merchants and capitalists were thoroughly alarmed and did their best, unsuccessfully, to counter the proposition with a far sounder one of their own. Nevertheless, in spite of the opposition of the governor and of the members of the upper house, the assembly insisted upon its course, and as there was no law preventing the issue of circulating notes by individuals or associations, the steps taken by the "sound-money" advocates to prevent the circulation of the Land Bank notes were to a considerable extent extralegal and exceedingly irritating to the paper-money advocates, who called themselves the "popular party." To prevent what seemed to portend the utter ruin of the moneyed interests of the colony, and in the long run of all the

---

[1] A. McF. Davis, "Provincial Banks: Land and Silver," Colonial Society of Mass., *Publs.*, III, 2-40.

people, the conservatives appealed to the privy council in England, and Parliament intervened by making the "Bubble Act," passed twenty years before at the time of the South Sea scandals, apply retroactively to the colonies, to the extreme confusion of the Land Bankers. The hardship of having their actions, which however ill-advised had been strictly legal, now made criminal was unquestioned, and the feeling between the two parties, which extended all over the colony, was intense. Affidavits affirmed that from five thousand to twenty thousand desperate advocates of the Land Bank scheme were preparing to march upon Boston from the country districts. Although the figures may be exaggerated there seems no reason to doubt a substantial substratum of truth in the belief that an armed rising was contemplated which was frustrated by prompt action on the part of the governor.

The larger political aspects of the episode do not concern us in the present narrative, for which the interest lies rather in its social results and implications. It had become evident to the conservatives in the colony that at last the radicalism which had been slowly developing almost unnoticed beneath the surface of society, evidenced only by complaints against specific groups of grasping speculators or vaguely against general economic conditions, had now become embodied in a political party which, both within the legislature and by armed force without, had violently threatened the accustomed control of colonial life. Local political action had become more and more the expression of radical sentiment and in assuming some of its modern aspects had proved the seedbed for the growth of the politician. Governor Shirley's description of a Boston town meeting has a singularly modern ring when he says that one of them "may be called together at any time upon the Petition of ten of the meanest Inhabitants, who by their constant attendance there generally are the majority and outvote the Gentlemen, Merchants, Substantial Traders and all the better part of the Inhabitants; to whom it is Irksome to attend at such meetings, except upon very extraordinary occasions." [1]

The change of interests which we have already noted in New England life was thus beginning to bring not only the lawyer, the great merchant, the speculator and others of the more fortunate or favored economic classes, but the professional politician who based his leadership upon voicing the ills of a common people growing more self-conscious. Popular grievances, the forum of the public meeting and the apathy or self-confidence of the upper classes combined to open his way. The upper economic group, in spite of their numerical inferiority, had hitherto remained in comfortable control partly because of the extremely limited franchise and partly because of the lack of grievances, leaders and cohesion among the common people. Grievances were now accumulating and leaders, though still obscure, were developing. The strength recently displayed by the "popular party" had seriously alarmed the merchant-capitalist group and they now realized, what had apparently escaped them before, that there was danger in the constantly increasing numbers of the assembly, owing to the fact that as each new town was incorporated it became entitled to send two representatives. Already there were eligible three hundred and twenty assemblymen as against only the permanently fixed number of twenty-eight members of the council. Steps were immediately taken, therefore, by the conservatives to prevent further increase in popular representation, and it was arranged by orders from the lords of trade that thereafter the privilege of sending repre-

[1] William Shirley, *Correspondence* (C. H. Lincoln, ed., N. Y., 1912), I, 418.

sentatives from newly incorporated towns should depend upon the governor's consent.

Evidence of the growing sectionalism and fear of losing control on the part of the entrenched groups appears just as clearly in Pennsylvania, where the rapid increase in population of the newer counties was threatening the control of the old "East," and the increasing number of citizens in Philadelphia was threatening that of the old municipal ruling class. Efforts therefore were made to prevent the intrusion of these new elements both by suffrage qualifications and the representation of counties. When Lancaster was formed in 1729 it was allowed only four votes in the assembly instead of the eight which were enjoyed by the older ones. For the next twenty years, in spite of great increase in population in the outlying districts, no new counties were erected, and when in 1749 and 1750 two were created, they were allowed but two members each, and two years later two others were given but one vote each.[1]

From the brief and inadequate surveys in these last two chapters, in the course of which we have merely, as it were, let down our line here and there to take soundings, it is evident that the social and economic life of the period, in both the South and the North, was marked by a more distinct difference between rich and poor, by the increase and concentration of wealth, and by the resultant growth of economic and social grievances upon the part of considerable sections of the population. There had never been entire equality or harmony but in the comparative simplicity of the earlier periods and under the rigid discipline of unsubdued wilderness, wild beast, savage foe and the ever present specter of stark hunger, the differences in both rank and opportunity had been reduced to a minimum. With the change from

[1] C. H. Lincoln, *The Revolutionary Movement in Pennsylvania* (Phila., 1901), 45-46.

forest to field, the rapid growth of wealth and the development of a more complex society, there had also come into play forces tending to cleave that society into sections and classes. The poor whites of the South, the foreigners of the Middle colonies and the depressed agriculturists and befooled frontier settlers of the North were among the groups which developed genuine and special grievances.

Back of all the colonies there was developing a frontier section in which the ideals, ways of living, hopes and animosities bore a common stamp from the woods of Maine to the mountain valleys of western Carolina. Within the older tidewater sections themselves there was no longer comparative unity of interest in the several localities but growing diversity and conflict, with an increasingly sharp alignment between classes and an increasing self-consciousness on the part of both the upper and lower. We are too apt to picture the life of the eighteenth century from the dignified homes of the rich, the literature found in their libraries, and the dull and stately if withal somewhat boisterous and coarse lives carried on within their walls and scented gardens. Beneath all this there was fermenting a new life among classes largely illiterate, without leadership and with but little voice in legislative halls. As individuals they had been bent upon making their own way in a new world where they found few of the restraints of the old, but when they began to feel that, one by one, hindrances and restraints were again appearing to tangle their way they began to turn restive, to become conscious of their aims and their common grievances, and to follow those who here and there essayed the rôle of leaders or of demagogues. The traces of this aspect of colonial life are far harder to disinter than are those of imperial conflict or of high social life. They are, as it were, written in invisible ink, but they cannot be ignored if we wish to understand rather than merely to recount the greater social movements of the later period of which they were the forerunners. That they were far from being ignored by the upper classes in their own day is shown by the various political moves that were made to thwart the awakened consciousness and the frequently crude efforts at self-assertion of the farmers and artisans.

In addition to such cleavages as were common to all the colonies, we have also to note the rise during this period of the two contrasted types of civilization in the North and the South, the one mainly agricultural and based upon slavery, the other becoming commercial and based upon free labor. In the past two chapters we have been for the most part concerned with forces which tended to divide the colonists into classes and sections, to set off the rich against the poor, the exploiters against the exploited, the East against the West. It is now time to examine those other forces which developed from the rise of an indigenous colonial culture and which tended to unite the various colonists by a common intellectual outlook, even as the frontier sections had been united in a common outlook upon the practical life of suffering, work and effort.

CHAPTER X

THE GROWTH OF A COLONIAL CULTURE

1713-1745

WE have spoken of the three periods of distinct cultural difference in the colonies. First that characterized by a purely transplanted growth, subject to slow modification and disintegration under the influences of the wilderness. Next the short period of extreme declension and of hesitation succeeding upon the withering of this imported culture, and thirdly the period of development of a native-born one. It is with the beginnings of this last that we have now to deal.

In spite of the many tendencies which were making for cleavages of one sort and another in the provincial society of the several colonies, we have nevertheless already noted several which were of considerable unifying power. So long as the colonies, and the innumerable villages and settlements in them, were separated from one another by long stretches of wilderness, and communication of any sort was scanty, there could be no development of a common consciousness or of a common public opinion. These are essentially growths of common interests and of interchange of ideas. The steadily increasing intercolonial trade was a factor of prime importance in this regard, as, in their narrower range, were the itinerant peddler, shoemaker, candle dipper and other petty tradesmen or artificers who made their way from neighborhood to neighborhood, weaving from the news and gossip of one and another a web of common thoughts and knowledge. The traveling preacher, and particularly the Quakers who were constantly on the move from one community to another, often with unpleasant encouragement from the citizens, were additional influences in bringing various groups into contact, as were also the intercolonial migrations which we have noted.

Throughout this period, the improvement in the roads and the enlarged size of vessels did much to facilitate traveling and thereby to promote intercourse. It is true that even the main highways were none too good and that once off these the traveler fared badly even on horseback, but well before the end of this period there was a much traveled system of roads connecting the different colonies with one another and the principal places in each. By 1732 there was enough public demand to warrant publishing the first American guidebook, which gave with much other useful information, the location and dates of the chief fairs in the Northern colonies and the roads and distances between the more important points.[1] It gave the road from Boston through Providence, New London, New York and Philadelphia to Jamestown, Virginia, in all seven hundred and eleven miles, and a number of branches from this main artery. This road continued as far south as Charleston, and traveling overland was now becoming frequent both for business and pleasure.

In 1744, for example, we have, among others, the extremely entertaining account of his trip overland from Annapolis to New Hampshire and back, entirely for amusement, by Doctor Hamilton, and the following year two accounts of a business journey by a Philadelphia merchant following the road from Philadelphia to Charleston and thence by boat to Frederica. At the

---

[1] *The Vade Mecum for America or a Companion for Traders and Travellers* (Boston, 1732).

beginning of the period such a commercial trip as the latter would undoubtedly have been made by sea, with no valuable intercolonial contacts except at the two ends of the journey. Wagons and carriages were coming into common use in the neighborhoods of all the larger coast towns and even to some extent in the back country. By the middle of the century the estate inventories in such a remote frontier as Augusta County, Virginia, show numerous wagons which had probably been in use many years before they were thus listed among the effects of their deceased owners. They were not, however, used for long journeys, and the travels of such men as have come down to us in written accounts were all made on horseback. There were as yet no stage coach lines, except here and there a very short and wholly local route, and even along the main highway of the Atlantic seaboard the wayfarer rode his own horse and traveled independently of any established transportation. The carrying of the post, however, gradually improved, although it was not until 1732 that Virginia agreed to enter the general postal system of the colonies.

One of the notable social movements of the period, and one which had a marked effect upon the dissemination of news and upon the formation of a public opinion, was the establishment of innumerable and now mostly forgotten organizations for social, intellectual and other purposes. We have noted how immigration from Europe to the colonies necessarily broke most of the ties uniting individuals in the social structure, which itself thus disintegrated, and how time was required for a new integration. That the time had now come for a coalescing of the individual atoms of society into a new social order is shown by the numerous voluntary organizations which sprang up in all the colonies. The simplest of these was the club, which was also just entering upon its great vogue in England. These colonial clubs, which we find mentioned in surprisingly large numbers from the second decade of the century, were groups of individuals, mostly although not always men only, which met at stated intervals, frequently once or twice a week, at a tavern or private residence for social intercourse, the interchange of ideas, and the generous absorption of liquor. Made up of men of a common trade or profession, of a single racial group, of a special social set, or merely of congenial spirits, they must have been of vast influence in helping to overcome the extreme individualism of society and to form public opinion.

Travelers were welcomed at their gatherings if properly introduced, and it is from such guests that we get many glimpses of clubs that would otherwise be forgotten. Thus in 1710 John Fontaine, as a visitor in New York, amused himself with frequent evenings at the Irish Club and the French Club; Hamilton on his journey north in 1744 mentions a "drunken club" at a tavern near Joppa, Maryland, the "Governor's Club" and Musick Club at Philadelphia, the Hungarian Club in New York, the Philosophical Club at Newport, and the Physical Club and the "club at Withered's" in Boston; Black, in the same year, speaks of the Beefsteak Club of Philadelphia; and we have also mention of a fishing club of the same town formed in 1732 as the Schuylkill Fishing Company, the Hum Drum Club in New York in 1734, the Tuesday Club of Annapolis, founded in 1745, the South River Club near that town and already called "antient" in 1747, the Maryland Jockey Club established 1745, the French Club of Charleston, 1737, and many others. In fact they sprang up everywhere and evidently answered to a genuine social need.

The name, whether serious or playful, was often

belied, and the main object was usually conviviality and talk. Thus Black tells us that the "Beef Stake Club" was so called because the members gathered to eat steaks but that when he attended and the dinner came on there were over twenty other dishes. At the Philosophical Club in Newport, Hamilton says that they drank punch and smoked tobacco and that at their meeting he "was surprised to find that no matters of philosophy were brought upon the carpet. They talked of privateering and the building of vessels." [1] This failure to cling to high matters was evidently a common one. In 1747 a club member of Chestertown in Maryland wrote to the *Gazette* saying that "when Clubs (consisting of Men rightly sorted) meet together, to hear and impart News, communicate Thoughts and improve one another by Conversation, they pass away their spare Hours agreeably, and to good Purpose; but the Intention is wholly frustrated by an *Omnium Gatherum*, who are neither capable of improving or being improved." He asks for a copy of the rules of any good club as he hears that there is one in practically every county on the western shore.[2]

The fact that the philosophers of Newport preferred to discuss privateering rather than philosophy and that the affairs of the day were the topics at most of such gatherings elsewhere was not a serious drawback. The important thing was that everywhere, from Salem to Savannah, there were coming into existence focal points for the creating and sharpening of a common consciousness and a new social organ for the formation of common views.

In this period we have another instance of the same cohesive forces at work in the establishment of numerous lodges of Free Masons. The first reference to Masonry

[1] Dr. Alexander Hamilton, *Itinerarium*, 185.
[2] *Md. Gazette*, March 24, 1747.

in America seems to have been a letter from the collector of the port of Philadelphia in 1715 in which he speaks of spending "a few evenings in festivity" with his Masonic brethren. By 1730 there appear to have been several lodges established in Pennsylvania, and in 1735 one was established at Savannah, one at Charleston, one at Portsmouth in 1737, one at Norfolk in 1741, and within this period Masons were meeting regularly in Boston and New York, though there is much uncertainty as to a number of these early dates. That, however, is not essential, our main interest being in the establishment of an order which had ramifications in more than one half the colonies, soon to appear in a number of the others. By the middle of the century, a Mason traveling through America instead of being a lonely stranger would have found himself among an organized band of his brothers in the principal town of every one of the colonies with the exception of North Carolina. Here was another thread in the growing pattern of Americanism.[1]

To what an extent colonial boundaries were disappearing in social and intellectual relations is shown by the membership of one of the most interesting organizations which was founded within this period. In 1727 Franklin had organized the "Junto," a debating society of young men who met to read papers and discuss them afterward. This seems to have declined in interest and in 1743 Franklin, together with Cadwallader Colden and others, formed the first "American Philosophical Society." In the proposal he put out he suggested that such a society should be "formed of the *virtuosi* or ingenious men residing in the several colonies, to be established in the city of Philadelphia as the most

[1] R. F. Gould, *The History of Free Masonry* (London, 1887), VI, chap. xxxi; Ossian Lang, *History of Freemasonry in the State of New York* (N. Y., 1922), chaps. i-iii.

central place." [1]   Although the society at that time
languished, and Franklin had to confess that the members were "very idle gentlemen," nevertheless, the
membership included men from the colonies of New
York, New Jersey, Pennsylvania, Maryland, Carolina,
and several from New England, representing the best
intellectual elements in America.   Its mere formation
indicates that communication, culture and common interests had at least progressed sufficiently to make such
a combination seem feasible to so practical a man as
Franklin.   That it was formed is far more significant
of the new conditions than that it failed.

The growth of population in the several colonies
which made practically a continuous line of settlements
up and down the coast brought people together by the
mere physical fact of being neighbors.   Commerce,
travel, better roads, the post and other elements we have
mentioned were all adding their share in the formation
of a common life and thought for all the colonies.   Another and most important factor was the growth of a
periodical press.   Various things combined to make such
a growth possible in the period.   There was first the
physical problem of distribution and this was greatly
facilitated by the improvement in the roads and the
establishment of many postal riders on local routes about
the main centers.   By means of these it became possible
to extend the circulation of the journals beyond the
mere house-to-house delivery for the townsmen.   There
was also essential a public demand for news.   Man is a
gregarious and conversational animal.   If he talks about
what he is interested in, he is also apt to grow interested
in what he talks about.   Talking first and learning
afterward is by no means a rare dialectical process.   It
is probable, therefore, that the innumerable clubs which

[1] *An Historical Account of the Origin and Formation of the American
Philosophical Society* (Phila., 1914), 178.

came into existence at every cross-roads tavern were by
no means negligible in stimulating the demand for the
news sheets which had their rise within the same period.

Although the circulation remained small—as a rule
only a few hundred copies of any of the journals established being printed—this by no means represented
the public which they reached as they were handed about
from one to another and became stained and torn from
use in many a tavern and coffee house. In the preceding
period only one small journal, the innocuous *Boston
News-Letter*, had represented the entire periodical press
of the colonies, whereas in the one now under review
twenty-two weekly publications were started, of which
six were in Massachusetts, one in Rhode Island, four
in New York, six in Pennsylvania, two in Maryland,
one in Virginia and two in South Carolina.[1] A few of
these died untimely deaths or were merged in more prosperous contemporaries or successors but by the end of the
period the weekly newspaper was firmly established in
the six leading colonies of Massachusetts, New York,
Pennsylvania, Maryland, Virginia and South Carolina.
Of the six journals noted as having been started in Pennsylvania, three were in German, of which Christopher
Sauer's *Der Hoch-Deutsch Pennsylvanische Geschicht-
Schreiber* founded in 1739 was the earliest in the field.

In breadth of interest these new publications marked
a great advance upon the bare bones of scanty news
purveyed in the *News-Letter*. Beginning with the *New-
England Courant*, founded by James Franklin in Boston
in 1721, they developed a distinctively literary quality.
The *Courant*, indeed, lived only a few stormy years
until 1727 but the type had been successfully established, and although much of the literature in which the

---

[1] The first *Maryland Gazette* ran from 1727 to 1736, to be revived
in 1745. The *South-Carolina Gazette* was begun in 1732, lasted only
a few months, and began a new and long career again in 1734.

various journals indulged was either copied from English models such as the *Spectator* or was frankly inferior native growth, nevertheless it did provide the colonists with reading matter of some literary interest. [1]   Young Benjamin Franklin had worked with his older brother on the *Courant* but the well-known episode of his flight from Boston to Philadelphia resulted in establishing the latter town as the journalistic center of the colonies. Not only did his paper, the *Pennsylvania Gazette* (1729) become the most important and entertaining journal in America but his influence both directly and indirectly extended to those of other colonies in which he financed many journals. With the *South-Carolina Gazette* his relations were close and his influence is easily detected.

The make-up of these various semiliterary, seminews journals was much the same for all. In its first year, 1736, the *Virginia Gazette,* for example, published mainly brief news dispatches from other colonies, local items, letters from Europe, reprints of English articles or literary productions, original poems, essays and advertisements. In the latter part of the period the literary interest of the Virginia and South Carolina journals was rather greater than that of any published in New England, and the culture of both those colonies cannot be appreciated without a careful study of the files of their two gazettes. The old tradition of the continuous literary preëminence of New England was largely based upon mere ignorance of conditions and sources in the other colonies. Indeed, in original verse no other colonial journal can equal the *South-Carolina Gazette,* with the *Virginia Gazette* second, and the prose articles of the latter were quoted throughout all the colonies.

If the literary quality, meager as it was, of the many

[1] C. S. Brigham, "Bibliography of American Newspapers, 1691-1820," Am. Antiq. Soc., *Proceeds.*, new ser., XXV, 193 ff.

newspapers of this period was influential in molding public taste, it was to their news columns that the growth of public opinion was most indebted. The failure of the attempt to indict the elder Franklin in Boston for libel on account of certain articles in the *Courant* in 1723 cleared the way in that colony for the complete freedom of the press, as did the case of John Peter Zenger for New York eleven years later. In the latter case although the whole influence of the governor and court was against the publisher, the brilliant pleading of Andrew Hamilton, the most noted lawyer in America, who had been induced to travel from Philadelphia to appear for the defendant, won a verdict of not guilty from the jury, and Zenger continued to publish the *Journal* until his death. Hamilton's speech showed profound learning, and although some of the propositions which he advanced were not tenable as points in Anglo-American law at that time, they became permanently grafted into our political jurisprudence, and the speech, which was frequently reprinted in England, established his reputation abroad.[1]

Aided by these two victories, the evidently growing interest in intercolonial news, and better communications, the news elements in the journals increased, and when the largely literary *New England Journal* was merged with the *Boston Gazette* in 1741, the new organ was distinctly more of the modern newspaper type than any which had thus far appeared. That the colonists were taking a considerable interest in the affairs, political as well as commercial, of other colonies than their own is shown by the increasing number of items copied from other papers, such as speeches of the governors, acts of legislatures, and brief notes of murders, drownings, cases of arson, infanticide and other crimes or accidents. The fact that such items from New England found their

[1] Livingston Rutherfurd, *John Peter Zenger* (N. Y., 1904), chap. iii.

way into the *Maryland Gazette* or that similar happenings in South Carolina appeared in the Northern papers was of itself indicative of a growing solidarity of acquaintance and knowledge.

That the press was already being used as a means of influencing public opinion in other than political matters is shown in some of the entries in the diary of William Seward, who preceded Whitefield on his revivalistic tour of the colonies in 1741 and who may be called the first press agent in America. For example, we find him recording that he "wrote Paragraphs for the News, where our Brother was to preach and had preached," and again, from New Brunswick, "wrote Paragraphs for the News, of our Brother's Preaching, etc., particularly the following, to be published in New York," it being an article describing the remarkable success of the missionary in Philadelphia.[1] This work he continued, even editing Whitefield's own contributions, and preparing the way for him as he advanced by an adroit manipulation of articles in the press.

The success of the newspapers which had to a considerable extent filled their columns with literature rather than news seemed to indicate that there was a public which was ready for that sort of fare and the trend toward a pure news sheet of the modern type, which we have just noticed on the one hand, was balanced on the other by an attempt to segregate the purely literary portion of the papers and to establish magazines of the sort becoming popular in England. The time was not quite ripe for this ambitious effort and although three monthly publications were started none succeeded. The *American Magazine and Historical Chronicle* published in Boston from 1743 to 1746 lasted longest, but it was merely a close imitation of the *Lon-*

---

[1] William Seward, *Journal of a Voyage from Savannah to Philadelphia, 1740* (London, 1740), 10, 17, 18.

don Magazine, and was largely devoted to the republication of English articles. The most interesting attempt was that of the *General Magazine and Historical Chronicle for all the British Plantations in America,* started by Franklin in Philadelphia in 1741.[1] The advance from the extreme parochialism of earlier days was indicated by the scope of its contents. It was distinctly a production by Anglo-Americans for Anglo-America, including not only the continental colonies but also the West Indies. One department was devoted to the reprinting of essays from colonial papers—instead of from English journals—including selections from publications so far apart as Massachusetts and Virginia. Poems by colonials were also reprinted from the papers of New York, Pennsylvania, Virginia and South Carolina. In the department called "Accounts of or Extracts from new Books, Pamphlets, &c. published in the Plantations" we have not only the first attempt at systematic book reviewing in the colonies but a reviewing devoted entirely to the products of the colonial presses. It is evident that we are entering upon a period in which there was not only a distinct colonial culture developing but a culture which was becoming self-conscious. The content of this culture calls for a brief examination before considering other unifying forces in operation at the close of this period.

Its beginning was marked by a fierce conflict between science and religion in connection with the introduction of the new method of inoculation for the smallpox, which conflict started in London and spread thence to the colonies. Beginning with 1714 several articles ap-

---

[1] In the same year there was also started in Philadelphia the *American Magazine, or a Monthly View of the Political State of the British Colonies.* It has been stated that there is only one copy of this known and that it ran for only three numbers. It ran for at least twelve copies, all of which are in the Library of Congress. The *Boston Weekly Magazine* and the *Christian History* both belong to this period also.

peared in the *Transactions* of the Royal Society and else-where on the results of inoculation as practised in Turkey. These called forth denunciatory sermons by clergymen who called it "a Diabolical Operation, which usurps an Authority founded neither in the Laws of Nature or Religion, which tends to anticipate and banish Providence out of the World and promotes the Increase of Vice and Immorality." [1]   In the course of a serious epidemic of the disease in Boston in 1721 the articles fell into the hands of Cotton Mather who saw their importance and communicated them to the physicians of that town.   Dr. William Douglass, who was the only doctor there entitled to the degree, was deeply opposed to the innovation which was as warmly espoused by the American Zabdiel Boylston, who tried the process.   At once the town was in a ferment, and the people were so enraged that his life and Mather's were both threatened, and it was said that if any patient died the doctor should be considered a murderer.   In spite of a prolonged and violent opposition, Boylston won the day, backed by the two Mathers and three others of the leading clergy of Boston.   The conflict, however, was repeated at intervals in other colonies.

Within this period Cotton Mather, Paul Dudley and John Winthrop of Massachusetts and Jared Eliot of Connecticut all continued to interest themselves in science, and in 1738 Winthrop was appointed to the new chair of mathematics and natural philosophy at Harvard.   There was also evidence of a certain amount of popular interest in such matters.   In 1734 Pro-fessor Isaac Greenwood gave "astronomical lectures" twice a week in Boston, apparently successfully.   In the early death of Edward Bromfield that town lost a scientist of some promise, and it is interesting to observe

---

[1] Sermon by Mr. Massey [England] quoted in the *Am. Wkly. Mercury*, Jan. 1, 1722.

that this lad of twenty-three, who graduated at Harvard in 1742, was building a pipe organ of twelve hundred pipes, had made excellent maps, and had ground some remarkable lenses with which he was experimenting when he died. By the combined use of these last and a lantern he had projected on a screen the magnified image of a drop of water so as to show the animalculæ magnified to the length of half an inch, and by the same method had magnified a louse to proportions of several feet and shown all its digestive processes on the screen.[1]

In spite of these few men, however, the primacy in scientific research had passed to the Middle and Southern colonies. In New York, Cadwallader Colden suggested to Dr. William Douglass in Boston that a scientific and literary society be formed of men in both colonies, and in 1736 papers were published by the medical men of Boston who seem to have acted on the suggestion, although the society was short-lived. From medicine and philosophy, Colden passed to botany which seems to have been the favorite colonial science of the day, and became a correspondent of Linnæus, Peter Collinson and others in Europe. In Philadelphia James Logan was the first to carry on investigations in America in physiological botany, and in 1739 published the results of his experiments on maize in support of the Linnæan theory of sex in plants. John Bartram, who unlike most of the colonial scientists of the day was native born, started his famous botanical garden at Philadelphia in 1718 and established a European reputation as a botanist and collector.[2]

In Virginia, John Mitchell, the able and versatile doctor of medicine, wrote the first American treatise on the principles of science, published ten years later at

[1] Account in the *Am. Mag.*, Boston, Dec., 1746.
[2] *Colden Papers*, N. Y. Hist. Soc., *Colls.*, *1917*, 271-273; *1918*, 146-147; Wm. Darlington, *Memorials of John Bartram and Humphrey Marshall* (Phila., 1849)

Nürnberg in 1748. His study of the causes of coloration in races was written from the standpoint of an evolutionist, and he also contributed a number of scientific studies to the Royal Society, but his scientific fame rests chiefly on his investigations of the yellow fever epidemic of 1737 which were not published until after his death. John Tennent also wrote on medicine and botany from Virginia, as did John Clayton, and William Byrd was made a fellow of the Royal Society for his scientific interests. Mark Catesby, who was in Virginia from 1712 to 1721, going thence to South Carolina, published his magnificent work on the *Natural History of Carolina, Florida, and the Bahama Islands* in 1731, and the remarkable colored plates are a revelation of what work could be done in commercial publishing at that time. In Charleston, Dr. John Lining wrote his *Observations on the Weather of Charlestown*, and some medical essays; Dr. Lionel Chalmers was studying the same problems, the results to appear in two volumes in a later period; and Dr. William Bull, as we have seen, was the first colonial to receive a genuine degree of Doctor of Medicine, which was bestowed on him at Leyden in 1734.

It was just at the very close of this period that interest developed in electricity; Franklin's scientific services belong to the next. Nothing was done in the rapidly developing sciences of chemistry and geology. If American contributions to science were as yet slight, the foundations were being laid, and in all the principal colonies there were now men who were in close touch by correspondence with the foremost men in Europe, and who were contributors to a number of the leading scientific societies of the Old World.

Of even more importance than the work actually being done was the temper with which the scientific attainments of the age, meager as they seem to us, were infusing the people. All progress is relative, and to the men of that time the advance they had made seemed as great to them as that made since appears to us. A new optimism and sense of power were beginning to show themselves. In an article in the *Virginia Gazette* in 1737, reprinted six years later in the Bostonian *American Magazine,* we read that "the World, but a few Ages since, was in a very poor Condition, as to Trade, and Navigation. Nor, indeed, were they much better in other Matters of useful Knowledge. It was a Green-headed Time, every useful Improvement was hid from them; they had neither look'd into Heaven nor Earth; into the Sea, nor Land, as has been done since. They had Philosophy without Experiment; Mathematics without Instruments; Geometry without Scale; Astronomy without Demonstration. . . . They went to Sea without Compass; and sail'd without the Needle. They view'd the Stars without Telescopes; and measured Latitude without Observation. . . . They had Surgery without Anatomy, and Physicians without the Materia Medica. . . . As for Geographic Discoveries, they had neither seen the North Cape, nor the Cape of Good Hope. . . . As they were ignorant of Places, so of Things also; so vast are the Improvements of Sciences, that all our Knowledge of Mathematics, of Nature, of the brightest Part of humane Wisdom, had their Admission among us within the last two Centuries. . . . The World is now daily increasing in experimental Knowledge, and let no Man flatter the Age, with pretending we are arrived to a Perfection of Discoveries." [1]

In the arts, we have to note the continuance of the two tendencies mentioned in an earlier chapter, a decline in the folk art and a gradual advance in that for the rich. The moderate increase in manufactured articles kept pace with a decrease in their home or individual

[1] *Va. Gazette,* Jan. 14, 1736; *Am. Mag.,* Oct., 1743.

production. Among the comparatively poor, for example, crude manufactured pottery tended to replace
the few pieces of treasured pewter. In other articles,
cast iron was beginning to be substituted for the hand-
wrought work of the smith, and in architecture, carving
completely disappeared from the houses of the small
farmer or artisan, which were losing their picturesque
quality and tending to become the hopeless square boxes
with which the countryside is too familiar today. The
graceful Windsor chair, which although it may have
originated in England became far more characteristic of
the colonies, began its vogue about 1725 and was found
everywhere, with slight local differences throughout the
colonies, but in general there was a distinct decline in
the æsthetic quality of the furniture of the people.

On the other hand, the number of painters and of
pictures in the houses of the well-to-do increased. In
Charleston, B. Roberts, Alexander Gordon and Jere-
miah Theuss were all at work in this period, Theuss
being the painter of the Ravenels, Porches, Manigaults,
Izards, Allstons and other social leaders there. In
Virginia, Charles Bridges, from 1730 to 1750, was
painting many of the portraits—including that of
Evelyn Byrd—which have often hopefully been as-
cribed to Sir Godfrey Kneller. In Maryland, Hesselius,
whom we have already mentioned, besides much portrait
work, executed in 1721 the first ecclesiastical decoration
in North America in a painting of the Last Supper for
the Church of St. Barnabas in Queen Anne's Parish.
Philadelphia, New York, Boston and Newport, all had
their favorite portrait painters; Robert Feke of the last
named town is now recognized as the best, certainly
among those of American training. In Boston Smibert
seems occasionally to have imported and sold pictures as
well as painted them. In 1735 he offered for sale a large
collection of valuable engravings after Raphael, Michel-

angelo, Poussin, Rubens and others, including the principal artists of England, Holland, France and Italy. The mere fact of naming the artists in this period indicates an increasing interest in art. Sculpture makes its first appearance in the inventory of Smibert's estate in 1752 in which there was included £4 worth of "Bustoes and figures in Paris plaster."

Music and the drama showed a more noteworthy advance than did painting. The execrable church singing in New England was defended against attempted improvement by recalcitrant deacons and other conservative persons who claimed that the suggested new singing by note would grieve good men, exasperate them and cause them to "behave disorderly," that it was popish, that it might—horrible thought!—introduce instruments, that the names of the notes were blasphemous, and for other equally good reasons. Finally the new method won its way, and the change to Watts' psalms in many churches and the doing away with the old system of "lining out" greatly improved the music. New England, however, was not musical, and even in cultivated and wealthy Newport the organist of Trinity Church complained in 1739 that any musician was metaphorically buried alive there.

There may have been a concert in Boston as early as 1732, and a notice in the *Boston News-Letter* of the postponement of one in 1734 indicates that they may have become more or less frequent by that time "in the Consort Room in Wing's Lane." [1] The first recorded one in New York was given in 1733, but we have no notice of any in Philadelphia during this whole period, although there is a trace of a musical society in 1740 and we have already noted Hamilton's attendance at the "Musick Club" four years later. Nevertheless, there was apparently more interest in music in the Middle and

[1] Issue of Jan. 24, 1733.

Southern colonies than in New England. The best to
be heard at this time was undoubtedly that at the Mora-
vian settlement of Bethlehem, founded in 1741, and
which was destined to become the center of the Bach cult
in America. In addition to the organ, the concerts at
Bethlehem employed the violin, *viola de braccio, viola
de gambia,* flutes and French horns, and the fame of the
concerts became so great as to attract as visitors Franklin, Washington and others of the most prominent men
in the colonies.

For the current discussion of music we can turn to the
Virginia Gazette and there find several of the leading
articles devoted to it, one of them being a long disquisi-
tion on Italian opera.[1] Charleston, however, probably
had the best public musical life in the colonies. Good
concerts were frequent there after 1732, the first song
recital in America was given there the following year,
and in 1735 the first ballad opera.

Sporadic efforts were also made during this period to
establish the drama, but the real beginnings of the
American theater belong to the decade following 1750.
There was certainly a theater in Williamsburg, Virginia,
by 1722 and possibly earlier, but it was not successful,
although occasionally used. In New York, the "New
Theater" was used from 1732 to 1734, among other
performances given being "The Beaux' Stratagem" and
"The Busybody." It appears to have been opened again
in 1739 but there is nothing known of it definitely.
In Charleston, the successful concert season to which we
have just alluded was followed by the building of a
theater, which opened in January 1735, with the performance of Otway's "Orphan." In 1737 a performance was given by the Free Masons, but no play is heard
of again for another dozen years. Philadelphia had
puppet shows in 1742 but no dramatic performance

---

[1] Issues of Oct. 15 and 29, 1736.

during this period, and New England throughout the whole colonial time was negligible in the history of both drama and opera.

Science and the arts, however, affected but a small part of the population. Science was only for the intellectually élite and the arts as they were developing were mainly for the rich. The mental life of the mass of men, outside of the daily routine of living, ran almost wholly in the two channels of politics and religion, which were subtly intermingled. In politics the period witnessed the steady advance in the theory of natural rights and the law of nature. We have already spoken of the important work of John Wise which was published just as the period opened, and the doctrines which he had so ably put forth were springing up almost spontaneously throughout the colonies. Thus Samuel Mulford in his speech before the New York assembly in 1714 invoked "the Law of God and Nature," as protection for the rights of the people against the unjust attitude of the customs officials. He added that the law complained of was "settled upon the Subject by Act of Parliament," but as the century advanced, Parliament retreated into the background in the popular theory, which more and more posited natural rights and a natural law superior to any made by man.

The belief that there were fundamental legal principles deducible from nature was beginning to take firm hold of the popular mind. From these it was thought that the rights of individuals and the constitutions of states could be readily drawn and embodied in bills of rights. But in practice these rights were naturally those which seemed best to satisfy the desires of the people of the day, and in the early eighteenth century the people were living a simple agricultural or frontier existence. These "rights" thus tended to become identified with the common-law rights of Englishmen and to give to the

conception of the common law a rigidity and immuta-
bility which was invalid and alien to its true spirit.
That law, which was reasonable and adaptable, thus
became largely bound to the intellectual outlook and the
social needs of a transient phase of colonial life.   The
flexibility which other phases of colonial development
tended to give to law, as we noted in an earlier chapter,
was beginning to be counteracted by the new philosophical notions coming into vogue.

Another notable characteristic of our American legal
development was being fostered in this period by the
increasing acceptation among the colonists of the political doctrine of contract.   That of covenants—of a covenant with God, of a covenant with the ruler, of covenants with one another—was peculiarly characteristic of
the Puritan faith, and as we have pointed out, there was
a strong Puritan tinge in practically all the colonies.
Through the writings of Locke, Sidney and others, however, the doctrine was absorbed throughout colonial
America.   One of the obviously implicit points in such a
doctrine was the dependence of legal consequences upon
an individual act of will, and hence it tended to impress
deeply upon colonial legal theory that individualism
which was also emphasized by the life of the frontier
and which became one of the main features in American
legal development.   The seeds of this doctrine had been
present in many of the colonies from the start, but the
increasing interest in law, the establishment of systems
of courts, the gradual taking shape of a colonial jurisprudence and the immense importance which legal
theories had for political disputes in the period, all made
the ideas which were becoming embedded in the popular
consciousness of the time of immense importance for the
colonists and their successors.   Those ideas were of certain inalienable rights, of an abstract liberty of contract,
and of immutable legal principles, laying the entire stress

upon the rights of the individual and of property instead of upon those of society or of man as a unit in social life. Many of the difficulties with which we meet today in the administration of justice, in the treatment of criminals, and in the securing of legislation aiming at social welfare are traceable to that Puritan doctrine and influence which in this period were uppermost in forming the mold of colonial legal theory, just when it was taking the shape it was to retain for more than a century longer.[1]

Although one of the chief influences in legal development was thus derived from the legalistic aspects of religious doctrine, we have already several times had to note the decline in religious interest among the people. The original fervor of the New England Puritans had long since passed, and throughout all the colonies the growing variety of life, the economic struggles and opportunities, the encroachments of Deism, Arminianism and other first fruits of the growing rationalism notable in the period, turned men's thoughts away from the old doctrines. There was everywhere not only a secularizing of interests but a growing coldness and formalism in religious life. Within the period of this chapter, however, the colonists were to be caught up in a movement, the sources of which were in Europe, that was to sweep through America, completely altering the outlook of the people and leaving behind results of the first importance in every department of colonial life.

Since the account of the Great Awakening written by Joseph Tracy in 1840, which was devoted mainly to the movement in New England, there was no volume published on the subject for eighty years, and the tendency has been to overstress the New England as-

[1] H. D. Foster, "International Calvinism through John Locke and the Revolution of 1688," *Am. Hist. Rev.*, XXXII, 475-499.

pects of it and to limit it largely to the dramatic events about 1740. That portion, however, was a mere episode in what was in fact a long-continued evangelistic movement, extending over many years and present in all the colonies, closely linked with and influenced by contemporary movements in England and on the continent of Europe. Long before the coming of Whitefield in 1739, there had been stirrings here and there which presaged a change in spirit and a deep discontent with the stereotyped and formal religion which had become the type of no one church alone. Among the varied sects of the German immigrants to Pennsylvania there were many Pietists and a deep infusion of the pietistic spirit, and throughout the century these settlers were peculiarly liable to religious excitement. Before the Awakening in its narrower sense, there had been a number of revivals in that colony which had converted to a more zealous religious life many of the Lutherans and Reformed, whose churches had been largely neglected.

In New Jersey, the Dutch who had settled on the Raritan, finally felt themselves strongly enough established to secure a pastor from Holland, and applied for one through Domine Freeman of Long Island. They secured the young Theodorus J. Frelinghuysen, who was a member of the minority evangelical party at home and who looked forward to spreading his view in the colony. Arrived in New Jersey in 1720 he at once set to work there with passionate earnestness, proclaiming the vital necessity of conversion, and roundly denouncing the formalism of mere outward observance of religious duties. His zeal and ability made a profound impression not only on the local churches of his own denomination but upon the Presbyterians of the valley, and his influence spread to other places. In 1726 he held a notable revival, and in that year the Presbyterians of the valley decided to call a minister, whom they secured in the person of young Gilbert Tennent and who was greatly encouraged by Frelinghuysen. Indeed, his close association with the young Presbyterian became one of the chief complaints against the Reformed pastor who, like the evangelicals of all denominations, soon became a storm center of religious controversy.

Gilbert Tennent, who was to be one of the leaders in the movement, was the son of the Reverend William Tennent, a minister of the church in Ireland and a graduate of the University of Glasgow. The father had immigrated to America and in 1718 had become a member of the Presbyterian synod. After settling in several places he finally became pastor of the Presbyterian Church at Neshaminy, Pennsylvania. The number of Presbyterians had increased enormously by the exodus from Ireland, but the removal to the frontier had resulted in a lowering of both moral and religious tone. Hardened by their experiences in the old country and the new, as well as by their creed, they lacked the gentler qualities of Christianity, and like the Puritans of contemporary New England, tended to fall into mere formalism and a gloomy insistence upon outward observance. A minority, however, had become imbued with evangelical principles and there had been as a result a division into conservative and innovating parties, both in Pennsylvania and New England, before Tennent began his work.

Powerful exhorter as he was, his influence was mainly as an educator of a remarkable group of boys who were, later, in the evangelical party to be of enormous influence on the life of the colonists. In 1726 he built the little shack which became widely known as the "Log College," and there, in addition to his four sons, he taught Charles Beatty, John Roan, William Robinson, Samuel and John Blair, Samuel Finley and John Row-

land.   Whitefield pronounced the education given as
superior to that obtainable in the schools of New England or Europe.   On the other hand it was held up to
derision by the ministers of the conservative party who
feared that the men who went forth from it to preach
were mere ignorant enthusiasts.   The truth lies between
these two extreme estimates, and the after work of the
small body of graduates proves that their training in
languages, logic and theology was of no mean quality.
Young Gilbert Tennent began his own work in 1726,
his brother John three years later, and between 1730
and 1735 the others as well were preaching to deeply
moved congregations.   Other evangelists also came into
the Raritan Valley and a John Cross held a notable revival there in 1734 and 1735.

There had been installed as pastor in Northampton,
Massachusetts, one of the most remarkable Americans of
the day, who was to be a leading figure in the great
movement although it is absurd to speak of him as having initiated it both in the colonies and in Europe.   Jonathan Edwards was unquestionably one of the greatest
intellects which this country has produced.   Interpret-
ing the universe solely in logical terms, however, he was
led to the seemingly inevitable conclusion that God was
the author of evil, that He was a monster of wrath, and
that man was utterly helpless in his moral strivings
against the incomprehensible predestination of the Deity.
In spite of much original sweetness both of mind and
character, Edwards deliberately preached the most dam-
natory doctrine in the name of Christ which it is possible to conceive.   Content neither to rest in suspense
upon the insoluble problem of the existence of evil, nor
to accept as an act of faith the doctrine of God as love,
which was preached by the founder of that religion of
which Edwards had been ordained a minister, he described God as a being with no more pity than a fiend,

holding those who had striven for righteousness, as well as the abandoned, "over the pit of hell, much as one holds a spider, or some loathsome insect, over the fire" and rejoicing, in a manner which would shock the most degenerate human criminal, over the consequences of the evil of which He was himself the author. To this had New England Puritanism come at last. There had been a revival, the most important which had then occurred, in Enfield under his preaching in 1735, with many of the frenzied physical manifestations which were to become common as the movement continued, and Edwards wrote an account of it which was widely read both in the colonies and England.

All of these, and other scattered manifestations of revival, were destined to be swept up together in the great movement which was initiated by the preaching of Whitefield on his several tours through the colonies, beginning in 1739. Accounts of the marvelous influence of his preaching in England and the astounding size of his audiences had been described in a number of the colonial newspapers, such as the *South-Carolina Gazette*, the *Virginia Gazette* and the Philadelphia *Mercury*, and when he landed the way had been prepared for similar results here. Wherever he went the people poured out to hear him and the new evangelism swept like a fire across the colonies.

It is impossible to describe in detail the continuance of the movement in the several localities. There was a renewed outburst in Northampton and all New England was in a frenzy, the wave of enthusiasm diminishing in intensity from Maryland southward. Congregations and whole denominations were split into "Old Light" and "New Light" parties and there was much that was inherently baneful, as well as deeply shocking to taste, in certain of the manifestations. The ultrareligious excitement of the emotions produced a reaction, and by

1744 the movement had everywhere largely spent its force. The frenzy of those years and the abusive recriminations to which it gave rise, however, had been only the culmination of forces and desires which had been present for some preceding years and the effects were deep and lasting.[1]

The repressed emotions and the longing for a religious life that should be something more than intellectual assent to creeds and outward observances had been stirring the breasts of vast numbers of the people who, asking for bread, had been handed polished stones by the ministers of the established churches. If the inevitable reaction carried many with it, nevertheless the ebb of the movement left in all the colonies large bodies of evangelical congregations to whom religion had become something far more vital than it had been before and which called for expression not merely in church attendance but in all the activities of life.

Whitefield himself had been almost as deeply influenced by pure humanitarianism as by religion, and the humanitarian movement in the colonies may be traced mainly from this time forward. One of his main interests in his first and later visits to America was the home for orphans, of which he laid the corner stone in 1740, and where he soon had over a hundred children in his charge. On his journeyings through the colonies much of the money which he raised went to the upkeep of this "House of Mercy," Bethesda, as he named it. When John Wesley came over in 1735 on his mission to Georgia to convert the slaves and Indians, he wrote that he hoped by doing so to come "to know what it is to love my neighbor as myself"; and outside of the New England leaders of the movement, or rather the succession of movements, this note of love for humanity is a constantly recurrent one.

[1] Joseph Tracy, *The Great Awakening* (Boston, 1842), chaps. ix-xiv.

Moreover, in spite of the many ignorant preachers who were thrown up by the popular nature of the revivals, there was really given a permanent impetus to the cause of both sectarian and popular education. The movement also brought a new sense of pity and responsibility for the Indian. There had, indeed, already been sporadic attempts to minister to him, but with the services of the two Brainerds there may be said to have begun the continuing tradition of missionary service. Of the young men who had been trained in the Log College, Samuel Blair established a classical and theological school at Fogg's Manor which numbered among its pupils at least four colonial leaders of note. John Blair became a professor at Princeton; Samuel Finley, who was later to become president of Princeton, established an academy which taught, among others, two subsequent governors and the celebrated Dr. Rush of Philadelphia; and as results of the general movement may be traced the later founding of the four colleges of Presbyterian Princeton, Congregationalist Dartmouth, Baptist Brown, and Dutch Reformed Rutgers.

The ascendancy of the old established churches had been shaken, and the people had to a great extent won the right to such a religious life as seemed to them best for themselves. Underneath the purely religious aspects of the movement, there was a deep undercurrent of democracy and individualism. The control of the conservative element was everywhere shattered, and the evangelicals of all denominations felt themselves in far closer sympathy with one another than with the "Old Lights" of their several churches. The intellectual as well as the emotional life of the colonies had been stirred deeply, and the residents of them all had watched the phenomena of the others with rapt attention. It was the first movement which had embraced them all and for the first time they found themselves caught up together in a single wave of emotion. Not only the rigid distinctions between colonial churches but boundary lines and provincial prejudices had been swept aside, and when the movement passed, the new evangelistic denominations were to a considerable extent no longer provincial but American.[1]

Within the same years in which these events had been occurring, two others had taken place which were of influence in the formation of a common colonial consciousness. In 1740 the English government decided to ask for volunteers in the colonies for an expedition directed against the Spanish settlements in the Caribbean incidental to the "War of Jenkins' Ear." The colonists responded with enthusiasm and considerably more than the three thousand asked for volunteered, the recruits coming from all the colonies, North and South, which thus found themselves interested in another common topic of an entirely different sort from that which we have just been considering. The management of the expedition was atrociously bad and the casualties unnecessarily and appallingly heavy. The colonial troops not only received worse treatment than the English regulars, but the incapacity of both branches of the English military services made a lasting impression upon the colonial mind, so that the Cartagena expedition became another milestone in the development, by contrast, of colonial self-confidence.

By 1744 England found herself drawn into the larger operations of the War of the Spanish Succession and in consequence declared war against France. The following year there took place the well known capture of Louisburg by a combination formed of the English fleet and New England land and naval forces. Although the English contingent rendered invaluable service and the operation could not have been successful without it, the

---

[1] J. T. Adams, *Revolutionary New England*, 177-178.

plans had all originated in Boston and the New Englanders not only took a well justified pride in the result but were inclined to assume the entire credit for the capture. It was, indeed, a notable achievement and tended enormously to increase the fast growing self-confidence of the colonists. The news as it spread through the other colonies to the south stirred their pride also, although they had had no part in the undertaking. For example a long ode by a native rimester in the *Maryland Gazette* asks

> Shall brave New England's Glory fly
> Thro' Earth, Air, Sea, and fill the Sky,
>   Resounding loud Applause;
> Shall distant Poets raise the Strain,
> And neighboring Muses on the Main
>   Be silent in the Cause? [1]

There was still, indeed, much provincial jealousy and lack of understanding and no prevision of a common destiny. Separation from England was undreamed of and, as the next period was to show, the colonies were yet far from being able to unite even in self-defense. Moreover, most of the culture was imported. Many of the artists and scientists whom we have spoken of earlier in the chapter were either recent immigrants or mere birds of passage. Nevertheless, the period marks the beginning of a strong colonial sense of self-confidence, of native culture, and of the many unifying forces which were steadily to grow in power. In a dispatch home to England, Colonel Blakeney, the recruiting officer in charge of colonial volunteers for the Cartagena expedition, wrote that "from the highest to the lowest, the Inhabitants of these Provinces seem to set a great Value upon themselves, and think a Regard is due to them,

[1] *Md. Gazette*, Jan. 14, 1746.

especially in the Assistance they are able to give the Mother Country on such Occasions." [1]

The growing wealth, population and stability were beginning to have their effect, and Franklin could speak of the pioneering period as being past, at least for the seaboard, and that the time had come to think of other things than merely subduing the wilderness. Indeed, mere lapse of time was beginning to have its effect, and the age of some of the colonists' institutions was of influence in developing a sense of an established social structure. Harvard, although young as compared with the Spanish universities in Mexico and Peru, was nevertheless over a century old by the end of this period. In the South, William and Mary College had nearly rounded its first half-century, and many schools and churches in the North and the South could boast of continuous existence of from seventy-five to a hundred and twenty-five years. If a large proportion of the men who were developing colonial scientific and artistic life were "foreigners," on the other hand there were many, like Mather, Edwards, Bartram and Franklin, who were native-born and racy of the soil. In many minor details, such as the samplers which we have mentioned, colonial life was striking out in this period into characteristic ways of its own. In furniture-making, for example, two distinctly American types were contributed by colonial cabinet workers about the middle of the eighteenth century.

It is also within this period that we begin to find comments upon "Americanisms" in our language making their appearance. For example, a traveler in 1745 notes the changed meaning in America of the term "ordinary" as applied to an inn, though the *New Oxford Dictionary* does not trace this divergence prior to

[1] Col. W. Blakeney to Newcastle, Aug. 21, 1740, Colon. Office Papers. 5, no. 41.

1774.[1] Similarly the word "branch" in the sense of "a stream running across the road" is found and defined by the same traveler, although the dictionary does not trace it before the nineteenth century. The use of "fall" for "autumn" appears so casually, in letters of William Logan in 1727 and Eliza Lucas in 1742, as to indicate that it was already an accepted form. Samuel Johnson in 1756 spoke of the "American dialect," and many of the words most familiar in the colonies must have been utterly strange to ears in the mother country.

Part of the new American vocabulary came from borrowing from other languages. *Skunk, hickory, squash, caribou, porgy, catalpa, raccoon, terrapin* and a host of other names now in common use came from the native Indian, as well as those used to designate the new implements of one sort and another which the colonists adopted, such as *canoe, toboggan, moccasin, tomahawk* and *wigwam*. By the middle of the century such French words as *bureau, gopher, bogus, portage, prairie* and *chowder* had become an integral part of "the American language." The Dutch had contributed *cruller, stoop, waffle, scow, boss, cookey, span* (of horses), *pit* (of a peach), and others unknown in England. More important than these borrowings were the new words which the colonists coined for themselves, such as *bull-frog, egg-plant, snow-plow, cold-snap, trail, pop-corn, shingle, back-log, sophomore, schooner, cat-boat,* to mention at random a few from the mass of terms which were beginning to make the common language of Americans sound strange and uncouth to their English cousins. Many new adjectives, such as *handy, kinky, chunky,* were well established before the Revolution. Many of the terms which were sound old English and which the colonists had brought with them were being

---

[1] [L. Campbell], *Itinerant Observations in America,* reprinted from the *London Mag.* (Savannah, 1878), 43.

retained here, whereas they were falling into disuse in England, so that they came later to be considered as "Americanisms" and added to the divergence between the two countries. Among these we may note *burly*, *cater-corner*, *likely*, *deft*, *scant* and *ornate*. *Bub*, for a boy, is very old English but has been retained only in America. In sounding the vowels, the colonists retained the flattened *a* which was then common in England and did not differ in this respect from the English until the latter began to use the broad *a* in the third quarter of the century.[1] In Maryland, however, traveling Englishmen already noted that, by association with the Negroes, the children unconsciously imitated their speech, and that Southern pronunciation was thus beginning to assume its peculiar characteristics.

Among the common people, if there was ample ignorance, bigotry and prejudice, there was a mental activity which had been much stirred by the experiences of newcomers in their immigration; and for the native-born, by life in the wilderness, the constant shift of many from one locality to another, the military expeditions, changing social conditions and the great revivals. For the most part, the farmers and artisans and petty tradesmen have left no written record of their thoughts, and it is only now and then that the veil lifts and allows us to see what these may have been. Conversation seems to have been one of the staple products of colonial life, and we have frequent reports of its subjects by the travelers now wandering about.

Hamilton was careful to note many such as he rode from Annapolis northward and helps us to fill in the outlines of a picture of popular thought and preoccupations. In one of the inns at which he stayed, the "learned company consisted of the landlord, his overseer and

[1] H. L. Mencken, *The American Language* (N. Y., 1923), 49 ff., 55 ff., 59, 63, 73.

miller and another greasy thumbed fellow," and the topics of dispute were "politicks, news, and the dreaded French War." Riding along a day or so after, he fell in with a Scotch-Irishman who "had a particular down-hanging look, which made me suspect he was one of our New-light bigots" and who told Hamilton, after a little preliminary religious discourse, that he "was damned without redemption." A little farther along, picking up the proprietor of the Principal Iron Works, the conversation turned from religion to politics. Crossing Elk Ferry, he says that the ferryman plied his tongue much faster than his oar, understood a few scraps of Latin and had heard of Terence. At the next inn the landlord again discoursed only of religion. On the next stretch he picked up three Pennsylvanians whose topic was "the insignificancy of the neighboring Province of Maryland" as compared to their own. At the inn in Philadelphia there were "several comical grotesque Phizzes . . . which would have afforded variety of hints for a painter of Hogarth's turn," but their possessors talked "upon all subjects,—politics, religion and trade. Some tolerably well, but most of them ignorantly," displaying, how-ever, that curiosity which was one of the characteristics of the American rustics everywhere. At the inn at Trenton, the conversation ranged from politics and re-ligion to physics, and at the next stop he was treated to a discussion between two Irishmen, a Scot and a French Jew about sacred history. At Saybrook Ferry, in Con-necticut, a rabble came in and began to discuss theology, and of the lower classes generally in that colony he says that they talked "so pointedly about justification, sancti-fication, adoption, regeneration, repentance, free grace, reprobation, original sin, and a thousand other such pretty chimerical knick-knacks, as if they had done noth-ing but studied divinity all their lifetime, and perused all the lumber of the scholastic divines, and yet the fellows look as much, or rather more like clowns than the very riff-raff of our Maryland planters.   To talk in this dialect in our parts would be like Greek, Hebrew or Arabick.'' [1]

In the constant recurrence of religion as a topic even five years after the main year of the great revival, we can see the influence which that movement was still exerting, and in the frequent reference to politics we can divine that there were many thoughts stirring among the lower classes besides the petty affairs of their households or villages.   Wherever we touch the life of the period, we get a sense of change, of restlessness, of commercial, political and intellectual activity, and yet of growing stability, prosperity, intercolonial acquaintance, unity and self-confidence.   In the next period a great war, which was to tax colonial resources to their uttermost, was to strengthen and bind together many of the strands which we have indicated in this rapidly developing colonial life and culture.

[1] Hamilton, *Itinerarium*, 6, 8, 20, 36, 40, 200.

CHAPTER XI

THE MID-CENTURY

1745-1763

ALTHOUGH the Peace of Aix-la-Chapelle in 1748 was supposed to end hostilities, and the Seven Years' War did not officially begin until 1756, nevertheless there was unofficial warfare between French and English during more than half of the intervening period, just as there had been much of the time between 1713 and 1739. Throughout the years covered by this chapter the life of the colonists was deeply affected by the military situation. This influence can be traced in the rise in speculation, the growth of radicalism, stimulation of the intellectual life, development of the idea of colonial union, and in other aspects, economic and social.

During the wars practically all the ports in the colonies fitted out their privateers to prey on the enemy's commerce, and the papers of the day are filled with exciting stories of rich captures. Thus in the earlier ones, we read of three New York privateers which took a Dutch ship with $38,000, one from Philadelphia capturing ten thousand pieces of eight, another taking a ship with $30,000 in cash, while ship and cargo were worth $40,000 more. Of two others, one made a haul of thirty-eight thousand pieces of eight and another took a boat worth £100,000.[1] In 1745 a letter from St. Kitt's to Annapolis says that "there is hardly anything to be seen now in the West Indies but English Men of

[1] *Md. Gazette*, May 10, 24, 31, 1745; *Am. Mag.*, Oct., 1745.

War and Privateers." [1]   In Rhode Island the number of
privateers rose from three in 1739 to twenty-one in
1744, from which figure there was a decline to five
by 1748.   In New York, however, the number steadily
increased to the end of the war, when that port had
sixteen.[2]

In the next war the privateers again swarmed out of
every port from Boston to Savannah, and in 1757 the
New York Gazette is full of stories of rich captures running from £9,000 to £15,000 sterling.   On the other
hand, it cost much to fit out the vessels engaged in the
business, there was trouble from desertions of crews, occasional difficulties with dishonest captains who appro-
priated prizes to themselves, and more especially was
there delay and loss due to the numerous appeals taken.
This was particularly true of the Dutch vessels, and
these appeals were not seldom sustained by the higher
authorities in England.   As the prize money had to be
distributed to the crews prior to appeal, a reversal usually resulted in heavy loss for the owner of the privateer.

During the whole war, the illicit trade with the
French West Indies was carried on with the enemy with
an entire disregard of the exigencies of the military situation.   This was shared in by the merchants of all the
colonies from Pennsylvania northward and to a lesser
extent by the Southerners.   Increasing as the war continued, it has been estimated that in 1760 between four
and five hundred Northern vessels carried French cargoes from the Spanish "free port" of Monte Cristi, where
the trade had centered and where the French secured
provisions and military stores and marketed their sugar
and molasses.

[1] *Md. Gazette*, May 17, 1745.
[2] These figures were kindly given to me by Mr. H. M. Chapin of the
Rhode Island Historical Society, who has been making a study of the
subject, and to whom I am also indebted for some suggestions as to the
unprofitableness of the ventures as a whole.

At the opening of the Seven Years' War insurance on ordinary commercial vessels was from twelve to fifteen per cent.[1] That the losses to the merchants on their normal business were heavy is indicated by a statement in the *Maryland Gazette* in 1745 that since the beginning of that war thirty ships, seventeen snows, twenty-five brigantines and twenty sloops, all belonging to the port of Philadelphia, had been cast away, lost or taken by the enemy.[2] In the cases of some colonies there was also marked dislocation of trade due to the war, as for example in Maryland which was mainly dependent, indirectly, upon France as a consumer of her inferior grade of tobacco, and which consequently suffered heavily, with great increase of poverty among the lower classes.

By the middle of the century, although the fur trade had declined in some colonies, it had increased in others, and in Pennsylvania and South Carolina it was an important factor in export trade. In the former it was becoming closely allied with frontier land speculation, and rich Philadelphia merchants, including some Jews, were already mingling dreams of far westward imperial expansion with the routine instructions given to their pack-horse trains and traders. The war, however, called an abrupt halt to all such plans, and in some cases the dealers lost heavily by the hostilities.

The commerce which was thus subject to these highly speculative influences had increased enormously from the earlier period which we considered in a preceding chapter. In 1754 Boston was obviously lagging behind her more prosperous rivals New York and Philadelphia, through the customs houses of which latter places there entered in that year three hundred and sixty-eight and four hundred and seventy-six vessels respectively as compared with only one hundred and ninety-six and one

---

[1] *Conn. Gazette*, July 24, 1756.
[2] Issue of May 31, 1745.

hundred and seventy-three twenty years previously.[1]
The increase in number of vessels, however, tells only
part of the story of enlarged commerce. If we examine
the cargo lists of the Virginia vessels engaged in the
West India trade we find that whereas those we listed
for the earlier period carried only about ten thousand
staves or shingles in their mixed cargoes, those of 1752
were carrying as much as forty-eight thousand staves
and a hundred thousand shingles.

With every increase in the size of the unit of trade it
becomes correspondingly difficult for the small man to
compete with the capitalist who possesses ample resources. When we consider, in addition, the heavy expenses incidental to conduct of business in war time—
one of the noteworthy features of the period was a rise
in interest rates—and the great risks involved, it becomes evident that what was an incidental loss to be
averaged out by the great merchant was ruin for the
small trader of the earlier day. In fact two of the most
marked characteristics of the period were the rampant
speculation and the rise of "big business" with its attendant ramifications into local politics.

To a certain extent all classes shared in the speculative
mania. Lotteries were set on foot for every conceivable
purpose, from the founding of churches or schools to
the extrication of bankrupts from their personal difficulties. The great speculations of the time, however,
were in privateering, commerce and land, and in all these
the scales were heavily weighted in favor of the capitalists and those influential in politics. As an example
of the intercolonial scope and methods of large-scale

---

[1] Tabulated from issues of the *N. Y. Gazette* and *Pa. Gazette*. The
file of the *Boston News-Letter* which I examined for that year lacked
about twelve issues. The incomplete entries totaled only 348 vessels to
compare with 578 in 1733. Eight of the missing weeks were from
Nov. 5 to the end of the year, so that even making all allowance the
total would not seem to have exceeded that of two decades earlier.

business as it was developing in those years of rapid mercantile aggrandizement, we may note the formation of the "United Company of Spermaceti Candlers" in Newport in 1762. About 1750 that town had received an accession of great importance in the arrival and settlement of numerous Jewish families from Spain, Portugal and Jamaica, including those of Lopez, Rivera, Hart and Hays, and its subsequent rapid rise in commerce was not a little due to the shrewd abilities and wealth of these newcomers. They had introduced the use of spermaceti candles and by 1760 there were seventeen factories for their manufacture in Newport alone. The price was exceedingly high, but not content with the rapid advance of the industry, the leaders in it entered into an agreement with all the manufacturers in New England and Philadelphia which for some time absolutely controlled the entire industry from the price of raw materials to that of finished product, including all phases of marketing both.[1]

In New England, partly because of the mercantile character of the life and partly because the records are more complete, the new tendencies can be more clearly traced than elsewhere, and in that section we note them in many lines of business. Until 1760 the great New England pine belt, which extended southwest from Nova Scotia to the Connecticut River, had been tapped only through New Hampshire, where lived Mark Hunting Wentworth, brother of the all-powerful governor, and himself one of the richest men in America and the "lumber king" of the day. The woods in that colony had been cut so far back from the coast that it was becoming increasingly costly to carry on operations. On the other hand, Connecticut had no staple. It carried on only a coasting trade and one of moderate size to the

[1] *Commerce of Rhode Island* (Mass. Hist. Soc., Colls., ser. 7, IX), 88-92, 97-100.

West Indies, all its European imports coming through the neighboring colonies. The customs house entries for 1775, as recorded in the *Connecticut Gazette,* fail to show the arrival of a single vessel from England. As articles in that journal about the middle of the century abundantly testify, this dependence upon their neighbors was becoming galling to the more ambitious mercantile leaders of the little colony.

A group of these decided to try to compete with New Hampshire by lumbering in the upper Connecticut Valley. In order, however, to forestall Wentworth's certain antagonism it appeared necessary to secure the appointment of a local admiralty judge, who also by virtue of his office would have ample powers in regard to the king's woods. An admiralty judge was one of the most hated of the royal officials in all the colonies, and Connecticut had always been the leader in attempting to maintain absolute independence of the home government. We cannot here develop the whole story of the intrigues which followed, but it is indicative of the growing influence of business over the colonial legislatures that that of Connecticut was finally induced to send an application for the appointment of such an official, whose good offices, if they could be obtained, would be of benefit only to the small group of capitalists interested in the logging scheme, and whose appointment would otherwise be inimical to the interests and deep prejudices of the great majority of the citizens of the colony.

The speculation in lands, which we have had occasion to note several times as influencing the social, or rather antisocial, outlook of the poorer classes, rose to new heights both during and after the wars. The most noteworthy case in New England was that of the Susquehanna Company, organized to exploit wild lands on the river of that name in Pennsylvania, and for which the stockholders had only a flimsy Indian title. Not only did the operations of this company threaten to embroil the colony of Connecticut in a war with that of Pennsylvania, but after a long period of protests and ill will, they did bring on hostilities with the Indians. So important was the persistent action of the stockholders with regard to the colony's relations with its neighbor, with England and with the natives, that the whole population of Connecticut became split into rival parties, the radicals favoring expansion, and the colony dividing sectionally between a radical east and a conservative west, as it happened to be in this case. In spite of bitter opposition, the company was finally successful in securing the majority of the members of the lower house of the legislature in their favor, and the whole unsavory affair became another evidence of the close connection which was developing between large-scale business and the legislatures.

Speculation in new townships, with all the attendant grievances on the part of actual settlers to which we have already called attention, became rampant toward the end of the war, and among the moneyed men of the old settlements shares in these ventures changed hands as readily as stocks today. Ezra Stiles, for example, who had a thirteen-thousand-acre interest in the Susquehanna purchase was also buying and selling shares in the towns of New Concord, Lempster, New Britain, Killington, Harwinton, Cornwall, North Haven, South Kingston, and others in New Hampshire, Connecticut and New York. He was careful as far as possible to buy proprietors' rights only, which, as in one recorded case, the speculators declared they intended to retain in as few persons as possible so as to prevent control of taxation and other local matters passing into the hands of the actual settlers.

Such speculation was by no means limited to the

North, and in 1749 two large companies, the Loyal and the Ohio, were granted respectively eight hundred thousand and five hundred thousand acres west of Virginia across the Alleghanies. Quarrels between the two rivals ensued, and although more or less land was disposed of to settlers by both, legal proceedings delayed settlement. Just before the opening of the Seven Years' War another company, the Greenbrier, was granted a hundred thousand acres by the Virginia legislature but, the war immediately ensuing, no advantage could be taken of the grant and a renewal was later refused owing to the new Western policy based upon the British proclamation of 1763. Both land companies and other corporations were frequently created in the colonies without direct resource to the crown, although the right to do so on the part of the local authorities was presumed to be derived, explicitly or implicitly, from the sovereign as the only ultimate source of such power. In the royal colonies, the governor as the direct representative of the monarch, generally considered that he had such a right, although there were exceptions and his exercise of it was not always unquestioned by the colonists. Occasionally a governor was himself sceptical of his power when called upon to exercise it. The right of the governors in the proprietary colonies was similar save in so far as it was specifically limited by the crown patents to the proprietaries. In the corporate colonies, the governor possessed no such power, and as the colonies themselves were corporations, it was extremely questionable whether their assemblies could create other corporations, and the question remained unsettled during the entire colonial period. Connecticut was particularly cautious in her action in this regard, although certain corporations such as Yale College were erected there. In general, however, the home authorities did not disallow such colonial incorporations, however questionable the technical rights of the various local authorities may have been.[1]

The actual military operations of the wars were either at sea or on the frontier, and the older seaboard settlements did not suffer. Indeed, in them, commerce, wealth and intercolonial travel, both for business and pleasure, all increased. These demanded better means of communication, which rapidly improved in the middle of the century. Many travelers of different sections comment on the excellence of the roads and the frequent advertisements for the sale of carriages indicate that their use was becoming much more general. In 1754 an advertisement in Boston offers "to let at a reasonable rate" a "handsome compleat coach" to go to Piscataqua, Rhode Island, or any other place with two or four horses.[2]

This, however, though better than horseback riding, was still an individualistic mode of travel. A new epoch in intercolonial communication and acquaintance came only with the establishment of stagecoaches and boats, running on regular schedules and carrying passengers at moderate tariffs. In 1753 an advertisement informs us that the Trenton Ferry has been "revived" and that a stage will run from Brunswick to Trenton, and a "Stage Boat" from that point to Philadelphia. The next year James Wells undertook to operate a combined stage and boat line twice a week "load or no load" between New York and Philadelphia. One or two other routes were added, and in 1757 as "the Stage-Boats and Waggons employed between Philadelphia and New York are found considerably advantageous to Travellers" it was announced that the line would be extended to Annapolis.[3]

[1] J. S. Davis, *Essays in the Earlier History of American Corporations* (Cambridge, 1917), I, chap. 1.
[2] *Boston Wkly. News-Letter*, July 25, 1754.
[3] *N. Y. Gazette*, June 4, 1753; June 3, July 8, 1754; April 14, Oct. 24, 1757.

Although these early lines seem to have met with some vicissitudes, the new method of travel persisted on the most important highway in the colonies, and in 1760 another line was advertised between the largest two Eastern towns.[1]

The postal service also reveals the increasing demands of the times, as well as the all pervading cultural influence of that mid-century American, Benjamin Franklin. The service had been declining for some years when he was appointed deputy postmaster-general jointly with William Hunter of Virginia in 1753. It had taken six weeks to make the trip between Philadelphia and Boston, and in winter the post set out only fortnightly. The new postmasters established weekly posts and cut the time in half. By 1757, during the summer months the mails passed between New York and Philadelphia twice a week, and their increasing use is indicated by the fact that whereas at the end of 1756 one hundred and fifty letters were advertised as held at the New York office, three years later the number unclaimed in Philadelphia was over five hundred.[2] With the general increase in communication there was a decided improvement in the character of the inns. The number of "clean, decent houses" increased, and occasionally they became notably good, as one described by that English traveler and chronic fault-finder George Fisher who found a tavern in Maryland full of fine mahogany furniture and the rooms "so stuft with fine large glaized Copper Plate Prints" that he fancied himself back in one of the best print shops in London.[3]

It would be interesting to trace all the various influences which were at work to account for the great increase in the demand for reading matter which is notable

---

[1] *Pa. Gazette*, March 20, 1760.
[2] *N. Y. Gazette*, Jan. 3, 1757; *Pa. Gazette*, Jan. 3, 1760.
[3] "Narrative of Geo. Fisher," *William and Mary Quar.*, XVII, 170.

in this period. That war, as always, stimulated the demand is probably unquestionable, and we may, perhaps, find two more humble contributing causes in the improved facilities for warmth and light. Although, as we have already noted, stoves of a Dutch type were occasionally used, most colonial households had been obliged to content themselves with the cheerful but not very satisfactory heat from the roaring log fire in one or two rooms. Although from at least as early as 1731 onward coal began to be imported and grates used to some extent,[1] the introduction of the new type of stove invented by Franklin in 1742 fairly revolutionized the heating of the colonial houses of the simple as well as the more expensive sort. The great majority of the early colonists had been without lights except for the flaming pine knot or the open fire. In 1761 the president of Harvard College made some experiments to calculate the cost of the various sorts of candles, including the greatly superior and newly introduced spermaceti. From his table we learn that the "common sale candles" cost one and three quarter pence per hour, or, translating this very roughly into the value of money today, perhaps we may say it cost about $8 a month for the use of one candle for a five-hour evening, an amount which obviously would have been prohibitive in most households. The spermaceti candles were a great improvement but they cost more than double the ordinary ones based upon light per hour. However, the increase in wealth and luxury, the introduction of several sorts of lamps from about 1750 onward, and the well heated rooms, must have added greatly to the number of winter-evening readers. One no longer had to choose between burning one's face and freezing one's back while hugging the fire in a half-dark room or go-

[1] *Cf.*, for example, *Boston News-Letter*, May 6, July 15, 1731; April 26, 1733.

ing to bed, but could sit in a well warmed apartment by a lighted table.

This increase in reading is evidenced in many ways. We have not only numerous lists of excellent private libraries but the advertising of books for sale in the news sheets, including those from Maryland southward, becomes more frequent and notable. The *Georgia Gazette* was not founded until 1763, but among its earliest issues are lists of books for sale including, besides many religious works, a good collection of the Latin classics and such modern writers as Milton, Hume, Shakespeare, Bacon, Congreve, Burnet, Dryden, Pope, Smollett, Gay and Bunyan as well as Molière, and songs set to music for the violin and flute.[1] Not only were the number of booksellers and that of imported books both rapidly increasing, but new trade methods indicate a widening interest. In 1760 James Rivington, recently arrived in Philadelphia from England, established a new store in that town and at once entered upon an energetic campaign of advertising. The enlarged scale of his operations is characteristic of the change in business methods in general. In December he stated in his first newspaper appearance not only that he had a large stock for retailing in Philadelphia but that "Country Shopkeepers may be furnished with a very great variety of such Books as are usually kept for the Supply of their Customers."[2] A few months later we find him making an offer in the papers of the other colonies, for example in the *Maryland Gazette*, to supply all public and private libraries on such reasonable terms "as to prevent the Managers of them sending to England for supplies," and renewing his bid for the trade of the country bookshops.[3] He also established branch shops of his own in some of the other colonies.

[1] *Ga. Gazette*, Feb. 9, 16, 1764.   [2] *Pa. Gazette*, Dec. 25, 1760.
[3] *Md. Gazette*, Aug. 6, 1761.

The public-library movement, now no longer as in Bray's time fostered from without but an indigenous growth from colonial needs, is another indication of the increased taste for reading and of the intellectual stimulation of the period. In the very closing years of the preceding era, five subscription libraries had been started, of which the most important was that organized by Franklin in Philadelphia, but between 1745 and 1763 there were no less than seventeen founded, of which one third were in Pennsylvania. These beginnings of a most important popular movement have not yet received the attention they deserve, and further research will undoubtedly add considerably to their number, for their wide distribution is indicated by the fact that a majority of those already known were not in the large centers but in small villages, and were scattered all the way from Portland, Maine, to Savannah, Georgia.[1]

The mental activity of the times is also clearly revealed in the increased circulation and better quality of the periodical press. In 1755 the *Connecticut Gazette* said that "the Utility of a publick News-Paper in an English

[1] As the following list, compiled from scattered sources, including manuscripts, contains more names than any other which I have seen, it may be given in full. The dates are either those of the known founding or the earliest recorded notice of the institutions. Library Company of Philadelphia, 1732; Useful Knowledge Library, Pomfret, Conn., 1732; Philogrammatican Library, Lebanon, Conn., 1739; Library of Friends, Philadelphia, 1742; Darby, Pa., a library, 1743; German Library at Germantown, Pa., 1745; Union Library of Philadelphia, 1746; Redwood Library, Newport, 1747; Library Society of Charlestown, S. C., 1748; Library at Providence, R. I., 1753; New York Society Library, 1754; Winyaw Society, Georgetown, S. C., 1755; Hatborough, Pa., 1755; Amicable Library, Philadelphia, 1757; Association Library, Philadelphia, 1757; Albany Society Library, 1758; Lancaster Library (name later changed to Juliana Library Company), Lancaster, Pa., 1759; Social Library of Salem, Mass., 1760; proposals for a circulating library, Annapolis, 1762; Blockley and Merion United Library Company, Pa., 1763; Portland, Me., 1763; Leominster Social Library, 1763; Georgia Society Library, mentioned 1764, probably in existence earlier. In the above list of public libraries founded during this period I have not included those of various institutions of learning.

country is now so universally acknowledged as scarcely
to admit of dispute," and during the years of the war
the press certainly reflected its growing prosperity.[1]
The *Maryland Gazette*, for example, greatly improved
with the beginning of hostilities and its news of the conflict was excellent. By 1758 it is noteworthy that the
general postoffice had to issue orders that whereas the
newspapers theretofore carried free had "of late years
so much increased as to become extremely burthensome
to the Riders, who demand additional Salaries" on that
account, a charge would have to be made.[2]

The time seemed ripe for attempting a new magazine,
and the publishers in Philadelphia were fortunate in
securing the Reverend William Smith, provost of the
new college, as editor. Arrangements were made to
receive subscriptions in Boston, Newport, New Haven,
New York and many other places, and the journal was
stated to be of "general use for all the British colonies,"
correspondents being secured in all of them on the continent and in several of the West Indies. It was also said
that it had been brought into existence by the war, and
from its first issue the new journal, called the *American
Magazine*, had a distinguished literary and financial success. Unfortunately after a year it had to be suspended
because its editor returned temporarily to England. A
successor, the *New American Magazine*, published at
Woodbridge, New Jersey, lacking editorial ability proved
a failure.

That the demand for literary fare of some sort was by
no means confined to the more cultivated circles is evident from the change which was coming over the almanacs. These little annual publications, which came
from the presses of every colony and which were
thumbed and read by the common people from year's
end to year's end, became almost small magazines them-

[1] Issue of April 12, 1755.   [2] *Pa. Gazette*, April 2, 1758.

selves. Although now by far the best known, Franklin's *Poor Richard* was only one of a host, and the *Pennsylvania Town and Country-Man's Almanack,* for example, contained many short stories, essays and articles on slavery and temperance. West's *Almanack* at Providence had tales, essays, poems and a little historical writing. Under the influence of the war, Hutchins' *Almanack* in New York became almost a miniature copy of the *Annual Register* in London, and besides the usual stock in trade of funny stories, poems and essays, contained each year excellent historical reviews of the progress of the war and the colonies, with maps and portraits.

An undertaking which illustrates the mercantile and scientific activity of the times, as well as the close cooperation in which men of different colonies were now acting together, was the attempt made in 1753 to find a northwest passage, and failing that to explore the coast of Labrador. Organized in 1752, mainly as a Philadelphia enterprise, it received subscriptions from merchants in Maryland, Pennsylvania, New York and Boston, and although unsuccessful as regards the passage did accurately map the coast from latitude 56 to 55. Another similar expedition set out from Rhode Island the same year, and in 1754, the Philadelphia vessel, the *Argo,* made a second attempt. The great scientific impulse of the time, however, came from the popular interest in the new developments in electricity. The discovery of the Leyden jar in Europe in 1745 had operated on the public mind much as the announcement of that of the X-ray or radium in our own day, only that the interest was then far more widespread and intense. Electrical experimenting became a fad with all people of fashion. Franklin's active mind at once fell under the spell, and his eleven experiments with the jar in 1747 covered all the "essential phenomena of the condenser" and stand almost without need of revision today. He devised a motor which could make fifty revolutions a minute and run half an hour from one discharge. His demonstration that lightning was electrical made the greatest impression upon laymen of any of his discoveries, but, scientifically, his rejection of the theory of action at a distance and his substitution of the theory of an all-penetrating fluid was of more significance. Perhaps even more significant, however, was the discovery both by America and Europe that the colonies had at last produced a scientific mind of nearly the first order, although we ought not to overrate the results of his researches.

In music, the theater, painting and the other arts, the activity of the period was as marked as in other respects. By 1753 New York and some of the other larger centers, both South and North, were having frequent concerts of the best music of the day, performed by orchestras large enough to render overtures, *concerti grossi* and symphonies. In 1759 the "Orpheus Club" was formed in Philadelphia and three years later was founded the celebrated "Saint Cecilia Society" at Charleston. With the coming of the professional Murray-Kean theatrical company, probably by way of the West Indies from England, the history of the theater in America entered upon a new phase. The event of greatest importance, however, was the arrival in 1750 of Mr. and Mrs. Lewis Hallam, both of whom were artists of note in London and whose company, joining with a part of the earlier one, remained together for twenty years and gave the residents of the colonies, outside of New England, opportunities to see performed by an excellent company all the plays which were on the stage at that time in London—Shakespeare, Addison, Rowe, Congreve, Farquhar and Steele. The repertoires of plays given in such towns and villages as New York, Philadelphia, Williamsburg, Annapolis, Norfolk, Hobb's Hole, Port Tobacco, Upper Marlborough, Petersburg and Fredericksburg would put most theaters of the present day to shame. Playing three days a week in New York, from September, 1753, to March, 1754, they gave twenty-one plays of the very cream of English dramatic literature, a theatrical season which in that respect that town has never equaled since. New theaters were built in several places, but such in New England were still called "Houses of Satan," and that section lay wholly outside the history of the art.

In painting, John Singleton Copley, who began his American period in 1753, was the fashionable painter of the time, and Benjamin West, the only American to become president of the Royal Academy, was just beginning his career in Philadelphia in the same year. Not only were portraits of the colonists being painted, but artists also gave some attention to the landscapes about them.[1] In 1757 we find the first exhibition of colonial paintings being held in New York, and the beginnings of colonial sculpture belong to the same period. These first appear in the form of portrait busts in churches, commemorative of the dead; importation of sculpture now becomes more frequent also. The effect of Washington's interest in the art, evidently influenced by the martial ideals of the war, is seen in an order which he sent in 1759 for busts of Cæsar, Alexander the Great, the Duke of Marlborough, Charles XII of Sweden and other generals. Instead of filling the order his London correspondent sent him statues of Bacchus and Flora. Unfortunately the comments of the not unemphatic Father of his Country have not been preserved.

The impulses following the religious revival, of which we spoke in the last period, found expression in this one in the founding of the College of New Jersey (later Princeton College) in 1746, of Wheelock's Indian School in 1754 (later to develop into Dartmouth College), of King's (later Columbia) College in the same

[1] Cf. *Md. Gazette*, Nov. 16, 1752.

year, and of Rhode Island College (afterwards Brown) in 1764. The nonsectarian institution which was to become the University of Pennsylvania was also established during these same years, in 1751, so that, including the three more ancient colleges, by the middle of the seventeen sixties there were institutions of higher learning established in seven of the ten colonies north of the Carolinas. As in so many other respects, we can trace in education during these years of the mid-century the distinct turn in tendencies long at work to change the transplanted culture derived from England into one more genuinely colonial. In the North, the grammar school of the traditional English type had been slowly declining, and in this period we mark the first beginnings of that distinctively American type, the academy, which was to have so great and so characteristic an influence later. In the South, the factors which we have noted tending to depress the poor white and to develop an aristocratic or, more accurately, plutocratic-planter type, were beginning to result in a decline educationally as compared with the North. Among the rich, the use of tutors, combined with a few years of English university training, continued to produce individuals of high cultural attainments, but even among them we note a change, for although the South Carolinians continued to go abroad for their education, both the Virginians and the Marylanders now began to some extent to attend the new colleges in the North. Between 1757 and 1763 we find no less than seventeen rich Maryland lads, including the Pacas, the Dorseys and the Chews, entered as students at Princeton, and a number of Virginia boys both there and at the new college in New York. It is probable that the risks at sea incidental to the war had much to do with this by no means unimportant change.

Closely connected with education and with the new humanitarian movement following upon the Great

Awakening was the new attitude toward children and child life. In the earlier periods, natural affection had of course always been in evidence in spite of Puritan doctrine and economic exploitation, but the difference between the old and the new is exemplified by the writings of the Puritan Jonathan Edwards and the Anglican Samuel Johnson, both of Connecticut. Whereas the former collected and published a selection of the most infamous passages from the Old Testament to show God's wrath against infants, the latter insisted upon the intellectual light to be found in children and asserted that we owed them the utmost reverence—*pueris maxima reverentia debetur*. The increased interest in the youngsters is shown not only by the increasing number of their portraits which were painted but by numerous advertisements in the newspapers of the different colonies, and even in the almanacs, of "English and Dutch Toys," "a large assortment of curious Toys for Children," "a great Variety of Play-Books for Children," or of "lotteries or small prints" for them.[1]

The same humanitarian impulse is found, more particularly among the Quakers, with reference to the Negroes, and in the writings of Anthony Benezet and John Woolman, found expression at once sweet and strong. The evils of drunkenness prevalent among all classes, and indeed all ages—for even small children were given raw rum to drink—also began to meet with frequent reprobation in the press. The opening of the Pennsylvania Hospital, which owes its origin to Dr. Thomas Bond, in 1751, inaugurated a new era in the treatment of the insane, who now began to be considered as sufferers whom it was possible to relieve rather than as criminals whom it was necessary to restrain. Through-

[1] *Boston Wkly. News-Letter*, June 6, 1754; *Va. Gazette*, July 11, 1751; *Warner's Almanack* (Williamsburg, Va.), 1762; *Ga. Gazette*, Oct. 18, 1764.

out the colonies societies sprang up having as their object the alleviation of the distresses or sufferings of the poor, such as "The Society for encouraging Industry and employing the Poor" in Boston, or the "Corporation for the Relief of poor and distressed Presbyterian Ministers, their Widows and Children" in Philadelphia. South Carolina had been an early leader in charitable work, and in 1764 an organization was founded in Savannah to relieve "every poor person without distinction," reference being made to the great good that such societies had accomplished in the other colonies and to an earlier one in Georgia itself.[1]   Charity, indeed, was intercolonial in its scope, and at the time of the great Boston fire of 1760, collections among all the counties of Maryland netted £2004, and Virginia contributed £1340 sterling for the sufferers.

In one way and another, in the life of the colonists, we have noted the many strands which little by little were being woven into one common fabric. The purely political movements toward governmental union lie outside the limits of our survey, and of the meeting at Albany in 1754 under stress of the common danger from the enemy, we need only say that its vain attempt to frame a political union of all the colonies was indicative at once of the fact that sentiment had advanced sufficiently far to make such an attempt appear feasible but not far enough to make it successful. Had the various intercolonial influences which began mainly to be important toward the middle of the century—such as commerce, the press, better means of travel, improved postal facilities, the education of Southern boys in Northern schools, and all the rest—been in operation longer by the time that the leaders met at Albany the results might have been different. However, the meeting there of twenty-five delegates from seven different colonies, an as-

[1] *Ga. Gazette*, Nov. 8, 1764.

semblage, as Hutchinson said, the "most deserving of respect of any which had been convened in America," attracted wide notice and focused attention upon the common interests of all the colonies and tended to familiarize the colonists with the thought of such interests transcending the old boundary lines.   The journals in different colonies followed the proceedings, and many articles advocating union appeared all up and down the coast, affording, with the military events of the war a little later, subjects which inevitably widened the colonists' visions.

Among the Albany delegates were numbered some of the ablest lawyers in the colonies, and it is from this mid-century that we may date the rise of the lawyer in American political life.   There had before been able lawyers who had been influential in their several communities, and as a class they had been slowly coming into greater social prominence.   As early as 1730 there had been thirty practitioners in New York City, but the quality of some was less than doubtful.   The year before six of the leaders had formed a little bar association, pledging themselves not to appear in any case with those whose certificates bore recent dates, it being alleged that standards had sadly declined within the past four years. The charter of the city granted in 1730 restricted the practice in its courts to eight lawyers.   The supreme court judges in the same year ruled that a seven years' apprenticeship would be requisite for candidates who applied for certificates to practice before them.   All this showed a growing professional consciousness within the ranks.[1]   But from about the time of the conference of 1754 their advance into political prominence continued rapidly, until in the next period they will be found to

[1] N. Y. Assembly Journal, I, 600-601; Jay Papers in N. Y. Historical Society Library; Minutes of the Common Council, IV, 7; Supreme Court Records, June 9, 1730.

have taken the leading place in directing public opinion. We have already spoken of the rise of new and unknown men to leadership in industrial and political life, and this was a movement which, as always, was intensified by the war.   The serious dislocation which war always brings to established business and the great speculative opportunities it affords invariably alter to a very great extent the personnel of the leaders in every field.   Colden in New York in 1765 wrote that there "the most opulent families, in our own memory, have arisen from the lowest rank of the people," and this was true to a considerable extent of all the mercantile communities.[1] The rise of business on a large scale, the increasingly complicated forms of association, partnership and company promotion, the large land grants, the growing close connection between business and the legislatures and courts, all made legal advice and legal influence more and more necessary to the business men, many of whom had themselves recently emerged from an unlettered obscurity.   The alliance thus naturally formed between the lawyers, large capitalists and landowners was beginning to make a new alignment in social life, and the extremely powerful groups thus formed were beginning to be a cause for alarm to the crown officials and the poorer classes alike.   If, on the one hand, the somewhat vague association into which the lawyers of New York had entered by 1765 resulted in warnings to the English government of their growing power by Colden, no less was there widespread comment inimical to the legal profession in the more radical news sheets and almanacs.[2]

At the same time that the lawyers were thus coming into the lead, there was an equally marked decline in

---

[1] *N. Y. Col. Docs.*, VII, 705.
[2] Cadwallader Colden, *The Colden Letter Books* (N. Y. Hist. Soc., *Colls.*, X), 61-62, 71, 92.

the position of the clergy. The rough camp life of the war and the added impulse given to the spread of deism and even atheism by the English troops and officers who came over imbued with rationalistic principles, undoubtedly had some effect on the religious life of the colonies. The decline in political influence of the clergy, however, had been going on for decades. In some sections this was partly due to the inferior quality of the clergy themselves, but on the whole somewhat the same influences seem to have been at work as in our own day, the growth of an educated laity and distrust of clerical leadership in lay affairs. In 1758 the Reverend Jonathan Boucher, recently arrived in Virginia from England, wrote home that the clergy "generally speaking, are the most despis'd and neglected Body in the Colony; and to do the Virginians Justice, Candor I'm afraid w'd be oblig'd to confess, that none have less reason than they to complain of Injustice." [1] Although this may have been somewhat exaggerated, the drift away from clerical leadership is shown by a number of incidents as well as by the obvious absence of ministers as leaders of opinion in other than religious matters. Thus the Reverend Jonathan Mayhew of Boston felt it necessary to preface a sermon dealing with political matters with an apology for a minister's trespassing upon such ground. Just after the close of our period, two theses submitted at Harvard for the Master's degree on the topic "Ought ministers of the Christian religion to preach politics" were decided in the negative. One of the notable rules of the subscription library founded at Albany was that no clergyman should ever be a trustee.

A sign of the times indicating the passing of the old simple conditions may be found in the marked decrease in marriage. Both spinsters and bachelors, so rare in the early days, now became more numerous, and this new

[1] Letters of Rev. Jonathan Boucher, *Md. Hist. Mag.*, VII, 17-18.

situation called forth not a little comment, humorous and serious, in the papers of New York, Maryland and the other colonies. With the passing of almost universal marriage came an increase in prostitution in the larger towns.

In spite of the bitterness against the French, which on account of their inhuman employment of the Indians against the settlers was growing in all the frontier sections, the inhabitants of the tidewater country seem to have felt little active animosity. Whatever poverty and hardship the war might bring to the frontiersmen and the poorer classes in the older settlements, the merchants in many of the colonies were fattening on profitable war contracts, on illicit trade with the enemy, and on speculation of various sorts. As the war progressed and large bodies of English troops were employed in ever greater numbers, the funds sent over for their maintenance actually turned the customary unfavorable balance of trade into a favorable one for the colonists. Most of the upper classes were in one way or another involved in mercantile affairs, and for them, remote for the most part from the scene of actual operations, the war was far from being an unmixed evil. In fact, it seems to have brought about a marked accenting of French influence both in styles and literature, which was to become even greater in the next period, although it is easy to overrate its importance. Indeed, it may be noted that just before the beginning of the war in 1754 a poem in a New York newspaper ends with

> But mount on French Heels when you go to a Ball,
> Tis the Fashion to totter and shew you can fall;
> Throw Modesty out from your Manners and Face,
> A la Mode de François, you're a Bit for his Grace.[1]

In 1746 the *American Magazine* had had a long article to show that the English had followed French fashion

[1] *N. Y. Gazette*, Jan. 7, 1754.

for a half century, but the vogue of the enemy seemed to grow greater with the war.[1] French teachers and even French tutors frequently appear in the advertisements, and the number of French books in the booksellers' notices increase notably. In 1762 and 1763 works by Montesquieu, Voltaire, Rabelais, Racine and other French authors were offered for sale in the principal journals in the North and South. Of these works the most popular appear to have been Rousseau's *Emile* and *Nouvelle Héloise* and Montesquieu's *Spirit of Laws,* the last usually in the enormously popular two-volume English translation. Rousseau's *Contrat Social* did not appear in the colonies until the very end of 1764 and seems never to have achieved a wide sale or notable influence.[2] On the other hand, Montesquieu was advertised everywhere, from the Massachusetts to the Georgia *Gazettes.*

Although the war was thus stimulating the intellectual life and lining the pockets of certain classes and fortunate individuals, there were others who were beginning to suffer severely before its close. For a while wage-earners benefited greatly owing to the advance in wages. Free labor had always been scarce and this situation was emphasized by the number of men drawn away for military service. High wages, the scarcity of labor and its inefficiency become notes which are heard with increasing frequency in all the colonies. In North Carolina Governor Arthur Dobbs wrote that labor was so scarce that the workmen would do only about a half-day's real work, yet that wages had gone to such high figures that between the two conditions building and improvements to plantations had to be wholly suspended, except by slave labor. The same story came from Virginia, where

[1] Reprinted in *Md. Gazette,* Feb. 17, 1747.
[2] The first notice which I have found of it in either a private library list or a bookseller's advertisement is in the *Mass. Gazette,* Dec. 13, 1764.

it was stated that wages had become so high that for less than a third more than a year's wages of an inefficient, bungling free laborer, one could buy a slave for life, the comparison being made by one who was opposed to slavery and dreaded its increase. In Maryland the numerous advertisements for labor of all sorts offered inducements far above those formerly prevailing, and in one notice we read that the price of the advertiser's goods have had to be vastly increased because workmen are "very difficult to be met with even at the most extravagant wages." [1] In Pennsylvania, employers advertised not only that "high wages" would be paid but liberal tips and cash every week, and the same conditions prevailed farther north. It is evident that labor was temporarily in a position to demand almost anything it wished, and that its great improvement in relative status would make the reaction more bitterly felt when labor should come to suffer in the general collapse incidental to the pricking of the bubble of fictitious wartime prosperity.

On the other hand, heavy taxes and high prices due both to real needs and to profiteering, caused much suffering among those who were not in a position to increase their incomes as rapidly. The war debts of the colonies rose to previously unheard of figures— £818,000 in Massachusetts, £385,000 in Virginia, £313,000 in Pennsylvania, and proportionately large sums in the others. [2] Even early in the war a writer in Connecticut complained that "people groan under heavy Taxes; we have no fixed Medium of Trade; and Poverty rushes in, like an armed Man." [3] It is noteworthy that in this most independent of all the colonies he lays much of the trouble to the unnecessarily large number of public of-

[1] *Md. Gazette*, April 23, 1761.
[2] "State of the Debts," Brit. Mus. Add. MSS. 35909.
[3] *Conn. Gazette*, March 20, 1756.

ficials.   Just after the close of the war Peter Fontaine, in
Virginia, wrote that "things wear but a gloomy aspect,
for the country is so excessively poor, that even the industrious, frugal man can scarcely live, and the least
slip in economy would be fatal." [1]   Complaints of profiteering by the rich in war contracts and trade were constant.   The contracts were enormous for that day, one
of the first to be filled in New York amounting to over
two million pounds of bread, two million pounds of beef
and other supplies in proportion.[2]   Even in the smaller
colonies there were allegations by the people of fraudulent profits.[3]   Complaints of the poor are heard with
increasing frequency as hard times followed on the heels
of prosperity.   "Wood at Three pounds Ten Shillings
a Cord," writes a contributor to the *Pennsylvania Gazette* "a Price never before heard of!   The country man
says, We have Wood enough.   The Boatman says, I
could fetch two Loads while I am bringing and unload-
ing one" but "the Rich engross—when perhaps two
Hundred Families have not a stick to burn." [4]

In many of the colonies a heavily depreciated paper
currency with attendant inflation in prices added to the
distress of many, and was a fertile source of discontent.
In Massachusetts and Connecticut the issues had been
redeemed in 1750 under pressure from the British government, with the cash received to reimburse those colonies for the expenses incurred on the Louisburg expedition, and hence they were thereafter on a sound money
basis.   This change, however, was bitterly opposed by
the debtor class and the ignorant, and when Parliament
passed an act in 1751 forbidding the further issue of

[1] Jacques Fontaine, *Memoirs of a Huguenot Family* (Ann Maury,
tr., N. Y., 1872), 374.
[2] "Investigation of Baker & Kilby's Contracts," Brit. Mus. Add. MSS.
35909.
[3] *E.g., A Regulator for Crazy Will's Death-Watch, or P— J—'s
Witchcraft explain'd* (Connecticut broadside, July 30, 1761).
[4] Issue of Jan. 10, 1760.

paper money in any of the New England colonies, except in certain cases, it met with violent opposition.

By the end of the war, the farmers were feeling the reaction in general business, and the price of all agricultural produce fell rapidly.[1]   In Connecticut, of the two hundred and sixty-five law suits in the New Haven County court in 1761 most were for debt, and "the general inability of People to make due Payments" became the subject of comments in the broadsides as well as of legislative action.[2]   Although the war did not actually end until 1763, operations in the American continental sphere were practically over by 1759, and the opening of new frontier lands to settlement, combined with the poverty of many in the old sections, caused fresh emigration to the outlying regions on an enormous scale.   This, in turn, reacted upon prices of lands in the old settlements and caused a severe decline.   By 1762 the value of farms in many sections of New England, for example, had fallen one half, and the farmers' equities in their mortgaged properties were practically wiped out.   Those who left them and went to seek new homes in the wilderness did so smarting under the sense of economic injustice, only to encounter those other causes of irritation of which we have already spoken in the new speculative towns.   In some sections, more particularly in Pennsylvania, the seaboard settlements had shown themselves unable or unwilling to protect the frontiersmen in the earlier stages of the conflict, and to the economic resentment was added a burning anger against the classes or the governments which exploited the frontier while refusing it assistance.

In the two generations which we have covered from 1691 to 1763, the growth of the colonies had been most

[1] A. M. Schlesinger, *Colonial Merchants and the American Revolution* (Columbia Univ., *Studies*, LXXVIII), 56-57.
[2] *Cf. Obstructions of Trade* (Connecticut broadside of 1764).

extraordinary, the population increasing nearly seven-fold. Instead of the scattered settlements in the nearly unbroken forest, separated from one another by leagues of Indian trails, there was now almost continuous settlement from Maine to Georgia, connected by a network of roads over many of which wheeled traffic was constant and on not a few of which stagecoaches plied regularly several times weekly. When our story began, there was not a single newspaper in America and no public means of conveying letters from one isolated settlement to another. At the end, there was a score of well established and able journals carrying the news of all the colonies, and a post which brought even the most remote settlements into fairly economical touch with one another. In most of the colonies, with the increase of communication and papers, there had developed not only a local public opinion but some glimpse of a larger common life and destiny. In all of them, the formation of opinion had largely passed from religious to lay leaders, and politics had freed itself from clerical control. The transplanted culture, which we found slowly dying of inanition at the beginning of our survey, had given place to a vigorous development of native growth, and the content of colonial life had become vastly enriched. In commerce, the imports of manufactured goods from England had risen from approximately £140,000 in 1697 to £1,630,000 in 1763. Even local manufactures had begun to compete with agriculture as a leading factor in at least one section. The frontier, which had been merely at the backdoor of the tidewater sections at the beginning, had been pushed far across the back country, even over the mountains, and in the whole tidewater section there was now a stability and an immunity from danger almost as great as in the mother country itself.

On the other hand, these very facts had brought into

existence new animosities and divisions, and a sectionalism of deeply disruptive tendency.   Although the tidewater sections of all the colonies had been brought far
closer to one another than had been the case at the opening of the century, almost every colony now had its own
problem in the conflict—economic, political and cultural
—between its older portion and its newer frontier.
Moreover, with the increased wealth and the fullness of
cultural life, had also come an alignment between the
rich and poor which was far more marked than anything
which can be observed in the simpler days of the beginnings.   Wealth had concentrated, and whereas the capitalist of the older towns was far richer than his grandfather had ever dreamed of becoming, the poor settler
was no better, if as well, off as *his* grandfather had been.
His house was no better, nor his food, nor his educational facilities, and on the other hand he was apt to be
much farther removed from the centers of culture, was
more despised by the rich, and was exploited by them in
a way which the earlier frontiersmen had not been when
they planted their homes on free land and but a short
distance from tidewater.   In the South the great planter,
by the use of slave labor, had enormously increased the
productive capacity of his plantation, but his poorer
neighbor had gone down in the struggle, or moved away
beyond the mountains where the blight of the comparison of Negro slavery with his own free labor did not fall.
In the towns, theaters, concerts and art exhibitions added
steadily to the amenities of life for those who dwelt in
the ever enlarging stately Georgian mansions, but in the
small houses of the farmer or mechanic the art of the
people had deteriorated.   New blood, also, had come
into colonial life, and with the influx of Germans and
Scotch the old racial solidarity and sentimental allegiance
of the colonists had to a marked degree been lost.   Nevertheless, the disappearance of the French power from

Canada and the West by the Treaty of 1763 seemed for the time to offer boundless opportunity for expansion and to open new lands where the discontented and the exploited might find a freer and less hampered life.

CHAPTER XII

Critical Essay on Authorities

PHYSICAL SURVIVALS

THERE are two points of view from which objects of historical interest may be collected and exhibited—the artistic and the utilitarian. Until recent years museums adopted, almost wholly, the first standpoint; but now efforts are being made to broaden the collections so as to include the second, and, notably in the collections of the Pocumtuck Valley Memorial Association at Deerfield, Massachusetts, and the Bucks County Historical Society at Doylestown, Pennsylvania, the student may study the kitchen utensils, farm implements, and all the paraphernalia of daily life.

The best collections of colonial silver are in the Museum of Fine Arts, Boston, and the Metropolitan Art Museum, New York. Painting of the period was practically confined to portraiture and the portraits are fairly well scattered through a great number of museums, historical societies and libraries up and down the seaboard. The best collection of pottery is at the Pennsylvania Museum, Philadelphia. Furniture is also widely scattered in exhibitions of specimen pieces, as at the Morgan Memorial at Hartford, Connecticut, or arranged in completely furnished rooms or houses. This latter form of display was first given impetus by the Essex Institute in Salem, Massachusetts, in 1907, in an arrangement of three livable rooms dating from 1750 to 1800. In 1904 the Rhode Island School of Design at Providence erected a dwelling of Georgian type and furnished it carefully and completely but this is not a literal reproduction. The Pennsylvania Museum has furnished three early American rooms, the Chicago Art Institute has opened one, and the Boston Museum of Fine Arts has opened a wing of American decorative art in which are three rooms from the

Derby-Rogers house from Salem. By far the most important exhibition of such period rooms, however, is that in the American wing of the Metropolitan Museum in New York.

In addition to these museum exhibits many individual colonial houses are now being preserved furnished. Washington's home at Mount Vernon is well known. The Society for the Preservation of New England Antiquities, 2 Lynde Street, Boston, controls twelve old houses, all appropriately furnished, which are listed in their publication *Old Time New England*. In the various boroughs of New York are the Van Cortlandt Manor, the Dyckman House and the Ditmars House. The Pennsylvania Museum of Mt. Pleasant on the Schuylkill is installed in a house built by John McPherson in 1761, representing the best period of Pennsylvania architecture and contains a fine collection of contemporary furnishing. Recently, the Harwood Mansion in Annapolis has been purchased for preservation, and this movement is steadily growing.[1]

Considerable authentic picture material on the early part of the eighteenth century may be found in standard histories such as Winsor's and Avery's and in many monographs; but the most serviceable collection is R. H. Gabriel, ed., *The Pageant of America* (15 vols., New Haven, 1926——). The volumes are topical in treatment; seven volumes have appeared.

BIBLIOGRAPHIES

The best guide to printed material available down to the time of its publication is Justin Winsor, *Narrative and Critical History of America* (8 vols., Boston, 1884-1889). The *Bibliography of American Historical Societies*, edited by A. P. C. Griffin and issued as the second volume of the *Annual Report* of the American Historical Association for 1905, is invaluable for material published by historical societies down

[1] The author is indebted for most of the above facts to Mr. H. W. Kent, Secretary of the Metropolitan Art Museum, and to Mr. R. F. Bach, Associate in Industrial Arts in the same institution.

to that time. The *General Index to Papers and Annual Reports of the American Historical Association, 1884-1914,* was issued in 1918 as the second volume of the *Report for 1914.* The *Writings on American History,* an annual guide to current material, is now brought out by the American Historical Association, and the latest volume brings the material down to 1923. Special bibliographies may be found in many of the volumes listed below, such as *The Cambridge History of American Literature.*

DOCUMENTARY SOURCE COLLECTIONS

The data for social and economic history are voluminous but scattered through innumerable and varied sources. A prime general source for each colony is its public records. Among these are the *New Hampshire Provincial* (or *State*) *Papers* (N. Bouton and others, eds., 31 vols., Concord, 1867-1907) ; *Acts and Resolves of the Province of Massachusetts Bay* (from 1692) (17 vols., Boston, 1869-1910) —containing many valuable notes; *Records of the Colony of Rhode Island and Providence Plantations in New England* (J. R. Bartlett, comp., 10 vols., Providence, 1856-1865)— somewhat unreliable; *Public Records of the Colony of Connecticut* (J. H. Trumbull and C. J. Hoadly, comps., 15 vols., Hartford, 1850-1890) ; *Documents Relating to the Colonial History of the State of New York* (E. B. O'Callaghan and B. Fernow, eds., 15 vols., Albany, 1856-1887) ; *Archives of the State of New Jersey* (W. H. Whitehead and others, eds., ser. 1, 27 vols., Newark, 1880-1906) ; *Pennsylvania Archives* (Samuel Hazard and others, comps., ser. 1, 12 vols., ser. 2, 19 vols., ser. 4, 12 vols., Phila., 1852-1907) ; *Minutes of the Provincial Council of Pennsylvania* (6 vols., Phila., 1860) ; *Archives of Maryland* (41 vols., Balt., 1883-1922) ; *Calendar of Virginia State Papers* (11 vols., Richmond, 1875-1893) ; *Colonial Records of North Carolina, 1662-1776* (W. L. Saunders, ed., 10 vols., Raleigh, 1886-1890)—with many British documents; *Colonial Records of the State of Georgia* (A. D. Candler, ed., 17 vols., Atlanta, 1904-1906). The legislative journals of a few of the colonies are now being published separately, e.g., the *Journals of the House of Burgesses of Virginia, 1727-1776* (H. R. McIlwaine and J. P. Kennedy, eds., 8 vols., Richmond, 1905-1910), and the *Journals of the House of Representatives of Massachusetts, 1715-1727* (Cambridge, 1919-1926), of which seven volumes have been published down to 1727. In addition to the records of the colonies much material may be found in the collections of colonial laws.

The earlier part of the period for all of the colonies is also covered by the *Calendar of State Papers, Colonial Series, America and West Indies* (I-XIX, London, 1860-1925), for the years from 1691 to 1712. *The Acts of the Privy Council* (W. L. Grant and James Munro, eds., 4 vols., Hereford, Eng., 1908-1911), covers the entire period but is less useful for our purpose. *The Journal of the Commissioners for Trade and Plantations, 1709-1722* (4 vols., London, 1925), briefly calendars or lists thousands of papers dealing with colonial conditions. Some material on the American customs may be found in the *Calendar of Treasury Papers* (11 vols., London, 1868-1903).

Among the most valuable collections of papers and correspondence we may note: William Shirley, *Correspondence* (C. H. Lincoln, ed., 2 vols., N. Y., 1912); the *Belcher Papers* (Mass. Hist. Soc., *Colls.*, ser. 6, VI, VII); *Correspondence of the Colonial Governors of Rhode Island* (G. S. Kimball, ed., 2 vols., Boston, 1902); Jared Ingersoll, *Correspondence and Papers* (F. B. Dexter, ed., New Haven Colony Hist. Soc., *Papers*, IX); *Law Papers, 1741-1750* (3 vols., Conn. Hist. Soc., *Colls.*, XIII-XV); *Wolcott Papers, 1750-1754* (2 vols., *ibid.*, XV-XVI); *Fitch Papers, 1754-1766* (2 vols., *ibid.*, XVII-XVIII); Cadwallader Colden, *Papers* (6 vols., N. Y. Hist. Soc., *Colls.*, III-VII); *Correspondence between William Penn and James Logan, 1700-1750* (2 vols., Pa. Hist. Soc., *Memoirs*, IX-X); Alexander Spotswood, *Official Letters* (2 vols., Va. Hist. Soc., *Colls.*, I-II); *Dinwiddie Papers* (2 vols., Va. Hist. Soc., *Colls.*, III-IV); *Historical Collections of South Carolina* (B. R. Carroll, ed., 2 vols., N. Y., 1836).

Of the publications of historical societies and of historical magazines, all of the following should be carefully searched in addition to specific articles referred to in the later paragraphs: Massachusetts Historical Society, *Collections*, 75 vols.; Massachusetts Historical Society, *Proceedings*, 55 vols.; Colonial Society of Massachusetts, *Publications*, 24 vols.; Historical Society of Pennsylvania, *Memoirs*, 14 vols.; *Pennsylvania Magazine of History and Biography*, 46 vols.; *Maryland Historical Magazine*, 17 vols.; *Virginia Magazine of History and Biography* (published by the Virginia Historical Society), 30 vols.; *William and Mary College Quarterly*, 30 vols.; *South Carolina Historical and Genealogical Magazine* (published by the South Carolina Historical Society), 23 vols.; Georgia Historical Society, *Collections*, 9 vols. Most of these are continuing publications.

Of the very highest importance for the second half of the period are the various colonial newspapers, notably the almost perfect files of the Maryland and South Carolina *Gazettes*. The *Virginia Gazette* is of unique importance for commerce in that it lists the cargoes of the vessels entering and clearing. Unfortunately, although there are known to have been two complete files in existence, they have both been destroyed by fire and we have only those for 1736-1739 and 1751-1752.

GENERAL AND LOCAL HISTORIES

In *The American Nation: a History* (Albert Bushnell Hart, ed., 28 vols., N. Y., 1904-1918), E. B. Greene, *Provincial America, 1690-1740* (N. Y., 1905), covers the earlier part of the period, but it is notable that the next volume, G. E. Howard, *Preliminaries of the Revolution, 1763-1775* (N. Y., 1905), leaves a gap of twenty-three years, although R. G. Thwaites, *France in America, 1497-1763* (N. Y., 1905), fills it in partially. The second volume of Edward Channing, *History of the United States* (6 vols., N. Y., 1905 —), covers the whole period and is especially valuable on the commercial side. For South Carolina an excellent history may be found in the first two volumes of Edward McCrady, *History of South Carolina* (4 vols., N. Y., 1897-1902). J. T. Adams, *Revolutionary New England, 1691-1776* (Boston, 1923), covers the period for that section. Justin Winsor, *Memorial History of Boston* (4 vols., Boston, 1880-1881), although written forty years ago, remains one of the best histories of the larger towns. S. Judd, *History of Hadley* (Springfield, 1905); J. H. Trumbull, *The Memorial History of Hartford County* (2 vols., Boston, 1886); G. Sheldon, *A History of Deerfield* (2 vols., Deerfield, 1895-1896); Frances M. Caulkins, *History of New London* (New London, 1895); W. DeL. Love, *The Colonial History of Hartford* (Hartford, 1914); H. R. Stiles, *The History and Genealogies of Ancient Windsor* (2 vols., Hartford, 1891); and Gertrude S. Kimball, *Providence in Colonial Times* (Boston, 1912), all contain valuable economic and other data. The following half dozen, among others, have material bearing upon the land troubles of the colonists: Ellen D. Larned, *History of Windham County, Connecticut* (2 vols., Worcester, 1874); W. S. Heywood, *History of Westminster, Massachusetts* (Lowell, 1893); D. W. and R. F. Wells, *History of Hatfield, Massachusetts* (Springfield, 1910); J. H. Temple, *History of the Town of Palmer* (Palmer, 1889); Arthur Chase, *History of Ware, Massachusetts* (Cambridge, 1911) and G. W. Chase, *History of Haverhill* (Haverhill, 1861). O. J. Harvey, *History of Wilkes-Barre, Pa.* (2 vols., Wilkesbarre, 1909), is essential for the Susquehanna Land Company. J. F. Watson, *Annals of Philadelphia* (2 vols., Phila., 1857), is still useful for much information as to social manners and customs. *The Ancient City* (Annapolis, 1887), by E. S. Riley, has a good deal of social data for Annapolis.

For the western frontier of Virginia, J. A. Waddell, *Annals of Augusta County, Virginia, 1726-1871* (Richmond, 1886), and the earlier *History of Augusta County* (Staunton, 1882) by J. L. Peyton, are both valuable. J. H. Clewell, *History of Wachovia, North Carolina* (N. Y., 1902), and Reverend Alexander Gregg, *History of the Old*

Cheraws (Columbia, S. C., 1905), both have good material for the more southern colonies.

BIOGRAPHIES AND AUTOBIOGRAPHIES

Biographical material is notably scant as compared with the period immediately succeeding. The standard lives of Oglethorpe and Penn should be consulted for the two colonies founded by them. In Everett Kimball, *The Public Life of Joseph Dudley (Harvard Hist. Studies*, XV, 1911), and G. A. Wood, *William Shirley* (Columbia Univ., *Studies*, XCII, 1920), we have excellent pictures of royal governors, the one colonial and the other English-born. Alice M. Keys in *Cadwallader Colden* (N. Y., 1906) draws another royal official who was also a leading intellectual figure. The life of an early scientist is that of the botanist Bartram in William Darlington, *Memorials of John Bartram and Humphrey Marshall* (Phila., 1849). Franklin touched colonial life on every side and John Bigelow, *The Life of Benjamin Franklin* (3 vols., Phila., 1893), and the other biographies are essential. Both intellectual and religious life are illustrated in Barrett Wendell, *Cotton Mather* (N. Y., 1891); A. V. G. Allen, *Jonathan Edwards* (Boston, 1889); E. E. Beardsley, *Life and Correspondence of Samuel Johnson* (Boston, 1887); and H. W. Smith, *Life and Correspondence of Rev. William Smith* (2 vols., Phila., 1880). W. L. Stone, *Life and Times of Sir William Johnson,* (2 vols., Albany, 1865), and J. S. Walton, *Conrad Weiser and the Indian Policy of Colonial Pennsylvania* (Phila., 1900), deal with Indian relations and two of the most important figures of the colony in that regard.

There is very little biographical material relating to the business men and local public officials of this period, although there are many of importance from the social and economic standpoint, who await their biographers. For this field, L. H. Gipson, *Jared Ingersoll* (New Haven, 1920), is a model. West Indian contacts in the social life are illustrated in H. H. Ravenel, *Eliza Pinckney* (N. Y., 1902), and in S. F. Batchelder, "Colonel Henry Vassall,"

Cambridge Hist. Soc., *Proceeds,* X (1915), 5-78. The former, an account of one of the most charming women of colonial times, may be supplemented by the *Journal and Letters of Eliza Lucas* (Mrs. H. P. Holbrook, ed., Wormsloe, Ga., 1850). One of the typical Puritan figures of the earlier part of the period, Samuel Sewall is described in N. H. Chamberlain, *Samuel Sewall and the World He Lived in* (Boston, 1897). The student, however, must have recourse to the famous diary itself, one of the most important of all the social documents of the time—*Diary of Samuel Sewall, 1674-1729* (Mass. Hist. Soc., *Colls.,* ser. 5, V-VI, VII). This should be supplemented by the *Letter-Book of Samuel Sewall* (Mass. Hist. Soc., *Colls.,* ser. 6, I-II). Two other notable diaries are John Adams, *Works* (10 vols., Boston, 1850-1856), I-II, and the *Diary of Joshua Hempstead of New London* (New London County Hist. Soc., *Colls.,* I)—the latter a mine of information as to the lives of the simple people. The *Extracts from the Itineraries of Ezra Stiles* (F. B. Dexter, ed., New Haven, 1916) has miscellaneous data of value.

LOCAL GOVERNMENT AND TAXATION

The reader will find indispensable H. L. Osgood, *The American Colonies in the Eighteenth Century* (4 vols., N. Y., 1924). G. E. Howard, *An Introduction to the Local Constitutional History of the United States* (Johns Hopkins Univ., *Studies,* extra vols., IV-V, 1889), has much detailed information as to local governmental units although the theories of origins in vogue when the book was written are now discredited. Among other special studies of particular colonies we may note the following in the Johns Hopkins University, *Studies:* J. S. Bassett, *The Constitutional Beginnings of North Carolina,* XII (1894, no. 3); Edward Ingle, *Local Institutions of Virginia,* III (1885, nos. 2-3); same author, *Parish Institutions in Maryland,* I (1883, no. 6); L. W. Wilhelm, *Local Institutions of Maryland,* III (1885, nos. 5-7); W. P. Holcomb, *Pennsylvania Boroughs,* IV (1886, no. 4). Although dealing with the seventeenth century, P. A. Bruce, *Institutional History of Virginia in the Seventeenth Century* (2 vols., N. Y., 1910), is of first importance. The following works are essential: W. H. Fry, *New Hampshire as a Royal Province* (Columbia Univ., *Studies*, XXIX, 1908); E. P. Tanner, *The Province of New Jersey, 1664-1738 (ibid.*, XXX, 1908); E. J. Fisher, *New Jersey as a Royal Province, 1738-1776 (ibid.*, XLI, 1911); W. R. Shepherd, *History of the Proprietary Government in Pennsylvania (ibid.*, VI, 1896); N. D. Mereness, *Maryland as a Proprietary Province* (N. Y., 1901); C. L. Raper, *North Carolina: a Study in English Colonial Government* (N. Y., 1904); J. R. McCain, *Georgia as a Proprietary Province* (Boston, 1917). They vary much in interest and value, but each is, as yet, the only work in its field. E. B. Greene, *The Provincial Governor (Harvard Hist. Studies*, III, 1898), is a thoroughly scholarly treatment of its topic. F. R. Jones, *History of Taxation in Connecticut* (Johns Hopkins Univ., *Studies*, XIV, 1896, no. 8), has some material for this period, as has E. W. Capen, *The Historical Development of the Poor Law of Connecticut* (Columbia Univ., *Studies*, XXII, 1905). For the topics indicated the students should also consult William Hill, *First Stages of the Tariff Policy of the United States* (Am. Econ. Assoc., *Publs.*, VIII, 1893, no. 6), and A. A. Giesecke, *American Commercial Legislation before 1789* (Univ. of Pa., *Publs.*, 1910).

THE NON-ENGLISH STOCKS

E. E. Proper, *Colonial Immigration Laws* (Columbia Univ., *Studies*, XII, 1900), may well be read as an introduction to this section, as also St. G. L. Sioussat, *Economics and Politics in Maryland, 1720-1750* (Johns Hopkins Univ., *Studies*, XXI, 1903, nos. 6-7), which has a chapter on Dulany's relation to organized immigration.

SCOTCH. C. A. Hanna, *The Scotch-Irish* (2 vols., N. Y., 1902), has much matter badly arranged. C. K. Bolton, *Scotch-Irish Pioneers* (Boston, 1910), deals almost entirely with the movement before 1720. H. J. Ford, *The Scotch-*

Irish in America (Princeton, 1915), is good, but far from adequate. George Howe, *The Scotch-Irish and Their First Settlements in the Tyger River and Other Neighboring Precincts in South Carolina* (Columbia, 1861), deals with that colony. The papers in the *Proceedings* of the Scotch-Irish Society Congresses (10 vols., Nashville, 1889-1901) vary greatly in value, but there is much material in the best of them.

IRISH. There is little material on the Celtic-Irish immigration. The papers in the *Journal of the American-Irish Historical Society* (1897——), are disappointing. M. J. O'Brien in *A Hidden Phase of American History* (N. Y., 1919) has gathered interesting data but, as is almost invariably the case with the historians of these racial groups, makes sweeping claims which are not substantiated. In connection with this the student should read J. F. Jameson's review in the *American Historical Review*, XXVI (1921), 797-799.

GERMANS. At once the most ample and most scholarly treatment of the Germans is A. B. Faust, *The German Element in the United States* (2 vols., Boston, 1909). This also contains an exhaustive bibliography. *Falckner's Curieuse Nachricht* (J. F. Sachse, ed., Phila., 1905) is valuable for the early immigration literature. *Gottlieb Mittelberger's Journey to Pennsylvania, 1756* (C. T. Eben, tr., Phila., 1898) contains information as to the difficulties encountered by the immigrants. One of the best brief accounts of the movement is Oscar Kuhns, *The German and Swiss Settlements of Colonial Pennsylvania* (N. Y., 1914). The reader may also consult Friedrich Kapp, *Geschichte der Deutschen Einwanderung in Amerika* (Leipzig, 1868); Herrmann Schuricht, *History of the German Element in Virginia* (2 vols., Balt., 1898-1900); and J. W. Wayland, "The Germans of the Valley," *Va. Hist. Mag.*, IX (1901-1902), 337-352, X (1902-1903), 33-47. S. H. Cobb, *The Story of the Palatines* (N. Y., 1897), is a good account of that phase; and Lucy F. Bittinger, *The Germans in Colonial Times* (Phila., 1901), is a good popular account. M. D. Learned, *Life of Francis Daniel Pastorius* (Phila., 1908),

is a biography of the most important early leader.   V. H.
Todd has translated and edited *Christoph Von Graffenried's Account of the Founding of New Bern* (*Publications
of the N. C. Hist. Com.*, Raleigh, 1920) ; this tells the story
of the Palatines in Carolina.   The volumes of the *Proceedings* of the Pennsylvania-German Society are a mine of important articles, many of which have been published separately.   J. P. Hoskins has an interesting article on "German
Influence on Thought and Culture in the Colonial Period,"
in the *Princeton Theological Review*, V.

SWEDES.   We have two contemporary descriptions of the
Swedish settlement, of which the latter is of considerable
importance: T. C. Holm, *A Short Description of the Province of New Sweden, 1702* (Hist. Soc. of Pa., *Memoirs*, III,
1834) ; and Israel Acrelius, *A History of New Sweden*
(Stockholm, 1759, reptd. in Hist. Soc. of Pa., *Memoirs*,
XI, 1876).

SWISS.   Examples of emigrant literature may be found in
G. P. Voight, "Swiss Notes on South Carolina," *S. C. Hist.
and Geneal. Mag.*, XXI (1920), 93-104, and *Proposals
of Mr. Peter Purry of Newchatel for Encouragement of such
Swiss Protestants as should agree to accompany him to Carolina* (B. R. Carroll, comp., *Hist. Colls. of S. C.*, II, 1836),
121-140.   The best account of the movement is by A. B.
Faust, "Swiss Emigration to the American Colonies in the
18th Century," *Am. Hist. Rev.*, XXII (1916), 21-24, and
*List of Swiss Emigrants in the 18th Century to the North
American Colonies* (Wash., 1920).

FRENCH.   L. J. Fosdick, *The French Blood in America*
(Boston, 1911), is unscientific and has the usual characteristics of the literature of these groups, but is the only single
volume dealing with the subject.   There are many valuable
papers in the *Proceedings* of the Huguenot Society of America, 1883-1909, and in the *Transactions* of the Huguenot
Society of South Carolina (16 vols., 1889 —).   The *Documents Relating to the Huguenot Emigration* (R. A. Brock,
ed., Va. Hist. Soc., *Colls.*, n.s., V, 1886), has good material
relating mainly to Virginia.   Jacques Fontaine, *Memoirs of
a Huguenot Family . . . 1715 and 1716* (Ann Maury, tr.,

N. Y., 1872), is much the best single contribution to this subject.

JEWS, WELSH, DUTCH. There is no volume dealing with the Jews in the colonial period, but there is a good deal of data in the many papers of varying merit in the *Publications* of the American Jewish Historical Society (Balt., 1893——). C. H. Browning, *Welsh Settlements in Pennsylvania* (Phila., 1912), contains a good deal as to their original emigration and their land arrangements in the colony. In spite of a considerable literature, little work of a scientific character has been done regarding Dutch influence and the Dutch settlers themselves. H. T. Colenbrander, "The Dutch Element in American History," Am. Hist. Assoc., *Rep. for 1919*, 193-201, and Ruth Putnam, "The Dutch Element in the United States," *ibid.*, 205-218, should be consulted as checks on extravagant claims.

LAND

Lois K. Mathews, *The Expansion of New England* (Boston, 1909), is an excellent exposition of the gradual spread of settlement and the opening up of new lands. For the land systems of the various sections and colonies, the student may advantageously consult: Melville Egleston, *The Land Systems of the New England Colonies* (Johns Hopkins Univ., *Studies*, IV, 1886, nos. 11-12); Edward Channing, *The Narragansett Planters (ibid.*, IV, 1886, no. 3)—a study of a section of Rhode Island affording a unique type of land development in New England; C. W. Spencer, "The Land System of Colonial New York," N. Y. State Hist. Assoc., *Proceeds.*, XVI (1917), 150-164, dealing mainly with excessive grants and policies; C. P. Gould, *The Land System in Maryland, 1720-1765* (Johns Hopkins Univ., *Studies*, XXXI, 1913, no. 1), an important and scholarly treatment; J. S. Ballagh, "Introduction to Southern Economic History—the Land System," Am. Hist. Assoc., *Rep. for 1897*, 101-129, calling for revision as to size of holdings; T. J. Wertenbaker, *The Planters of Colonial Virginia* (Princeton, 1922)—of first importance for size of land

holdings; H. A. M. Smith, "The Baronies of South Carolina," *S. C. Hist. and Geneal. Mag.,* XI-XV (1910-1914),
XVIII (1917), *passim.* The only comprehensive work on
the quitrent is an excellent one by B. W. Bond, *The Quit-
Rent System in the American Colonies* (New Haven, 1919).
There is much material relating to the Susquehanna Company in *Pennsylvania Archives,* ser. 2, XVIII, and in the
excellent little monograph by Edith A. Bailey, "Influences
toward Radicalism in Connecticut, 1754-1776," Smith Col.,
Studies, V (1920), 179-252. W. C. Pendleton, *History of
Tazewell County and Southwest Virginia, 1748-1920*
(Richmond, 1920), contains material on the Virginia land
companies. The whole topic is closely bound up with local
government, local history and immigration, and should be
studied in conjunction with the works noted in those
connections.

LAW AND LEGAL INSTITUTIONS

The most important collections of the laws of the several
colonies are cited in E. Channing, A. B. Hart and F. J.
Turner, *Guide to the Study and Reading of American History* (revised edn., Boston, 1912). For courts and the administration of law, the various works cited under Local
Government and Taxation should be consulted. There are
also a few separate essays, such as John Noble, "Notes on
Admiralty Jurisdiction in the Colony and in the Province of
the Massachusetts Bay," Col. Society Mass., *Publs.,* VIII
(1903), 150-185; William Nelson, *The Law and Practice
of New Jersey from the earliest Times concerning the Pro-
bate of Wills,* etc. (Paterson, 1919); and Harrington Putnam, "The Early Administration of Equity in this Country,"
N. J. State Bar Assoc., *Year Book* (1918-1919). Of first
importance are the articles in *Select Essays in Anglo-American Legal History* (3 vols., Boston, 1907), by C. M.
Andrews and others. Two important short studies, the one
of the common law and the other of statute law in the colonies, are: St. G. L. Sioussat, *The English Statutes in Maryland* (Johns Hopkins Univ. *Studies,* XXI, 1903, nos.

11-12), and P. S. Reinsch, *English Common Law in the Early American Colonies* (Univ. of Wis., *Bull.,* no. 31, *Econ., Pol. Science and Hist. Series,* II, no. 4, 1899). A. H. Carpenter treats of another factor in "Habeas Corpus in the Colonies," *Am. Hist. Rev.,* VIII (1902), 18-27. Roscoe Pound, *The Spirit of the Common Law* (Boston, 1921), discusses the various influences in the development of American common law. C. J. Hilkey, *Legal Development in Colonial Massachusetts, 1630-1686* (Columbia Univ., *Studies,* XXXVII, 1910, no. 2), is valuable for the study of the foundations and has a selected bibliography. There are a number of works dealing with the relations of the colonial legislatures and judiciary to England, of which the most useful for our purpose is E. B. Russell, *The Review of American Colonial Legislation by the King in Council* (Columbia Univ., *Studies,* LXIV, 1915, no. 2); see also G. A. Washburne, *Imperial Control of the Administration of Justice in the Thirteen American Colonies* (*ibid.,* C V, 1923). The *Reports by Sir John Randolph and by Edward Barradall of Decisions of the General Court of Virginia, 1728-1741* (R. T. Barton, ed., 2 vols., Boston, 1909) and Josiah Quincy, Jr., *Reports of Cases Argued and Adjudged in the Superior Court of the Province of Massachusetts Bay between 1761 and 1772* (Boston, 1865), both have valuable material.

MORALITY AND THE FAMILY

There is no comprehensive essay dealing with the public or private morals of the colonists. The condemnatory sermons of the clergy, which are perennial, cannot be taken at their face value, but there is material scattered through the descriptions of travelers, the diaries of settlers, the local court records, the newspapers and other sources from which an illuminating exposition might be made. The first volume of A. W. Calhoun, *A Social History of the American Family* (3 vols., Cleveland, 1917), which deals with the colonial period, is somewhat disappointing, but it is the only serious work dealing with that topic and sheds some light on the subject of sex relations. Sexual morality, or immorality, in New England is now fairly well documented for the student. C. F. Adams, "Some Phases of Sexual Morality and Church Discipline in Colonial New England," Mass. Hist. Soc., *Proceeds.*, ser. 2, VI (1891), 477-516, was the first to call attention to the matter. H. R. Stiles, *Bundling, its Origin, Progress and Decline in America* (Albany, 1869), is inadequate, but is the only work dealing with a phenomenon which was far more widespread than the author knew. *A Covenant for Reformation Assented to in Long Meadow, in Springfield, Aug. 22, 1728* is among the broadsides in the Library of Congress.

Apart from Calhoun's work, no effort has yet been made to treat the topic of family life in other than a popular and romantic fashion. Alice Morse Earle, *Child Life in Colonial Days* (N. Y., 1899), and same author, *Home Life in Colonial Days* (N. Y., 1899), are delightful books and her material was mostly drawn from original sources. Rosalie V. Halsey, *Forgotten Books of the American Nursery* (Boston, 1911) deals with children's books as early as the seventeen fifties. Alexander Graydon, *Memoirs of a Life chiefly Passed in Pennsylvania* (Edinburgh, 1822), contains in its earlier chapters an excellent description of a Philadelphia boyhood at the close of our period. Elizabeth A. Dexter, *Colonial Women of Affairs* (Boston, 1924) presents a number of women in relation to concerns other than the family.

HUMANITARIANISM

In so far as the humanitarian spirit influenced legislation and public institutions it may be followed in: E. W. Capen, *The Historical Development of the Poor Law in Connecticut* (already cited); John Cummings, *Poor Laws of Massachusetts and New York* (Ithaca, 1895); H. E. Barnes, *A History of the Penal, Reformatory and Correctional Institutions of the State of New Jersey* (Trenton, 1918), which contains a brief treatment of the colonial period; T. G. Norton, *The History of the Pennsylvania Hospital, 1751-1895* (Phila., 1895); J. H. Benton, *Warning out in New England* (Boston, 1911); and H. M. Hurd, *The Institutional Care of the Insane in the United States and Canada* (4 vols., Balt., 1916). *The Constitution and By-Laws of the Scots' Charitable Society of Boston* (Boston, 1896) gives many extracts from one of the earliest voluntary charitable societies. Mary S. Locke, *Anti-Slavery in America, 1619-1908* (Radcliffe Col., *Monographs*, XI, 1901), traces the growth of antislavery sentiment in the contemporary literature. John Woolman, *Journal* (J. G. Whittier, ed., Boston, 1871), is also useful for this phase. For missionary endeavor, there are W. DeL. Love, *Samson Occom and the Christian Indians of New England* (Boston, 1899); Frederick Chase, *History of Dartmouth College and the Town of Hanover* (Cambridge, 1891)—the outcome of Wheelock's Indian School; Jonathan Edwards, *Memoirs of the Rev. David Brainerd* (New Haven, 1822); and Thomas Brainerd, *Life of John Brainerd* (Phila., 1865).

RELIGION AND THE GREAT AWAKENING

For the relations between the churches and the colonial governments we have: S. H. Cobb, *The Rise of Religious Liberty in America* (N. Y., 1902); M. Louise Greene, *The Development of Religious Liberty in Connecticut* (Boston, 1905); B. C. Steiner, "The Restoration of the Proprietary of Maryland and the Legislation against the Roman Catholics during the Governorship of Captain John Hart, 1714-1720," Am. Hist. Assoc., *Rep. for 1899*, I, 231-307; H. R. McIlwaine, *The Struggle of Protestant Dissenters for Real Religious Toleration in Virginia* (Johns Hopkins Univ., *Studies*, XII, 1894, no. 4); S. B. Weeks, *The Religious Development in the Province of North Carolina* (ibid., X, 1892, nos. 5-6); and same author, *Church and State in North Carolina* (ibid., XI, 1893, nos. 5-6). A. L. Cross, *The Anglican Episcopate and the American Colonies* (*Harvard Hist. Studies*, IX, 1902), is an able study of the topic indicated.

For the various denominations, the volumes of *The American Church History Series* (12 vols., N. Y., 1893-

1897) will be useful. Of the enormous literature on this subject, the following works may be specified: H. M. Dexter, *The Congregationalism of the Last 300 Years* (N. Y., 1880)—a valuable compendious work with a bibliography so extensive and so arranged as to be useless for the general reader; F. H. Foster, *A Genetic History of New England Theology* (Chicago, 1907)—an excellent study of the subject; Jonathan Edwards, *Works* (4 vols., N. Y., 1856); Cotton Mather, *Diary* (Mass. Hist. Soc., *Colls.*, ser. 8, VII-VIII); Williston Walker, *The Creeds and Platforms of Congregationalism* (N. Y., 1893); J. S. M. Anderson, *The History of the Church of England in the Colonies and Foreign Dependencies of the British Empire* (3 vols., London, 1845); F. L. Hawkes and W. S. Perry, *Documentary History of the Protestant Episcopal Church in the United States of America* (N. Y., 1863-1864); Isaac Backus, *A History of New England with Particular Reference to the Denomination of Christians called Baptists* (Newton, 1871); R. M. Jones, *The Quakers in the American Colonies* (London, 1911); J. G. Shea, *The Catholic Church in Colonial Days* (N. Y., 1880); J. F. Sachse, *The German Sectarians of Pennsylvania, 1742-1880* (Phila., 1900); same author, *The German Pietists of Provincial Pennsylvania* (Phila., 1895); Lucy F. Bittinger, *German Religious Life in Colonial Times* (Phila., 1906).

For the Great Awakening the only two general accounts are Joseph Tracy, *The Great Awakening* (Boston, 1842), mainly concerned with New England, and C. H. Maxson, *The Great Awakening in the Middle Colonies* (Chicago, 1920), with a useful bibliography. Of the events of the movement the best contemporary account is *The Christian History* (Thomas Prince, Jr., ed., 2 vols., Boston, 1744-1745)—a weekly publication devoted to describing the progress of the revival. The accounts in Jonathan Edwards, *Works*, should be consulted; also Charles Chauncy (who was opposed to the movement), *Enthusiasm Described and Caution'd Against* (Boston, 1742); same author, *A Letter from a Gentleman in Boston to Mr. Geo. Wishart* (Edinburgh, 1742, reptd. Clarendon Hist. Soc., 1883); same author,

Some Seasonable Thoughts on the State of Religion in New England (Boston, 1743).

EDUCATION

E. G. Dexter, *A History of Education in the United States* (N. Y., 1922 ed.), and E. P. Cubberley, *Public Education in the United States* (Boston, 1919), are useful as general outlines. E. E. Brown, *The Making of our Middle Schools* (N. Y., 1921), is excellent and gives the English background. There are also the histories of the earlier colleges such as Yale, Dartmouth, Harvard, Columbia, Princeton, University of Pennsylvania and William and Mary. The place of apprenticeship in education is developed by R. F. Seybolt in *Apprenticeship and Apprentice Education in Colonial New England* (Teachers Col., Columbia Univ., *Contribs.*, LXXXV, 1917). Clifton Johnson, *Old Time Schools and School Books* (N. Y., 1917), is a popular work with interesting data on textbooks. Among the most useful works on the lower schools of the different colonies are: W. H. Small, *Early New England Schools* (Boston, 1914)—a good work though with many minor errors and which paints the conditions too optimistically; Harlan Updegraff, *The Origin of the Moving School in Massachusetts* (Teachers Col., Columbia Univ., *Contribs.*, XVII, 1908)—a very able and suggestive study. Of the several histories of education in Rhode Island the best is Charles Carroll, *Public Education in Rhode Island* (Providence, 1918). B. C. Steiner, *The History of Education in Connecticut* (U. S. Bureau of Education, *Circular of Information No. 2*, XIV, 1893), is one of a series which cover most of the original colonies. Another is Sidney Sherwood, *The University of the State of New York* (N. Y., 1900). W. W. Kemp, *The Support of Schools in Colonial New York by the Society for the Propagation of the Gospel* (Teachers Col., Columbia Univ., *Contribs.*, XVI, 1913), is an excellent study. Another exceedingly good one from the same institution is Thomas Woody, *Early Quaker Education in Pennsylvania* (*ibid.*, CV, 1920). For the South the best general account is E. W.

Knight, *Public Education in the South* (Boston, 1922), which deals to some extent with the colonial period and has a bibliography.

MEDICINE AND SCIENCE

Far more interest has been shown in early medicine than in any other of the sciences in colonial times. A good comprehensive account is F. R. Packard, *The History of Medicine in the United States* (Phila., 1901). The best biographical account is H. A. Kelly, *Cyclopedia of American Medical Biography* (2 vols., Phila., 1912). Examples of early medical literature may be found in "Extracts from the Book of Physick of William Penn," *Pa. Mag. of Hist. and Biog.*, XI (1916), 472-479, and John Wesley, *Primitive Physic or an Easy and Natural Method of Curing Most Diseases* (Trenton, 1788), which was first published in 1747 and went through at least sixteen editions by 1788. Much scattered material may be found in such books and articles as the following: Horace Davis, "Dr. Benjamin Gott: a Family of Doctors," Col. Soc. Mass., *Publs.*, XII (1909), 214-219; O. W. Holmes, "The Medical Profession in Massachusetts," *Medical Essays* (Boston, 1883), 312-369; F. H. Brown, "The Practice of Medicine in New England before 1700," Bostonian Society, *Publs.*, VIII (1911), 94-120; J. M. Toner, *Contributions to the Annals of Medical Progress and Medical Education in the United States* (Wash., 1874); G. W. Russell, *Early Medicine and Early Medical Men in Connecticut* (Hartford, 1892); Henry Bronson, "Medical History and Biography," New Haven Colony Hist. Soc., *Papers*, II (1877), 239-388; Theodore Diller, *Franklin's Contributions to Medicine* (Brooklyn, 1912); Richard Dillard, *Some Early Physicians of the Albemarle* (Raleigh, 1911); G. W. Norris, *The Early History of Medicine in Philadelphia* (Phila., 1886). The article on "Edward Bromfield," *American Magazine* (Boston, 1746), is also of interest. Lyman Carrier, "Dr. John Mitchell," Am. Hist. Assoc., *Rep. for 1918*, I, 201-219, is the most recent and best notice of that physician and scientist.

Next to medicine, botany was the main scientific interest of the colonists. Besides Darlington, *Memorials of John Bartram* (cited under Biographies), there are H. A. Kelly, *Some American Medical Botanists* (Troy, 1914), and J. W. Harshberger, *The Botanists of Philadelphia and their Work* (Phila., 1899). W. T. Sedgick and H. W. Tyler, *A Short History of Science* (N. Y., 1917), gives a summary view of the other sciences, and G. B. Goode, *The Beginnings of Natural History in America* (Biological Society of Washington, *Proceeds.*, III, 1884-1886), is very useful. The articles in the first volume of the *Records of the Celebration of the 200th Anniversary of the Birth of Franklin* (Phila., 1906) should be consulted, and useful information is found in C. W. Parsons, "Early Votaries of Natural Science in Rhode Island," R. I. Hist. Soc., *Colls.*, VII (1885), 241-263; "Early Letters from South Carolina upon Natural History," *S. C. Hist. and Geneal. Mag.*, XXII (1920), 3-9—from Sloane MSS., British Museum; and G. L. Kittredge, "Cotton Mather's Scientific Communications to the Royal Society," Am. Antiq. Soc., *Proceeds.*, n.s., XXVI (1916), 18-57. The transition between the religious and scientific points of view may be found in Cotton Mather, *The Christian Philosopher* (London, 1721). For the founding of the American Philosophical Society, see *An Historical Account of the Origin and Formation of the American Philosophical Society* (Phila., 1914), and *Early Proceedings of the American Philosophical Society* (Phila., 1884).

LITERATURE, PHILOSOPHY AND LIBRARIES

The first volume of *The Cambridge History of American Literature* (N. Y., 1917) is the best general account of colonial literature and has extended bibliographies. It by no means, however, wholly supersedes M. C. Tyler, *A History of American Literature* (2 vols., N. Y., 1878-1879), II (1677-1765), which in some respects, even yet, is more satisfactory. These works will serve amply as guides and there is no need to specify here individual authors. The most extensive work on our early philosophy, and an excellent one, is

I. W. Riley, *American Philosophy, the Early Schools* (N. Y., 1907). The same author's *American Thought* (rev. ed., N. Y., 1923) is also useful. C. E. Merriam, *A History of American Political Theories* (N. Y., 1903), gives a good brief account of colonial political thought. Nothing in this field, however, will take the place for the student of a thorough first-hand study of the political writings of John Locke in any one of their several editions.

With regard to books and libraries, as to so many topics, the student will find much more scholarly material relating to New England than to the Southern colonies. There is a good deal of information as to the early bookshops in G. E. Littlefield, *Early Boston Booksellers* (Boston, 1900). T. G. Wright, *Literary Culture in Early New England, 1620-1730* (New Haven, 1920), is scholarly and extremely useful, though the evidence of culture presented must not be taken as typical of the community at large. Isaiah Thomas, *The History of Printing in America* (Am. Antiq. Soc., *Colls.*, V-VI, 1874), is still indispensable for this section, as for the next. Of the two most notable private libraries in the colonies the catalogue of Byrd's collection will be found in J. S. Bassett, *Writings of Colonel William Byrd* (N. Y., 1901), and that of Mather in J. H. Tuttle, "The Libraries of the Mathers," Am. Antiq. Soc., *Proceeds.*, n.s., XX (1909-1910), 269-356. The only general account of colonial public libraries is still H. E. Scudder, *Public Libraries a Hundred Years Ago* (in *Public Libraries in the United States*, pt. I, Wash., 1876), but much new material has come to light since its publication. A. B. Keep, *The Library in Colonial New York, 1698-1776* (N. Y., 1908), is of great value, and E. V. Lamberton, "Colonial Libraries of Pennsylvania," *Pa. Mag. of Hist. and Biog.*, XLII (1918), no. 3, is useful.

NEWSPAPERS, MAGAZINES AND ALMANACS

Thomas, *History of Printing* (already cited), is essential, and Elizabeth C. Cook has done a good piece of work in her *Literary Influences in Colonial Newspapers, 1704-1750* (Columbia Univ., *Studies in English and Comparative Lit-*

erature, 1912). Daniel Miller has a good account of the early foreign press in *Early German-American Newspapers* (Pa. German Soc., *Proceeds.*, XXIX, 1908, pt. xxii), and W. L. King gives extracts in *The Newspaper Press of Charleston, S. C.* (Charleston, 1872). A large amount of material from the *Boston News-Letter* down to 1707 is reprinted in L. H. Weeks and E. M. Bacon, *An Historical Digest of the Provincial Press, Mass. Series* (Boston, 1911, 1 vol.—all published) ; and volumes xi, xii and xix of the *Archives of the State of New Jersey* (W. A. Whitehead and others, eds., ser. 1, 27 vols., Newark and Paterson, 1846-1905) are made up of newspaper extracts. The student, however, can substitute nothing for a study of the original papers themselves. The best guide to their location is C. S. Brigham, "Bibliography of American Newspapers, 1690-1820," in recent volumes of Am. Antiq. Soc., *Proceeds.*, and still in progress.

The best account of the development of the freedom of the press is C. A. Duniway, *The Development of the Freedom of the Press in Massachusetts (Harvard Hist. Studies,* XII, 1906). The Zenger case is given by L. A. Rutherfurd, *John Peter Zenger, His Press, His Trial, and a Bibliography of Zenger Imprints* (N. Y., 1904).

There is no separate comprehensive study of the magazines of the period. A. H. Smyth, *The Philadelphia Magazines and their Contributors, 1741-1850* (Phila., 1892), has a good account of the *American Magazine* of 1757. Two guides to almanacs, both New England, are H. M. Chapin, "Check List of Rhode Island Almanacs, 1643-1850," Am. Antiq. Soc., *Proceeds.*, n.s., XXV (1915), 19-54, and C. L. Nichols, "Notes on the Almanacs of Massachusetts," *ibid.*, XXII (1912), 15-134. Sam Briggs, *The Almanacs of Nathaniel Ames, 1723-1775* (Cleveland, 1891), reprints much of their contents.

THE FINE ARTS

ARCHITECTURE. Fiske Kimball, *Domestic Architecture of the American Colonies and of the Early Republic* (N. Y.,

1922), is a thoroughly scientific account, but by no means covers the entire field. For the general reader perhaps the best introduction is H. D. Eberlein, *The Architecture of Colonial America* (Boston, 1921), an excellent little book which touches upon the non-English influences. Of special interest is the pictorial approach afforded by T. F. Hamlin, *The American Spirit in Architecture* (R. H. Gabriel, ed., *The Pageant of America*, XIII, New Haven, 1926). As samples of the English books on building which had such a vogue, the reader may consult Batty Langley, *The Gentleman or Builders Companion, containing Variety of useful Designs for Doors*, *Gateways, Peers, Pavilions*, etc. (London, 1739), or his *The Builder's Jewel or the Youth's Instructor and Workman's Remembrancer* (London, eleven editions between 1741 and 1768). On the architecture of the different sections there is a considerable literature which varies from excellence to rubbish. The work on *Old Houses of Connecticut* (Bertha C. Trowbridge, ed., New Haven, 1923), under the supervision of C. M. Andrews, with views and floor plans is excellent. Mary H. Northend, *Historic Houses of New England* (Boston, 1914), and A. G. Robinson, *Old New England Houses* (N. Y., 1920), and same author, *Old New England Doorways* (N. Y., 1920), are popular and have many good illustrations. For Philadelphia we have H. D. Eberlein and H. M. Lippincott, *The Colonial Homes of Philadelphia and its Neighborhood* (Phila., 1912), and Frank Cousins and P. M. Riley, *The Colonial Architecture of Philadelphia* (Phila., 1920), both popularly written texts. L. A. Coffin and A. C. Holden, *Brick Architecture of the Colonial Period in Maryland and Virginia* (N. Y., 1919), is by far the best book on any section of the colonies and has a wealth of fine illustrations. R. A. Lancaster, Jr., *Historic Virginia Homes and Churches* (Phila., 1915), is of the popular type, as is also Harriette K. Leiding, *Historic Homes of South Carolina* (Phila., 1921). Alice R. and D. E. Huger Smith, *The Dwelling Houses of Charleston, South Carolina* (Phila., 1917), is a more careful study and one of the very few works dealing with the utterly neglected colonial history of that important town.

SCULPTURE AND PAINTING. Practically no attention has been paid to the beginnings of colonial interest in sculpture. For painting, William Dunlap, *A History of the Rise and Progress of the Arts of Design in the United States* (Boston, 1918, first published 1834), is still useful. Many valuable reproductions may be found in *Early American Paintings, Catalogue of an Exhibition held in the Museum of the Brooklyn Institute of Arts and Sciences* (Brooklyn, 1917). All of the following are useful for biographical data: F. W. Bayley, *Little Known Early American Portrait Painters* (Boston, n. d.); J. H. Morgan, *Early American Painters* (N. Y. Hist. Soc., 1921); F. W. Bayley, *The Life and Works of John Singleton Copley* (Boston, 1915); W. H. Whitmore, "The Early Painters and Engravers of New England," Mass. Hist. Soc., *Proceeds.*, IX (1886), 196-216; R. A. Brock, "Virginia's Past in Portraiture," *William and Mary College Quart.*, II (1893-1894), 121.

MUSIC AND THE THEATER. By far the best two works on music are O. G. Sonneck, *Early Concert Life in America, 1731-1800* (Leipzig, 1907), and same author, *Early Opera in America* (Boston, 1915)—the latter being important for the theater also. In regard to the latter C. P. Daly, *First Theater in America* (Dunlap Soc., *Publs.*, n. s., I, N. Y., 1896), should not be overlooked. G. O. Seilhamer, *History of the American Theatre* (3 vols., Phila., 1888), is a voluminous work containing much material: the general account is summarized in Arthur Hornblow, *A History of the Theater in America* (2 vols., Phila., 1919). G. C. D. Odell, *Annals of the New York Stage* (2 vols., N. Y., 1927), is an elaborate and authoritative work which will run ultimately to six volumes; the first volume covers the early eighteenth century.

MINOR ARTS. H. D. Eberlein and Abbot McClure, *The Practical Book of Early American Arts and Crafts* (Phila., 1916), is good, but much of it deals with material beyond our period. Of the minor arts silver has received the most attention and there are a number of good works relating to it. The most readily accessible and best for general use is F. H. Bigelow, *Historic Silver of the Colonies and its Makers* (N.

Y., 1917). F. W. Hunter, *Stiegel Glass* (Boston, 1914), is the only work on that subject and has some beautiful colored reproductions. Lace is treated by Emily N. Vanderpoel, *American Lace and Lace-Makers* (New Haven, 1923), and samplers receive exhaustive and probably definitive treatment by Ethel S. Bolton and Eva J. Coe in *American Samplers* (Boston, 1921).

HOUSEHOLD FURNISHINGS AND WEARING APPAREL

The best book on furniture is L. V. Lockwood, *Colonial Furniture* (2 vols., N. Y., 1913). Esther Singleton, *The Furniture of our Forefathers* (N. Y., 1922), has a great deal of material and many illustrations, but is badly constructed and difficult to use except as a source book. Kate Sanborn, *Old Time Wall Papers* (N. Y., 1905), and Arthur Hayward, *Colonial Lighting* (Boston, 1923), are good treatments of their special topics. The best work on wearing apparel is Elizabeth McClellan, *Historic Dress in America, 1607-1800* (Phila., 1904). Alice Morse Earle, *Two Centuries of Costume* (2 vols., N. Y., 1903), is less satisfactory.

MANNERS AND CUSTOMS

The original material is widely scattered and much of it is to be found in works listed under other headings, more particularly Travels, and Biographies and Autobiographies. There is a vast quantity of secondary works dealing with the topics, frequently charmingly written. Almost invariably, however, they treat the entire colonial period as one, as if the decades brought no changes. Also, as a rule, it is the quaint or picturesque which is most stressed, so that the reader must use the books with considerable caution. The best small compendium is C. M. Andrews, *Colonial Folkways* (A. Johnson, ed., *The Chronicles of America Series*, 50 vols., New Haven, 1918-1921, XI). Mary N. Stanard, *Colonial Virginia, Its People and Customs* (Phila., 1917), is excellent for that colony, and Esther Singleton, *Social New York under the Georges, 1714-1776* (N. Y., 1902), has some very good material. W. B. Weeden, *Early Rhode Island*

(N. Y., 1910), is useful for that colony. Diaries, like that of Samuel Sewall previously cited, or the personal journals of more obscure men, some of which have come down to us, are important quarries of source material. E. S. Riley, *The Ancient City* (Annapolis, 1887), has a good deal of information on social clubs. H. L. Stillson, ed., *History of the Ancient and Honorable Fraternity of Free and Accepted Masons* (Boston, 1898), gives the best information as to that organization. J. H. Stiness, *A Century of Lotteries in Rhode Island, 1744-1844* (Providence, 1896), is the only volume on the lottery in the period. Much information on horse racing and breeding is in J. H. Wallace, *The Horse of America* (N. Y., 1897), and F. B. Culver, *Blooded Horses of Colonial Days* (Balt., 1922).

THE BUSINESS OF MAKING A LIVING

The best two general works are W. B. Weeden, *Economic and Social History of New England, 1620-1789* (2 vols., Boston, 1890), and P. A. Bruce, *Economic History of Virginia in the 17th Century* (2 vols., N. Y., 1896)—although the latter covers only the first decade of our period.

AGRICULTURE. Although it describes conditions just at the end of the colonial period, by far the most important source on colonial farming is *American Husbandry* (2 vols., London, 1775) which has been attributed to John Mitchell and also Arthur Young, and which has been used less than it deserves to be. For the economy of a large Southern plantation, both commercial and agricultural, there is much good material in the Letters of William Fitzhugh (*Va. Mag. of Hist. and Biog.*, I-VII) *passim;* Letters of William Byrd (*ibid.*, IX, 1901-1902), and Jared Eliot, *Essays on Field Husbandry* (reptd. from the first edition of 1747 in Mass. Soc. for Promoting Agriculture, *Papers*, 1911).

FUR TRADE. There is no satisfactory monograph on this subject. C. A. Hanna, *The Wilderness Trail* (N. Y., 1911), has valuable material, but is badly constructed. Sir William Johnson, *Papers* (J. Sullivan and A. C. Flick, eds., 4 vols., Albany, 1921-1925), contains much material, but as the wilderness of 3600 pages has not yet been provided with an index, its usefulness is impaired.   C. H. McIlwain's introduction to his edition of Peter Wraxall, *An Abridgment of the Indian Affairs (Harvard Hist. Studies,* XXI, 1915), is exceedingly good.   Unfortunately this volume also has no index.   There are some data in Benjamin Martyn, *An Impartial Inquiry into the State and Utility of the Province of Georgia* (London, 1741)—reptd. in Ga. Hist. Soc., *Colls.,* I (1840) ; Thomas Stevens, *A State of the Province of Georgia* (London, 1742)—reptd., *ibid.,* II (1842) ; Lord Percival, *A Brief Account of the Causes that have Retarded the Progress of the Colony of Georgia* (London, 1743)—reptd., *ibid.,* II (1842) ; E. G. M. Boutel-Dumont, *Histoire et Commerce des Colonies Angloises dans l'Amerique Septentrionale* (London, 1755) ; Alexander Spotswood, *Official Letters* (Va. Hist. Soc., *Colls.,* n. s., I-II, 1882) ; *Dinwiddie Papers (ibid.,* III-IV, 1883-1884) ; *Calendar of Virginia State Papers* (11 vols., W. P. Palmer and others, eds., Richmond, 1875-1893) ; *Baxter MSS. (Documentary History of the State of Maine,* IV-VI, Portland, Me., 1889-1900) ; and especially valuable among the colonial records, the *New York Colonial Documents,* the *Pennsylvania Archives* and the *North Carolina Colonial Records.*

TRADE AND COMMERCE.   For an understanding of the trade system and theory of the empire, G. L. Beer, *British Colonial Policy, 1754-1765* (N. Y., 1907), and same author, *The Old Colonial System, 1660-1754* (2 vols., N. Y., 1912), are fundamental.   The only criticism of Beer's brilliant work is that he tends occasionally to underrate the adverse effect of some of the English restrictions on colonial trade.   Gustav Schmoller, *The Mercantile System and Its Historical Significance* (N. Y., 1896), should be read for a general understanding of the mercantile theory.   Edward Channing, "The Navigation Laws," Am. Antiq. Soc., *Proceeds.,* n. s., VI (1889), 160-179, deals with the acts more specifically.   C. M. Andrews, "Colonial Commerce," *Am. Hist. Rev.,* XX (1914-1915), 40-64, describes the trade routes, and both that article and his "Anglo-French Commercial Rivalry, 1700-1750," *ibid.,* 39-556, 761-780, are essential studies. John Robinson and G. F. Dow, *The Sailing Ships of New England, 1607-1907* (Marine Research Soc., I, Salem, 1922), gives much information as to the ships which bore the commerce. The first volume of E. R. Johnson son and others, *History of Domestic and Foreign Commerce of the United States* (2 vols., Wash., 1915), is the most recent summary and has valuable references. For the illicit trade at the opening of the period, one of the most voluminous sources is R. N. Toppan, *Edward Randolph* (7 vols., Boston, 1898-1909).

Provincial and sectional treatments of commerce may be found in many of the works listed under General and Local Histories. In addition, Gipson, *Jared Ingersoll* (cited under Biographies), is indispensable for the lumber business of the North and business developments in the latter part of the period. R. G. Albion, *Forests and Sea Power (Harvard Economic Studies,* 1926), tells the story of the mast trade. Eleanor L. Lord, *Industrial Experiments in the British Colonies* (Johns Hopkins Univ., *Studies,* extra vol. xvii, 1898), also deals with lumbering and naval stores. M. S. Morriss, *Colonial Trade of Maryland, 1689-1715 (ibid.,* XXXII, 1914), is very important for that colony. C. P. Gould, *Money and Transportation in Maryland, 1720-1765 (ibid.,* XXXIII 1915, no. 1), is also excellent. Bassett's introduction to his *Writings of Colonel William Byrd,* previously noted, is useful for Virginia, as is also his "The Relation between the Virginia Planter and the London Merchant," Am. Hist. Assoc., *Rep. for 1901,* I, 551-573. W. J. Ashley, "American Smuggling, 1660-1760" (in his *Surveys Historic and Economic,* London, 1900), deals with that phase. For the West India trade, F. W. Pitman, *The Development of the British West Indies, 1700-1763* (New Haven, 1917), is invaluable. No attempt can be made here to deal with the voluminous pamphlet literature of the time. Sufficient reference for the ordinary student may be found in the footnotes to the works by Beer (cited above) and Adams, *Revolutionary New England.*

MANUFACTURING. V. S. Clark, *History of Manufactures in the United States, 1607-1860* (Wash., 1916), is the most recent general summary of our knowledge, but does not wholly supersede the still useful work by J. L. Bishop, *A History of American Manufactures, 1608-1860* (2 vols., Phila., 1861). Very considerable material on iron manufacture may be found in J. M. Swank, *History of the Manufacture of Iron in all Ages*, Phila., 1892); J. B. Pearse, *A Concise History of the Iron Manufacture of the American Colonies up to the Revolution* (Phila., 1876); and Mrs. Thomas Potts James, *Memorial of Thomas Potts, Jr.* (Cambridge, 1874). J. Stancliffe Davis, *Essays in the Earlier History of American Corporations* (*Harvard Economic Studies*, 1917) is the best work on the business organization of the time.

MONEY AND BANKS

A. McF. Davis, *Currency and Banking in the Province of Massachusetts Bay* (2 vols., Am. Econ. Assoc., *Publs.*, 1900-1901), is the most detailed study for any colony. The same author's *Colonial Currency Reprints, 1682-1751* (4 vols., Boston, 1910), is the only collection of the sort for the colonial period. In connection with the Land Bank episode in Massachusetts the same author's *Papers relating to the Land Bank of 1740* (Col. Soc. Mass., *Publs.*, IV, 1908), should be examined. C. J. Bullock, *Essays on the Monetary History of the United States* (N. Y., 1900), relates particularly to North Carolina and New Hampshire. I. W. Andrews, "McMaster on our Early Money," *Mag. of Western Hist.*, IV (1886), 141-152, has considerable information as to the currencies in use. Henry Phillips, Jr., *Historical Sketches of the Paper Money of the American Colonies* (Roxbury, 1865); Henry Bronson, *A Historical Account of Connecticut Currency, Continental Money and the Finances of the Revolution*, (New Haven Colony Hist. Soc., *Papers*), I (1865); E. R. Potter, *Rhode Island* (Providence, 1880); J. H. Hickox, *A History of the Bills of Credit or Paper Money issued by New York from 1709-1789* (Albany, 1866); and Gould, *Money and Transportation in Maryland* (previously cited), are all useful.

PIRACY AND PRIVATEERING

J. F. Jameson, ed., *Privateering and Piracy in the Colonial Period* (N. Y., 1923), has documents of the first importance. G. F. Dow and J. H. Edmonds, *The Pirates of the New England Coast, 1630-1730* (Marine Research Soc., II, Salem, 1923), is useful for that section. S. C. Hughson, *The Carolina Pirates and Colonial Commerce* (Johns Hopkins Univ., Studies, V-VII, 1894, nos. 5-7), treats of the important Southern conditions. Some of his deductions are criticized by McCrady, *History of South Carolina* (previously cited). C. N. Dalton, *The Real Captain Kidd* (N. Y., 1911), tries to rehabilitate the character of that somewhat maligned person, and gives extracts from his trial. The complete record is somewhat less favorable to him: *The Arraignment, Tryal and Condemnation of Captain William Kidd, for Murther and Piracy* (London, 1701).

FREE LABOR, SERVITUDE, SLAVERY

So far as the author is aware, there is not a single study of free labor in the colonies. J. R. Commons, ed., *Documentary History of American Industrial Society* (10 vols., Cleveland, 1909-1911), devotes two volumes to the colonial period, but the extracts are almost wholly from the better known printed sources for the South, and the work is disappointing. For servitude the following special studies may be recommended: T. D. Jervey, "The White Indented Servants of South Carolina," *S. C. Hist. and Geneal. Mag.*, XII (1911) 163-171; J. S. Bassett, *Slavery and White Servitude in the Colony of North Carolina* (Johns Hopkins Univ., Studies, XIV, 1896, nos. 4-5); J. C. Ballagh, *White Servitude in the Colony of Virginia (ibid.,* XIII, 1895, nos. 4-5); E. L. McCormac, *White Servitude in Maryland (ibid.,* XXII, 1904, nos. 3-4). K. F. Geiser, *Redemptioners and Indentured Servants in the Colony and Commonwealth of Pennsylvania* (New Haven, 1901), and C. A. Herrick, *White Servitude in Pennsylvania* (Phila., 1926), cover the subject for that colony.

For slavery two general works of importance are: W. E. B. DuBois, *The Suppression of the African Slave Trade to the United States, 1638-1870 (Harvard Hist. Studies, I, 1896)*, and A. W. Lauber, *Indian Slavery in Colonial Times within the Present Limits of the United States* (Columbia Univ., *Studies*, LV, 1913, no. 3). Specific studies for particular colonies are: G. H. Moore, *Notes on the History of Slavery in Massachusetts* (N. Y., 1886); W. B. Weeden, "The Early African Slave Trade in New England," Am. Antiq. Soc., *Proceeds.*, n. s., V (1887-1888), 13-128; E. V. Morgan, "Slavery in New York," Am. Hist. Assoc., *Papers*, V (1891, pt. iv), 335-350; Daniel Horsmanden, *The New York Conspiracy or a History of the Negro Plot, 1741-1742* (N. Y., 1810); H. S. Cooley, *A Study of Slavery in New Jersey* (Johns Hopkins Univ., *Studies*, XIV, 1896, nos. 9-10); J. R. Brackett, *The Negro in Maryland* (*ibid.*, extra vol. vi, 1899); J. C. Ballagh, *A History of Slavery in Virginia* (*ibid.*, XIII, 1913, no. 3; J. H. Russell, *The Free Negro in Virginia, 1619-1865* (*ibid.*, XXXI, 1913, no. 3); E. McCrady, "Slavery in the Province of South Carolina, 1670-1770," Am. Hist. Assoc., *Rep. for 1895*, 629-673. See also U. B. Phillips' valuable work on *American Negro Slavery* (N. Y., 1918).

TRAVEL

There are a few special works on the facilities for travel. The most pretentious is Seymour Dunbar, *A History of Travel in America* (4 vols., Indianapolis, 1915), which has a somewhat scant and generalized treatment of our period. A. B. Hulbert has gathered much valuable data on roads and trails in his *Historic Highways* (16 vols., Cleveland, 1902-1905). G. R. Putnam, *Lighthouses and Lightships of the United States* (Boston, 1917), lists those existing in the period, omitting one which apparently had been placed on Tybee Island about 1760. Alice Morse Earle, *Stage Coach and Tavern Days* (N. Y., 1922), is a readable account of the same character as her other works. W. H. Bayles, *Old Taverns of New York* (N. Y., 1915), has much miscellaneous information. Thomas Prince, *The Vade Mecum for*

America or a Companion for Traders and Travellers (Boston, 1732), is the first American guidebook.

The following list of travelers' journals and narratives, though far from complete, contains some of the main ones used in constructing the text of this volume: the *Journal of Madam Knight* (Boston, 1920)—an extremely entertaining account of a trip from Boston to New York in 1704; Rev. John Miller, *A Description of the Province and City of New York, 1695* (London, 1843)—containing some data on morals; "The Journals of Esther Palmer, in America," Friends Hist. Soc., *Journ.*, VI (1909), 38-40, 63-71, 133-139—good for Maryland and Virginia; the *Journal of Thomas Chalkley* (N. Y., 1808)—containing accounts of many voyages from Philadelphia from 1690 to 1730; John Archdale, "A New Description of that Fertile and Pleasant Province of Carolina" (London, 1707, reptd. in Carroll's *Hist. Colls. of S. C.*, II, 1836); Gabriel Thomas, *An Account of Pennsylvania and West New Jersey* (London, 1698, reptd., Cleveland, 1903); *Some Letters and an Abstract of Letters from Pennsylvania containing the State and Improvement of that Province* (London, 1691); George Howarth, "Early Letters from Pennsylvania 1699-1722," *Pa. Mag. of Hist. and Biog.*, XXXVII (1913), 330-340; Charles Wooley, *A Two Years Journal in New York and Part of its Territories in America* (London, 1701, reptd., N. Y., 1860); Jean Fontaine, "Journal, 1714-1715" (in Maury, *Memoirs of a Huguenot Family*, 245-310)—valuable for Virginia and New York; N. D. Mereness, ed., *Travels in the American Colonies* (N. Y., 1916)—a reprint of a number of journals of this period, mostly in the Indian country of the South; Hugh Jones, *The Present State of Virginia* (London, 1724, reptd. N. Y., 1865); John Lawson, *The History of Carolina* (London, 1718)—a well written account of a good observer of conditions about 1710; B. Martyn, *An Account Showing the Progress of the Colony of Georgia* (London, 1741, reptd. in Ga. Hist. Soc., *Colls.*, II, 1842); "Journal of William Black, 1744" (R. A. Brock, ed.), *Pa. Mag. of Hist. and Biog.*, I-II (1877-1878), *passim*—much good material for Maryland and Pennsylvania; Hamilton's *Itinerarium* (A. B. Hart, ed., St. Louis, 1907)—a trip from Maryland to Boston and back, by an excellent observer; William Logan, "Journal of a Journey to Georgia, 1745," *Pa. Mag. of Hist. and Biog.*, XXXVI (1912), 1-16, 162-186—overland from Philadelphia to Charleston, thence by sea; and "Visit to South Carolina in 1745," by James Pemberton—an important manuscript in the Library of Congress, written by the companion of Logan.

INDEX

Exports, of tobacco, 28, 49, 205; to Europe, 29; to West Indies, 29, 206; of furs, 36-37; total value of, 38; of fish, 42-43, 45; of rice, 49, 204-205; of staves, 205, 206. *See also* Commerce, Trade.

FAIRFAX FAMILY, and quitrents, 12.

Fairs, 43-44.

Falckner, Daniel, on Pennsylvania, 178.

Family life, unity of, 10-88; large families, 11; living conditions, 90-92.

Faneuil family, in Boston, 8; Benjamin advertises, 48.

Farmers, labor of, 2, 6, 11, 26, 194, 320; tools of, 26; as stock breeders, 26-27, 30, 32, 200; crops of, 194-201; mortgages of, 320; bibliography, 349. *See also* Agriculture, Labor, Land.

Ferries, use of, 46, 79, 301. *See also* Travel.

Finance. *See* Money, Wealth.

Finns, as immigrants, 10.

Fisheries, in New England, 42-43, 54, 232; and morals, 95; and Sabbath observance, 150.

Fitzhugh, Colonel William, orchard of, 27; plantation of, 30; legal training of, 60; and first Westover, 69; imports books, 114; employs local painter, 149; income of, 195.

Five Nations. *See* Indians.

Fletcher, Governor Benjamin, and land grants, 65.

Fontaine, John, on New York clubs, 261.

Fontaine, Peter, on poverty in Virginia, 319.

Food supply, fish, 42; embargoes on, 46; preparation of, 74; at inns, 76-79; farm-raised, 87; abundance of, 90.

Forests, primeval, 1; Southern, 26; fuel, 32, 39; naval stores from, 33; lumbering in, 298. *See also* Fuel, and colonies by name.

Fortunes. *See* Wealth.

France, effect of revocation of Edict of Nantes on, 7; illegal trade with, 52; brandies imported from, 52; bitter feeling towards, 316; influence of, on colonial life, 316-317. *See also* Canada, Huguenots, Indians.

Franklin, Benjamin, on making a living, 58; and friendship with Jared Eliot, 237; and Junto, 263 and American Philosophical Society, 263-264; and *Courant*, 265-266; and founding of *Pennsylvania Gazette*, 266; and the *General Magazine*, 269; attends concert at Bethlehem, Pa., 276; on colonial conditions, 288; invents stove, 303, and subscription library, 305; deputy postmaster-general, 302; and *Poor Richard's Almanac*, 307.

Franklin, James, and *New-England Courant*, 265-266.

Fraternal orders, Freemasonry, 262-263, 276. *See also* Associations.

Frelinghuysen, Reverend Theodorus J., and Presbyterian revival, 280-281.

French, Huguenots and Edict of Nantes, 7; as immigrants, 8; in Canada, 9; in Philadelphia, 10; and fur trade, 35-36; as silversmiths, 146; form clubs, 261; words in American language, 289; bibliography, 334-335.

Fruit. *See* crops.

Frontier, colonial, 3; dangers of, 13; and child labor, 92; and life of women, 93; effect of, on schools, 134; and effect of Indian wars, 153; and immigration, 183-184; and home life, 218-220, 256-257; effect of Seven Years' War on, 320; bibliography, 328-330, 335-336. *See also* Travel.

Furniture. *See* Home furnishing.

Fur trade, declines in New England, 34, 35, 38; from Canada to England, 36; and frontier immigration, 112; between Indians and South, 208; impor-

QUADRANGLE PAPERBACKS

American History

James Truslow Adams. *Provincial Society, 1690-1763*. (QP403)
Frederick Lewis Allen. *The Lords of Creation*. (QP35)
Lewis Atherton. *Main Street on the Middle Border*. (QP36)
Thomas A. Bailey. *Woodrow Wilson and the Lost Peace*. (QP1)
Thomas A. Bailey. *Woodrow Wilson and the Great Betrayal*. (QP2)
Charles A. Beard. *The Idea of National Interest*. (QP27)
Carl L. Becker. *Everyman His Own Historian*. (QP33)
Barton J. Bernstein. *Politics and Policies of the Truman Administration*. (QP72)
Ray A. Billington. *The Protestant Crusade*. (QP12)
Allan G. Bogue. *From Prairie to Corn Belt*. (QP50)
Kenneth E. Boulding. *The Organizational Revolution*. (QP43)
Robert V. Bruce. *1877: Year of Violence*. (QP73)
Roger Burlingame. *Henry Ford*. (QP76)
Gerald M. Capers. *John C. Calhoun, Opportunist*. (QP70)
David M. Chalmers. *Hooded Americanism*. (QP51)
John Chamberlain. *Farewell to Reform*. (QP19)
Arthur C. Cole. *The Irrepressible Conflict, 1850-1865*. (QP407)
Alice Hamilton Cromie. *A Tour Guide to the Civil War*.
Robert D. Cross. *The Emergence of Liberal Catholicism in America*. (QP44)
Richard M. Dalfiume. *American Politics Since 1945*. (NYTimes Book, QP57)
Carl N. Degler. *The New Deal*. (NYTimes Book, QP74)
Chester McArthur Destler. *American Radicalism, 1865-1901*. (QP30)
Robert A. Divine. *American Foreign Policy Since 1945*. (NYTimes Book, QP58)
Robert A. Divine. *Causes and Consequences of World War II*. (QP63)
Robert A. Divine. *The Cuban Missile Crisis*. (QP86)
Robert A. Divine. *The Illusion of Neutrality*. (QP45)
Elisha P. Douglass. *Rebels and Democrats*. (QP26)
Melvyn Dubofsky. *American Labor Since the New Deal*. (NYTimes Book, QP87)
Arthur A. Ekirch, Jr. *Ideologies and Utopias*. (QP89)
Harold U. Faulkner. *The Quest for Social Justice, 1898-1914*. (QP411)
Carl Russell Fish. *The Rise of the Common Man, 1830-1850*. (QP406)
Felix Frankfurter. *The Commerce Clause*. (QP16)
Edwin Scott Gaustad. *The Great Awakening in New England*. (QP46)
Ray Ginger. *Altgeld's America*. (QP21)
Ray Ginger. *Modern American Cities*. (NYTimes Book, QP67)
Ray Ginger. *Six Days or Forever?* (QP68)
Evarts B. Greene. *The Revolutionary Generation, 1763-1790*. (QP404)
Gerald N. Grob. *Workers and Utopia*. (QP61)
Louis Hartz. *Economic Policy and Democratic Thought*. (QP52)
William B. Hesseltine. *Lincoln's Plan of Reconstruction*. (QP41)
Granville Hicks. *The Great Tradition*. (QP62)
Stanley P. Hirshson. *Farewell to the Bloody Shirt*. (QP53)
Dwight W. Hoover. *A Teacher's Guide to American Urban History*. (QP83)
Dwight W. Hoover. *Understanding Negro History*. (QP49)
Frederic C. Howe. *The Confessions of a Reformer*. (QP39)
Harold L. Ickes. *The Autobiography of a Curmudgeon*. (QP69)
William Loren Katz. *Teachers' Guide to American Negro History*. (QP210)
Burton Ira Kaufman. *Washington's Farewell Address*. (QP64)
Edward Chase Kirkland. *Dream and Thought in the Business Community, 1860-1900*. (QP11)
Edward Chase Kirkland. *Industry Comes of Age*. (QP42)
Herbert S. Klein. *Slavery in the Americas*. (QP84)
Adrienne Koch. *The Philosophy of Thomas Jefferson*. (QP17)
Gabriel Kolko. *The Triumph of Conservatism*. (QP40)
Aileen S. Kraditor. *Up from the Pedestal*. (QP77)
John Allen Krout and Dixon Ryan Fox. *The Completion of Independence, 1790-1830*. (QP405)
Walter LaFeber. *John Quincy Adams and American Continental Empire*. (QP23)
Lawrence H. Leder. *The Meaning of the American Revolution*. (NYTimes Book, QP66)
David E. Lilienthal. *TVA: Democracy on the March*. (QP28)

American History (continued)

Arthur S. Link. *Wilson the Diplomatist.* (QP18)
Huey P. Long. *Every Man a King.* (QP8)
Gene M. Lyons. *America: Purpose and Power.* (QP24)
Neill Macaulay. *The Sandino Affair.* (QP82)
Ernest R. May. *The World War and American Isolation, 1914-1917.* (QP29)
Henry F. May. *The End of American Innocence.* (QP9)
Thomas J. McCormick. *China Market.* (QP75)
August Meier and Elliott Rudwick. *Black Protest in the Sixties.* (NYTimes Book, QP78)
George E. Mowry. *The California Progressives.* (QP6)
Allan Nevins. *The Emergence of Modern America, 1865-1878.* (QP408)
William L. O'Neill. *American Society Since 1945.* (NYTimes Book, QP59)
William L. O'Neill. *Everyone Was Brave.* (QP88)
William L. O'Neill. *The Woman Movement.* (QP80)
Frank L. Owsley. *Plain Folk of the Old South.* (QP22)
Thomas G. Paterson. *Cold War Critics.* (QP85)
David Graham Phillips. *The Treason of the Senate.* (QP20)
Julius W. Pratt. *Expansionists of 1898.* (QP15)
Herbert I. Priestley. *The Coming of the White Man, 1492-1848.* (QP401)
C. Herman Pritchett. *The Roosevelt Court.* (QP71)
Moses Rischin. *The American Gospel of Success.* (QP54)
John P. Roche. *The Quest for the Dream.* (QP47)
Arthur Meier Schlesinger. *The Rise of the City, 1878-1898.* (QP410)
David A. Shannon. *The Socialist Party of America.* (QP38)
Andrew Sinclair. *The Available Man.* (QP60)
Preston W. Slosson. *The Great Crusade and After, 1914-1928.* (QP412)
June Sochen. *The Black Man and the American Dream.* (QP81)
John Spargo. *The Bitter Cry of the Children.* (QP55)
Bernard Sternsher. *Hitting Home.* (QP79)
Bernard Sternsher. *The Negro in Depression and War.* (QP65)
Ida M. Tarbell. *The Nationalizing of Business, 1878-1898.* (QP409)
Richard W. Van Alstyne. *The Rising American Empire.* (QP25)
Willard M. Wallace. *Appeal to Arms.* (QP10)
Norman Ware. *The Industrial Worker, 1840-1860.* (QP13)
Dixon Wecter. *The Age of the Great Depression, 1929-1941.* (QP413)
Albert K. Weinberg. *Manifest Destiny.* (QP3)
Bernard A. Weisberger. *They Gathered at the River.* (QP37)
Thomas J. Wertenbaker. *The First Americans, 1607-1690.* (QP402)
Robert H. Wiebe. *Businessmen and Reform.* (QP56)
William Appleman Williams. *The Contours of American History.* (QP34)
William Appleman Williams. *The Great Evasion.* (QP48)
Esmond Wright. *Causes and Consequences of the American Revolution.* (QP31)

European History

William Sheridan Allen. *The Nazi Seizure of Power.* (QP302)
Hans W. Gatzke. *European Diplomacy Between Two Wars, 1919-1939.* (QP351)
Nathanael Greene. *European Socialism Since World War I.* (NYTimes Book, QP309)
W. O. Henderson. *The Industrial Revolution in Europe.* (QP303)
Raul Hilberg. *The Destruction of the European Jews.* (QP301)
Raul Hilberg. *Documents of Destruction.* (QP311)
Richard N. Hunt. *German Social Democracy.* (QP306)
John F. Naylor. *Britain, 1919-1970.* (NYTimes Book, QP312)
Steven E. Ozment. *The Reformation in Medieval Perspective.* (QP350)
Percy Ernst Schramm. *Hitler: The Man and the Military Leader.* (QP308)
Telford Taylor. *Sword and Swastika.* (QP304)
John Weiss. *Nazis and Fascists in Europe, 1918-1945.* (NYTimes Book, QP305)

See our complete catalog for titles in Social Science *and* Philosophy.